走向未來

Chinese for Tomorrow

新中文教程

A New Five-Skilled Approach

語法書第一冊

Volume 1 Grammar Book

Traditional and Simplified Characters

Wayne He, Dela Jiao, Qiuxia Shao,
Christopher M. Livaccari

CHENG & TSUI COMPANY
Boston

Chinese for Tomorrow
A New Five-Skilled Approach
Grammar Book

16 15 14 13 12 11 10 09 08   1 2 3 4 5

First Edition 2008

Published by
Cheng & Tsui Company
25 West Street
Boston, MA 02111-1213 USA
Fax (617) 426-3669
www.cheng-tsui.com
"Bringing Asia to the World"™

ISBN 978-0-88727-569-2

The *Chinese for Tomorrow* series includes student textbooks, grammar books, teacher's manuals, and online supplements. To learn more about the series, please visit www.cheng-tsui.com. ·

Printed in Canada

TABLE OF CONTENTS

PREFACE

The teaching of grammar has long been one of the most difficult challenges facing foreign language teachers. We take the view that new language can be acquired quickly and effectively without detailed grammatical explanation, but that a deep understanding of the language and its principles is crucial for developing a "feel" for the language and the way it works. We therefore offer our companion grammar book, which contains a systematic explanation of the basic grammatical principles of Mandarin Chinese. Each lesson explains some of the most basic grammar items selected from the Level A Grammar Program 甲级语法/甲級語法) of the Hanyu Shuiping Kaoshi (HSK, Chinese Proficiency Test Program, 中国汉语水平考试大纲/中國漢語水平考試大綱).[1]

This book begins with a brief, general explanation of some special features of Chinese grammar, followed by 10 lessons that comprise the main text. Grammar points are introduced in order of learning facility and usefulness—that is, concepts that are easier to grasp and patterns that are most useful are taught first. Based on our teaching experience, we believe that what is most helpful for beginning students is not detailed theoretical explanations of grammar principles, but rather practical information on how to use grammar correctly and appropriately. Therefore, the approach of this book is practical instead of theoretical: we show students exactly how to apply certain grammar points to reproduce their own sentences.

To facilitate learning, we present grammar items in terms of sentence patterns. Each item starts with a short explanation, followed by sentence patterns and multiple examples for the three main forms of sentences: affirmative sentences, negative sentences and interrogative sentences with answers. We also provide some functional explanation notes to some of the more complicated and difficult grammar points. These notes will help the students to understand how to use the grammar in everyday communication. The vocabulary used in the examples is limited to the new words of the current lesson or from previous lessons, with the exception of a few new words that are introduced, defined, and then used in the examples. Students can easily follow the sentence patterns to reproduce their own sentences. Such examples also serve to reinforce the vocabulary words learned in the textbook as they are used in a different context.

Each lesson concludes with an exercise section where students can practice the grammar items introduced in the lesson, and can also get additional practice using the vocabulary introduced in the corresponding textbook lesson together with the new grammar structures they have learned. Students should complete the exercises either orally or on a computer wherever possible, in accordance with the emphasis on Computer Chinese in this course. Answers to the exercises are provided at the end of the book.

[1] The HSK Chinese Proficiency Exam is the official standardized test of Chinese as a foreign language. Its grammar program is divided into four levels. Level A is the lowest of the four, and includes the most commonly used grammar items.

Why Present Grammar Separately?

The grammar book is based on the principle that the most effective way to teach a foreign language to adolescents and adults is by means of a two-track approach. One of these is the communicative approach, which is situational and builds competency in terms of using the target language to negotiate a wide range of topics and situations. The second approach is that of deeper knowledge and analytical understanding of the grammatical, phonological, and pragmatic systems of the language. The textbook follows the first track, the communicative approach, and the grammar book the second track.

For example, in a given lesson in the textbook, a student may be asked to learn how to say a small set of numbers, but as preparation for future growth, the student must also understand the workings of the number system and how to say all the numbers from one to one hundred. While the student may not be able to say all the numbers immediately, he or she will eventually gain mastery of the counting system. It makes sense to concentrate on the small set of numbers in the textbook lesson, but include the counting system in the grammar book.

How are the Grammar Book and Textbook Connected?

The textbook and the grammar book are closely connected. What students learn in the textbook is reinforced in the grammar book, and vice versa. Here are some specific ways in which the two books complement each other:

Vocabulary. The vocabulary used in corresponding lessons of the textbook and grammar book connects the two books. For example, the vocabulary introduced in Lesson 1 of the textbook is repeated and reinforced in Lesson 1 of the grammar book, to allow students and teachers to cover both books simultaneously in the same course.

Cross References. In the textbook, notes to the dialogues and passages refer to the points explained in the grammar book and indicate the lessons in which they can be found. In the grammar book, we also provide sample sentences selected from the textbook and explain certain grammar points by analyzing these sentences. It is important to note that the language items introduced in a given textbook lesson may or may not be covered in exactly the same lesson in the grammar book. In the textbook, vocabulary and sentence structures are presented in the order that students are likely to encounter them in their daily lives. In the grammar book, however, grammar items are presented in order of difficulty—the grammar items that are easiest to grasp are presented first. This two-track design is intentional, and it helps to strengthen students' language skills by providing broader exposure to language patterns and more repetition of vocabulary. For example, students may get a brief exposure to the use of the particle 了 "le" in Textbook Lesson 1, but may not learn 了 in detail until Grammar Book Lesson 6. This is because students will encounter 了 fairly early on in Chinese communication, but may not be ready to understand the range of uses of 了 until later. The grammar book serves to reinforce what was learned in textbook lessons, explain the new usage of familiar words at increasing levels of difficulty, and strengthen students' grasp of grammar.

Exercises. In the grammar book exercises, we provide at least one piece of conversation similar to what was introduced in the corresponding lesson in the textbook, but focusing on new grammar items explained in the grammar book. This way, the students can practice using the new grammar items in situations similar to the ones introduced in the textbook.

Suggestions for Teaching and Curriculum Planning

The companion grammar book has been designed to give teachers and students maximum flexibility and allow them to cover grammar at a pace that works best for their particular program. Students can study the grammar book together with the *Chinese for Tomorrow* textbook if they would like to have a better understanding of the grammar points introduced in the textbook. In addition, students using textbooks other than *Chinese for Tomorrow* can study this grammar book as an independent reference book because the grammar points discussed here are the most basic grammar points that every student is expected to know.

If you are teaching this book as part of the curriculum, we suggest teaching the relevant grammar points simultaneously with each corresponding lesson of the textbook. For example, if you are spending two weeks on Lesson 1 of the texbook, you might spend one full day or two half-days during that two-week period to cover the relevant grammar points discussed in the grammar book. Please see the suggested sample syllabi in the *Chinese for Tomorrow* Teacher's Manual for more detailed suggestions.

The authors
February 2007, New York

ABBREVIATIONS FOR GRAMMAR TERMS

A	Adjective
Ad	Adverb
AV	Auxiliary Verb
CE	Common Expression
Conj	Conjunction
CR	Complement of Result
CD	Compound Directional Complement
Exc	Exclamation
Int	Interjection
MW	Measure Word
N	Noun
Neg	Negation Word
NP	Noun Phrase
Num	Numerals
O	Object
Par	Particle
Pron	Pronoun
Prep	Preposition
PW	Place Word
QW	Question Word
S	Subject
TW	Time Word
V	Verb
VC	Verb plus Complement
VO	Verb plus Object

A Brief Introduction to Chinese Grammar

Every language has its own special features. To learn Chinese well, one needs to pay close attention to the similarities and differences between Chinese and one's native language.

In order to help elementary-level students better understand the special features of Chinese, we present the following brief introduction to Chinese grammar as a whole. Please note that like other languages, although there are grammar principles or rules in Chinese, almost every grammar principle or rule has exceptions. Therefore the introduction below is based on the most frequently seen Chinese sentences, and it may not apply to all sentences.

Chinese Sentence Structure

The word order of the most basic type of Chinese sentence is similar to that of English. Chinese sentences are made up of three component parts: subject (主语/主語 zhǔyǔ), predicate (谓语/謂語 wèiyǔ), and object (宾语/賓語 bīnyǔ), although some sentences do not contain objects. Many sentences also have some additional component parts, such as an adverbial modifier (状语/狀語 zhuàngyǔ), attribute (定语/定語 dìngyǔ) or complement (补语/補語 bǔyǔ).

Generally speaking, there are three main forms of sentences in Chinese: affirmative (肯定句 kěndìngjù), negative (否定句 fǒudìngjù), and interrogative (疑问句/疑問句 yíwènjù). Although some other special forms of sentences do exist, in this introduction we will focus on the three most common forms.

The most basic type of affirmative Chinese sentence consists of a subject, a predicate and an object. Time words are placed before or after the subject, as opposed to English, where time words are usually placed at the end of the sentence. Similarly, if there is a place word, it should precede the predicate (action verb) rather than follow it. For example: 今天我在家看书/今天我在家看書 (Jīntiān wǒ zài jiā kànshū. Today I'll read books at home).

Usually, a negative Chinese sentence is structured in the same way as an affirmative one, except that a negative adverb, such as 不 (bù) or 沒有 (méiyǒu) is inserted before the predicate. For example: 明天他不去学校/明天他不去學校 (Míngtiān tā bù qù xuéxiào. He is not going to school tomorrow).

The structure of a Chinese interrogative sentence is very different from that of English. In English, the verb and subject word order is reversed when making a question, but in Chinese, there is no need to do so. In most cases, the original word order of an affirmative or negative sentence is retained, and a question particle is added to the end of the sentence, or the expected answer can be replaced with an appropriate question word. For example: 你星期一看电影吗/你星期一看電影嗎 (Nǐ xīngqī yī kàn diànyǐng ma? Are you going to see a movie on Monday)? 你什么时候去中国/你什麼時候去中國 (Nǐ shénme shíhou qù Zhōngguó? When are you going to China)?

The Chinese Noun

In English, most nouns are countable, and can be distinguished as singular or plural by an "-s" or "-es" ending. Because Chinese characters are made of individual strokes rather than alphabetic letters, however, there is no way to mark nouns as singular or plural. A Chinese noun is always written the same way regardless of quantity. To determine the number of a Chinese noun, one must look at cues from context.

Furthermore, with very few exceptions, Chinese nouns are not classified or inflected as masculine, feminine or neutral, as in many other languages. Thus almost all nouns can be used freely, without modification and without the use of gender-specific articles, adjectives or other referents.

The Chinese Verb

Unlike English verbs, Chinese verbs never change their forms according to the gender or number of a subject, or the tense in the sentence. In other words, no matter whether the subject is male or female, singular or plural, or whether the action expressed by a verb took place in the past, is taking place right now, or will take place in the future, the verb is always written the same way.

第一课

LESSON 1

▶ I. Sentences with 是
(See Textbook I, Lesson 1)

Selected examples from the textbook:

格林是美国留学生。(Lesson 1)

他是我的中国朋友。(Lesson 1)

A sentence with 是 (shì, to be) as the verb is known as a "是 Sentence." At the most basic level, 是 is often used to identify people or objects. The negative form of 是 is 不是 (bù shì, to not be, no).

Affirmative sentence

Sentence structure:	S ＋ 是 ＋ 0

Examples:

Wǒ shì lǎoshī.

我是老师。

I am a teacher.

Nǐ shì liúxuésheng.

你是留学生。

You are a foreign student.

Tā shì Xiǎo Wáng.

他是小王。

He is Little Wang.

Zhè shì cāntīng.

这是餐厅。

This is the dining room (cafeteria).

第一課
LESSON 1

▶ **I. Sentences with 是**
(See Textbook I, Lesson 1)

Selected examples from the textbook:

格林是美國留學生。 (Lesson 1)
他是我的中國朋友。 (Lesson 1)

A sentence with 是 (shì, to be) as the verb is known as a "是 Sentence." At the most basic level, 是 is often used to identify people or objects. The negative form of 是 is 不是 (bù shì, to not be, no).

Affirmative sentence

Sentence structure: S ＋ 是 ＋ O

Examples:

Wǒ shì lǎoshī.

我是老師。

I am a teacher.

Nǐ shì liúxuésheng.

你是留學生。

You are a foreign student.

Tā shì Xiǎo Wáng.

他是小王。

He is Little Wang.

Zhè shì cāntīng.

這是餐廳。

This is the dining room (cafeteria).

Negative sentence

Sentence structure:	S ＋ 不是 ＋ 0

Examples:

Wǒ bù shì Měiguó lǎoshī.

我不是美国老师。

I am not an American teacher.

Nǐ bù shì Zhōngguó xuésheng.

你不是中国学生。

You are not a Chinese student.

Tā bù shì wǒ de péngyou.

他不是我的朋友。

He is not my friend.

Interrogative sentence

Sentence structure:	S ＋ 是 ＋ 0 ＋ 吗?

Examples:

Question: Nǐ shì xuésheng ma?

你是学生吗？

Are you a student?

Answers: (Shì,) wǒ shì xuésheng.

（是，）我是学生。

(Yes,) I am a student.

(Bù shì,) wǒ bù shì xuésheng.

（不是，）我不是学生。

(No,) I'm not a student.

Negative sentence

Sentence structure:	S + 不是 + O

Examples:

Wǒ bù shì Měiguó lǎoshī.

我不是美國老師。

I am not an American teacher.

Nǐ bù shì Zhōngguó xuésheng.

你不是中國學生。

You are not a Chinese student.

Tā bù shì wǒ de péngyou.

他不是我的朋友。

He is not my friend.

Interrogative sentence

Sentence structure:	S + 是 + O + 嗎？

Examples:

Question: Nǐ shì xuésheng ma?

你是學生嗎？

Are you a student?

Answers: (Shì,) wǒ shì xuésheng.

(是，) 我是學生。

(Yes,) I am a student.

(Bù shì,) wǒ bù shì xuésheng.

(不是，) 我不是學生。

(No,) I'm not a student.

Question: Xiǎo Wén shì lǎoshī ma?

小文是老师吗？

Is Little Wen a teacher?

Answers: (Shì,) Xiǎo Wén shì lǎoshī.

（是，）小文是老师。

(Yes,) Little Wen is a teacher.

(Bù shì,) Xiǎo Wén bù shì lǎoshī.

（不是，）小文不是老师。

(No,) Little Wen is not a teacher.

▶ II. Questions with 吗
(See Textbook I, Lesson 1)

Selected examples from the textbook:

你吃饭了吗？ (Lesson 1)

您好吗？ (Lesson 1)

In Chinese, there are many ways to form a question. The most common way is to add the question particle 吗 (ma) to the end of a statement. Note that unlike in English, the word order does not change.

Sentence structure:	S ＋ V （＋ O） ＋ 吗

Examples:

Question: Nǐ chī Zhōngguó fàn ma?

你吃中国饭吗？

Do you eat Chinese food?

Answers: (Chī,) wǒ chī Zhōngguó fàn.

（吃，）我吃中国饭。

(Yes,) I eat Chinese food.

(Bù chī,) wǒ bù chī Zhōngguó fàn.

（不吃，）我不吃中国饭。

(No,) I don't eat Chinese food.

Question: Xiǎo Wén shì lǎoshī ma?

小文是老師嗎？

Is Little Wen a teacher?

Answers: (Shì,) Xiǎo Wén shì lǎoshī.

(是，) 小文是老師。

(Yes,) Little Wen is a teacher.

(Bù shì,) Xiǎo Wén bù shì lǎoshī.

(不是，) 小文不是老師。

(No,) Little Wen is not a teacher.

▶ II. Questions with 嗎
(See Textbook I, Lesson 1)

Selected examples from the textbook:

你吃飯了嗎？(Lesson 1)

您好嗎？(Lesson 1)

In Chinese, there are many ways to form a question. The most common way is to add the question particle 嗎 (ma) to the end of a statement. Note that unlike in English, the word order does not change.

Sentence structure: S + V (+ O) + 嗎

Examples:

Question: Nǐ chī Zhōngguó fàn ma?

你吃中國飯嗎？

Do you eat Chinese food?

Answers: (Chī,) wǒ chī Zhōngguó fàn.

(吃，) 我吃中國飯。

(Yes,) I eat Chinese food.

(Bù chī,) wǒ bù chī Zhōngguó fàn.

(不吃，) 我不吃中國飯。

(No,) I don't eat Chinese food.

Question: Tā qù shàngkè ma?

他去上课吗？

Is he going to class?

Answers: (Qù,) tā qù shàngkè.

（去，）他去上课。

(Yes,) he's going to class.

(Bù qù,) tā bù qù shàngkè.

（不去，）他不去上课。

(No,) he's not going to class.

▶ III. Sentences with 有
(See Textbook I, Lesson 1)

Selected example from the textbook:

他有一个中国朋友，叫文国新。 (Lesson 1)

The verb 有 (yǒu) means to "have" or "possess." The negative form of 有 is always 没有 (méiyǒu), never 不有 (bù yǒu).

Affirmative sentence

Sentence structure:	S ＋ 有 ＋ 0

Examples:

Wǒ yǒu Měiguó péngyou.

我有美国朋友。

I have American friends.

Wáng lǎoshī yǒu Zhōngwén míngzi.

王老师有中文名字。

Professor Wang has a Chinese name.

Question: Tā qù shàngkè ma?

他去上課嗎？

Is he going to class?

Answers: (Qù,) tā qù shàngkè.

(去，) 他去上課。

(Yes,) he's going to class.

(Bù qù,) tā bù qù shàngkè.

(不去，) 他不去上課。

(No,) he's not going to class.

▶ III. Sentences with 有
(See Textbook I, Lesson 1)

Selected example from the textbook:

他有一個中國朋友，叫文國新。(Lesson 1)

The verb 有 (yǒu) means to "have" or "possess." The negative form of 有 is always 沒有 (méiyǒu), never 不有 (bù yǒu).

Affirmative sentence

Sentence structure:	S ＋ 有 ＋ O

Examples:

Wǒ yǒu Měiguó péngyou.

我有美國朋友。

I have American friends.

Wáng lǎoshī yǒu Zhōngwén míngzi.

王老師有中文名字。

Professor Wang has a Chinese name.

Negative sentence

Sentence structure: S ＋ 没有 ＋ 0

Examples:

Nǐ méiyǒu péngyou.

你没有朋友。

You don't have (any) friends.

Xiǎo Wén méiyǒu Zhōngwén lǎoshī.

小文没有中文老师。

Little Wen doesn't have a Chinese teacher.

Interrogative sentence

Sentence structure: S ＋ (没)有 ＋ 0 ＋ 吗

Examples:

Question: Lǐ lǎoshī yǒu Měiguó xuésheng ma?

李老师有美国学生吗？

Does Professor Li have American students?

Answers: (Yǒu,) Lǐ lǎoshī yǒu Měiguó xuésheng.

（有，）李老师有美国学生。

(Yes,) Professor Li has American students.

(Méiyǒu,) Lǐ lǎoshī méiyǒu Měiguó xuésheng.

（没有，）李老师没有美国学生。

(No,) Professor Li doesn't have American students.

Question: Nǐ méiyǒu Zhōngwén míngzi ma?

你没有中文名字吗？

You don't have a Chinese name?

Negative sentence

Sentence structure:	S + 沒有 + O

Examples:

Nǐ méiyǒu péngyou.

你沒有朋友。

You don't have (any) friends.

Xiǎo Wén méiyǒu Zhōngwén lǎoshī.

小文沒有中文老師。

Little Wen doesn't have a Chinese teacher.

Interrogative sentence

Sentence structure:	S + (沒)有 + O + 嗎

Examples:

Question: Lǐ lǎoshī yǒu Měiguó xuésheng ma?

李老師有美國學生嗎？

Does Professor Li have American students?

Answers: (Yǒu,) Lǐ lǎoshī yǒu Měiguó xuésheng.

(有，) 李老師有美國學生。

(Yes,) Professor Li has American students.

(Méiyǒu,) Lǐ lǎoshī méiyǒu Měiguó xuésheng.

(沒有，) 李老師沒有美國學生。

(No,) Professor Li doesn't have American students.

Question: Nǐ méiyǒu Zhōngwén míngzi ma?

你沒有中文名字嗎？

You don't have a Chinese name?

Answers: Wǒ méiyǒu Zhōngwén míngzi.

我没有中文名字。

I don't have a Chinese name.

Wǒ yǒu Zhōngwén míngzi.

我有中文名字。

I have a Chinese name.

Note: When 没有 is followed by an object, the short form 没 can be used.

For example:

Wǒ méi Zhōngwén míngzi.

我没中文名字。

Lǐ lǎoshī méi Měiguó xuésheng.

李老师没美国学生。

▶ IV. Cardinal numbers under 100
(See Textbook I, Lessons 1 and 2)

Selected examples from the textbook:

小文给他起了一个中文名字。 (Lesson 1)
我们家有五口人。 (Lesson 2)

Chinese numerals from zero to 10 are as follows:

零	(líng)	0
一	(yī)	1
二	(èr)	2
三	(sān)	3
四	(sì)	4
五	(wǔ)	5
六	(liù)	6
七	(qī)	7
八	(bā)	8
九	(jiǔ)	9
十	(shí)	10

Answers: Wǒ méiyǒu Zhōngwén míngzi.

我沒有中文名字。

I don't have a Chinese name.

Wǒ yǒu Zhōngwén míngzi.

我有中文名字。

I have a Chinese name.

Note: When 沒有 is followed by an object, the short form 沒 can be used.

For example:

Wǒ méi Zhōngwén míngzi.

我沒中文名字。

Lǐ lǎoshī méi Měiguó xuésheng.

李老師沒美國學生。

▶ IV. Cardinal numbers under 100
(See Textbook I, Lessons 1 and 2)

Selected examples from the textbook:

小文給他起了一個中文名字。(Lesson 1)
我們家有五口人。(Lesson 2)

Chinese numerals from zero to 10 are as follows:

零	(líng)	0
一	(yī)	1
二	(èr)	2
三	(sān)	3
四	(sì)	4
五	(wǔ)	5
六	(liù)	6
七	(qī)	7
八	(bā)	8
九	(jiǔ)	9
十	(shí)	10

The numbers from 11 to 19 are made by combining 十 (shí, 10) with the numbers 1 to 9.

For example:

十一	(shíyī)	11
十二	(shí'èr)	12
十三	(shísān)	13
十四	(shísì)	14
十五	(shíwǔ)	15
十六	(shíliù)	16
十七	(shíqī)	17
十八	(shíbā)	18
十九	(shíjiǔ)	19

Numbers from 20 to 99 are formed by saying the tens place number first, followed by 十 (shí, 10) and then the numbers 1 to 9.

For instance:

二十	(èrshí)	20
三十	(sānshí)	30
五十五	(wǔshíwǔ)	55
七十八	(qīshíbā)	78
九十四	(jiǔshísì)	94

Note: When counting numbers (e.g., 1, 2, 3, 4...), one should not use any measure words after the numeral (for a detailed discussion about measure words, please see the explanation in point V of this lesson). On all other occasions, however, one should insert a proper measure word between the numeral and the noun that is being modified.

"Two" is the only numeral that has two forms: 二 (èr) and 两 (liǎng), and they are different in usage. When counting numbers, we always say 二, but when stating the quantity of something or when "two" is followed by a measure word, we often use 两 instead. For example: 二十二 (èrshí'èr, 22), 两个老师 (liǎng gè lǎoshī, two teachers), 两个朋友 (liǎng gè péngyǒu, two friends). However, for "200 dollars," both 两百块钱 (liǎngbǎi kuài qián) and 二百块钱 (èrbǎi kuài qián) are acceptable.

The numbers from 11 to 19 are made by combining 十 (shí, 10) with the numbers 1 to 9.

For example:

十一	(shíyī)	11
十二	(shí'èr)	12
十三	(shísān)	13
十四	(shísì)	14
十五	(shíwǔ)	15
十六	(shíliù)	16
十七	(shíqī)	17
十八	(shíbā)	18
十九	(shíjiǔ)	19

Numbers from 20 to 99 are formed by saying the tens place number first, followed by 十 (shí, 10) and then the numbers 1 to 9.

For instance:

二十	(èrshí)	20
三十	(sānshí)	30
五十五	(wǔshíwǔ)	55
七十八	(qīshíbā)	78
九十四	(jiǔshísì)	94

Note: When counting numbers (e.g., 1, 2, 3, 4...), one should not use any measure words after the numeral (for a detailed discussion about measure words, please see the explanation in point V of this lesson). On all other occasions, however, one should insert a proper measure word between the numeral and the noun that is being modified.

"Two" is the only numeral that has two forms: 二 (èr) and 兩 (liǎng), and they are different in usage. When counting numbers, we always say 二, but when stating the quantity of something or when "two" is followed by a measure word, we often use 兩 instead. For example: 二十二 (èrshí'èr, 22), 兩個老師 (liǎng gè lǎoshī, two teachers), 兩個朋友 (liǎng gè péngyǒu, two friends). However, for "200 dollars," both 兩百塊錢 (liǎngbǎi kuài qián) and 二百塊錢 (èrbǎi kuài qián) are acceptable.

In spoken Chinese, when referring to such things as telephone numbers, room numbers, or bus route numbers, sometimes the number one can be pronounced in two ways: "yī" and "yāo." But in this case, often the number in question should be at least three digits. For example, 我的房间是 818 (my room number is 818) can be read "wǒ de fángjiān shì bā yī bā" as well as "wǒ de fángjiān shì bā yāo bā."

Sentences with a numeral

Sentence structure:	S ＋ V ＋ Num ＋ M ＋ O

Examples:

Wǒ yǒu liǎng gè hǎo péngyou.

我有两个好朋友。

I have two good friends.

（Incorrect: 我有二个好朋友。）

Lǐ lǎoshī yǒu shíjiǔ gè xuésheng.

李老师有十九个学生。

Professor Li has 19 students.

Gé Lín méiyǒu sì gè lǎoshī.

格林没有四个老师。

Green doesn't have four teachers.

▶ V. Measure Words
(See Textbook I, Lessons 1 and 2)

Selected examples from the textbook:

小文给他起了一个中文名字。(Lesson 1)
爸爸、妈妈开了一家中餐馆。(Lesson 2)

Measure words are used when expressing a quantity of people, objects or actions. In modern Chinese, a numeral alone cannot normally modify a noun directly. A proper measure word should be inserted between the numeral and the noun. Similarly, a demonstrative pronoun, such as 这 (zhè, this) or 那 (nà, that) alone cannot be immediately followed by a noun. Instead, a measure word is needed between the demonstrative pronoun and the noun. For example: 五个朋友 (wǔ gè péngyou, five friends), 那个学生 (nàge xuésheng, that student).

In spoken Chinese, when referring to such things as telephone numbers, room numbers, or bus route numbers, sometimes the number one can be pronounced in two ways: "yī" and "yāo." But in this case, often the number in question should be at least three digits. For example, 我的房間是 818 (my room number is 818) can be read "wǒ de fángjiān shì bā yī bā" as well as "wǒ de fángjiān shì bā yāo bā."

Sentences with a numeral

Sentence structure:	$S + V + Num + M + O$

Examples:

Wǒ yǒu liǎng gè hǎo péngyou.

我有兩個好朋友。

I have two good friends.

(Incorrect: 我有二個好朋友。)

Lǐ lǎoshī yǒu shíjiǔ gè xuésheng.

李老師有十九個學生。

Professor Li has 19 students.

Gé Lín méiyǒu sì gè lǎoshī.

格林沒有四個老師。

Green doesn't have four teachers.

▶ V. Measure Words
(See Textbook I, Lessons 1 and 2)

Selected examples from the textbook:

小文給他起了一個中文名字。(Lesson 1)
爸爸、媽媽開了一家中餐館。(Lesson 2)

Measure words are used when expressing a quantity of people, objects or actions. In modern Chinese, a numeral alone cannot normally modify a noun directly. A proper measure word should be inserted between the numeral and the noun. Similarly, a demonstrative pronoun, such as 這 (zhè, this) or 那 (nà, that) alone cannot be immediately followed by a noun. Instead, a measure word is needed between the demonstrative pronoun and the noun. For example: 五個朋友 (wǔ gè péngyou, five friends), 那個學生 (nàge xuésheng, that student).

In daily conversation, sometimes the number 一 (yī, 1) can be omitted if there is a measure word right after the number. For example: 这是（一）个中学 (zhè shì (yī) gè zhōngxué. This is a middle school).

Generally speaking, the association of a measure word with a noun is fixed according to the general meaning of the noun. Since different nouns should be collocated with different measure words, when learning a noun, one should also learn its corresponding measure word.

There are many measure words in Chinese. At the beginning level, students should learn the following most commonly used measure words:

个 (gè, for both people and objects)

位 (wèi, for people only)

张 (zhāng, for paper, tables, and other flat objects)

家 (jiā, for businesses, stores, restaurants, etc.)

本 (běn, for books, journals, etc.)

枝 (zhī, for pencils, pens, etc.)

件 (jiàn, for shirts, coats, and other clothing worn on top)

条 (tiáo, for pants, skirts, and other clothing worn on the bottom)

辆 (liàng, for vehicles)

口 (kǒu, for people in a family)

Examples:

Tā māma yǒu sān gè mèimei.

他妈妈有三个妹妹。

His mother has three younger sisters.

Wǒ jiā yǒu wǔ kǒu rén.

我家有五口人。

There are five people in my family.

Zhè bù shì (yī) jiā cāntīng.

这不是（一）家餐厅。

This is not a restaurant (cafeteria).

Wǒ méiyǒu sì gè Měiguó xuésheng.

我没有四个美国学生。

I don't have four American students.

In daily conversation, sometimes the number 一 (yī, 1) can be omitted if there is a measure word right after the number. For example: 這是(一)個中學 (zhè shì (yī) gè zhōngxué. This is a middle school).

Generally speaking, the association of a measure word with a noun is fixed according to the general meaning of the noun. Since different nouns should be collocated with different measure words, when learning a noun, one should also learn its corresponding measure word.

There are many measure words in Chinese. At the beginning level, students should learn the following most commonly used measure words:

個 (gè, for both people and objects)

位 (wèi, for people only)

張 (zhāng, for paper, tables, and other flat objects)

家 (jiā, for businesses, stores, restaurants, etc.)

本 (běn, for books, journals, etc.)

枝 (zhī, for pencils, pens, etc.)

件 (jiàn, for shirts, coats, and other clothing worn on top)

條 (tiáo, for pants, skirts, and other clothing worn on the bottom)

輛 (liàng, for vehicles)

口 (kǒu, for people in a family)

Examples:

Tā māma yǒu sān gè mèimei.

他媽媽有三個妹妹。

His mother has three younger sisters.

Wǒ jiā yǒu wǔ kǒu rén.

我家有五口人。

There are five people in my family.

Zhè bù shì (yī) jiā cāntīng.

這不是(一)家餐廳。

This is not a restaurant (cafeteria).

Wǒ méiyǒu sì gè Měiguó xuésheng.

我沒有四個美國學生。

I don't have four American students.

▶ 练习 Exercises

I. Change the following affirmative sentences into negative ones.

Example: 我是美国老师。 → 我不是美国老师。

1. 小王是新学生。
2. 他有中文名字。
3. 我是美国人。
4. 李老师有美国留学生。
5. 我去欢迎小张。
6. 我叫王美英。
7. 你去上课。

II. Change the following statements into questions.

Example: 我要吃饭？ → 你要吃饭吗？

1. 他要去出差。
2. 一会儿我去餐厅。
3. 新学生有中文名字。
4. 我去问王老师。
5. 他姓文。

III. Correct the errors, if there are any, in the following sentences.

Example: 我贵姓文。
Correction: 我姓文。

1. 我不有美国饭。
2. 新老师是不英国人。
3. 他姓张，叫小文张。
4. 请问，您是留学生？
5. 你快吃饭去餐厅吧！
6. 老师起给我了中文名字。

▶ 練習 Exercises

I. Change the following affirmative sentences into negative ones.

Example: 我是美國老師。 → 我不是美國老師。

1. 小王是新學生。
2. 他有中文名字。
3. 我是美國人。
4. 李老師有美國留學生。
5. 我去歡迎小張。
6. 我叫王美英。
7. 你去上課。

II. Change the following statements into questions.

Example: 我要吃飯？ → 你要吃飯嗎？

1. 他要去出差。
2. 一會兒我去餐廳。
3. 新學生有中文名字。
4. 我去問王老師。
5. 他姓文。

III. Correct the errors, if there are any, in the following sentences.

Example: 我貴姓文。
Correction: 我姓文。

1. 我不有美國飯。
2. 新老師是不英國人。
3. 他姓張，叫小文張。
4. 請問，您是留學生？
5. 你快吃飯去餐廳吧！
6. 老師起給我了中文名字。

IV. Rearrange the following words to make correct sentences.

1. 这/叫/名字/什么/个/人

2. 位/他/这/的/是/老师/朋友

3. 回来/他/了/那/好/了/太

4. 要/我/上课/去

5. 你/出差/中国/去/吗

V. Complete the following dialogue.

A: 你好！

B: _____！

A: 请问，您是美国学生吗？

B: _____。

A: 太好了！这位是……？

B: _____。

A: 您好！请问,您贵姓？

C: _____。

A: 很高兴 (gāoxìng, happy) 认识你们。对不起 (duìbùqǐ, excuse me), 我要去上课。
   一会儿见。

B: _____。

VI. Read the following numbers aloud in Chinese and write the first three in Chinese characters.

22, 38, 45, 97, 50, 14, 81, 78

VII. Fill in the blanks with the appropriate measure words.

我有一_____好朋友，叫文国新。小文有四_____朋友,三_____是
新学生，一_____是美国留学生。小文有四_____老师，两_____是
中国人，两_____是美国人。

IV. Rearrange the following words to make correct sentences.

1. 這/叫/名字/什麼/個/人
2. 位/他/這/的/是/老師/朋友
3. 回來/他/了/那/好/了/太
4. 要/我/上課/去
5. 你/出差/中國/去/嗎

V. Complete the following dialogue.

A: 你好！

B: 你好_____！

A: 請問，您是美國學生嗎？

B: _____。

A: 太好了！這位是……？

B: _____。

A: 您好！請問,您貴姓？

C: _____。

A: 很高興 (gāoxìng, happy) 認識你們。對不起 (duìbùqǐ, excuse me), 我要去上課。一會兒見。

B: _____。

VI. Read the following numbers aloud in Chinese and write the first three in Chinese characters.

22, 38, 45, 97, 50, 14, 81, 78

VII. Fill in the blanks with the appropriate measure words.

我有一_____好朋友，叫文國新。小文有四_____朋友, 三_____是新學生，一_____是美國留學生。小文有四_____老師，兩_____是中國人，兩_____是美國人。

VIII. Choose the right words to fill in the blanks, and then read the conversation aloud with a partner.

1.是　2.是　3.是　4.吗　5.吗　6.吗　7.有　8.有　9.有　10.没　11.个　12.个

A: 你好。

B: 你好。

A: 我＿＿＿＿美国留学生。请问，您＿＿＿＿＿老师＿＿＿＿＿？

B: 我＿＿＿＿王老师。你＿＿＿＿＿中文名字＿＿＿＿？

A: ＿＿＿＿＿有，您给我起一＿＿＿＿中文名字吧。

B: 好。你＿＿＿＿中国朋友＿＿＿＿？

A: 我＿＿＿＿三＿＿＿＿中国朋友。

B: 很好。哦，要上课了，一会儿见。

A: 一会儿见。

VIII. Choose the right words to fill in the blanks, and then read the conversation aloud with a partner.

1.是 2.是 3.是 4.嗎 5.嗎 6.嗎 7.有 8.有 9.有 10.沒 11.個 12.個

A: 你好。

B: 你好。

A: 我_____美國留學生。請問，您_____老師_____？

B: 我_____王老師。你_____中文名字_____？

A: _____有，您給我起一_____中文名字吧。

B: 好。你_____中國朋友_____？

A: 我_____三_____中國朋友。

B: 很好。哦，要上課了，一會兒見。

A: 一會兒見。

第二课

LESSON 2

▶ I. A-not-A Questions
(See Textbook I, Lessons 4 and 9)

Selected examples from the textbook:

你会不会写汉字？(Lesson 4)
你昨天有没有吃什么不好的食物？(Lesson 9)

Another way to ask a question is to put the affirmative form of a verb and the negative form of the verb right next to each other. This is called an A-not-A question. In most cases, in an A-not-A question, the questioner is not expecting an affirmative more than a negative answer, or vice versa.

Note that in an A-not-A question, other question particles, such as 吗, cannot also be used. Additionally, sentences that contain adverbs, such as 都 (dōu, all) or 也 (yě, also), should not be used with the A-not-A question pattern.

Sentence structure:	S ＋ Affirmative V ＋ Negative V ＋ O
Or:	S ＋ Affirmative V ＋ O ＋ Negative V
Or:	S ＋ Affirmative V ＋ O ＋ Negative V ＋ O

Examples:

Nǐ shì bù shì Zhōngguó rén?
你是不是中国人？

Or: Nǐ shì Zhōngguó rén bù shì Zhōngguó rén?
你是中国人不是中国人？

Or: Nǐ shì Zhōngguó rén bù shì?
你是中国人不是？
Are you a Chinese (person) or not?
（Incorrect: 你是不是中国人吗？）

第二課
LESSON 2

▶ I. A-not-A Questions
(See Textbook I, Lessons 4 and 9)

Selected examples from the textbook:

你會不會寫漢字？(Lesson 4)

你昨天有沒有吃什麼不好的食物？(Lesson 9)

Another way to ask a question is to put the affirmative form of a verb and the negative form of the verb right next to each other. This is called an A-not-A question. In most cases, in an A-not-A question, the questioner is not expecting an affirmative more than a negative answer, or vice versa.

Note that in an A-not-A question, other question particles, such as 嗎, cannot also be used. Additionally, sentences that contain adverbs, such as 都 (dōu, all) or 也 (yě, also), should not be used with the A-not-A question pattern.

Sentence structure:	S + Affirmative V + Negative V + O
Or:	S + Affirmative V + O + Negative V
Or:	S + Affirmative V + O + Negative V + O

Examples:

Nǐ shì bù shì Zhōngguó rén?

你是不是中國人？

Or: Nǐ shì Zhōngguó rén bù shì Zhōngguó rén?

你是中國人不是中國人？

Or: Nǐ shì Zhōngguó rén bù shì?

你是中國人不是？

Are you a Chinese (person) or not?

(Incorrect: 你是不是中國人嗎？)

Nǐ xiǎng bù xiǎng jiā?

你想不想家？

Do you miss home?

（Incorrect: 你想不想家吗？）

Nǐmen chī Zhōngguó fàn bù chī?

你们吃中国饭不吃？

Do you want to eat Chinese food or not?

Nǐ xué diànnǎo bù xué?

你学电脑不学？

Do you study computer science?

Nǐ hé mèimei dōu xué kuàijìxué ma?

你和妹妹都学会计学吗？

Do you and your younger sister both study accounting?

（Incorrect: 你和妹妹都学不学会计学？）

Nǐ mèimèi yě xué Zhōngwén ma?

你妹妹也学中文吗？

（Incorrect: 你妹妹也学不学中文？）

Note: When the predicate is preceded by an auxiliary verb, it is the affirmative and negative forms of the auxiliary verb, not the predicate verb, that are to be placed together. For example:

For example:

Question: Nǐ kěyǐ bù kěyǐ jiāo wǒ Zhōngwén?

你可以不可以教我中文？

Can you teach me Chinese?

Answers: Wǒ kěyǐ jiāo nǐ Zhōngwén.

我可以教你中文。

Yes, I can teach you Chinese.

Wǒ bù kěyǐ jiāo nǐ Zhōngwén.

我不可以教你中文。

No, I can't teach you Chinese.

Nǐ xiǎng bù xiǎng jiā?

你想不想家？

Do you miss home?

(Incorrect: 你想不想家嗎？)

Nǐmen chī Zhōngguó fàn bù chī?

你們吃中國飯不吃？

Do you want to eat Chinese food or not?

Nǐ xué diànnǎo bù xué?

你學電腦不學？

Do you study computer science?

Nǐ hé mèimei dōu xué kuàijìxué ma?

你和妹妹都學會計學嗎？

Do you and your younger sister both study accounting?

(Incorrect: 你和妹妹都學不學會計學？)

Nǐ mèimèi yě xué Zhōngwén ma?

你妹妹也學中文嗎？

(Incorrect: 你妹妹也學不學中文？)

Note: When the predicate is preceded by an auxiliary verb, it is the affirmative and negative forms of the auxiliary verb, not the predicate verb, that are to be placed together.

For example:

Question: Nǐ kěyǐ bù kěyǐ jiāo wǒ Zhōngwén?

你可以不可以教我中文？

Can you teach me Chinese?

Answers: Wǒ kěyǐ jiāo nǐ Zhōngwén.

我可以教你中文。

Yes, I can teach you Chinese.

Wǒ bù kěyǐ jiāo nǐ Zhōngwén.

我不可以教你中文。

No, I can't teach you Chinese.

Note: In the above sentences, 可以 is an auxiliary verb. See Lesson 5 in this grammar book for details on auxiliary verbs.

▶ II. Usage of Adjectives
(See Textbook I, Lessons 1, 2 and 3)

Selected examples from the textbook:

你是新学生吗？(Lesson 1)
这个名字很好。(Lesson 1)
我才到纽约，英文不好。(Lesson 2)

1. As Predicates

In Chinese, adjectives may function as predicates. In such cases, no other verbs, such as 是, are needed at the same time. The adverb 很 is usually used before the adjective.

Affirmative sentence

> **Sentence structure:**   S + A

Examples:

Wáng Xiǎonián de Zhōngwén hěn hǎo.
王小年的中文很好。
Xiaonian Wang's Chinese is very good.
（Incorrect: 王小年的中文是很好。）

Gé Lín de Zhōngwén míngzi hěn hǎo.
格林的中文名字很好。
Green's Chinese name is very good.
（Incorrect: 格林的中文名字是很好。）

Wáng Xiǎonián de Zhōngwén liúlì. Gé Lín de Zhōngwén bù liúlì.
王小年的中文流利，格林的中文不流利。
Xiaonian Wang's Chinese is fluent; Green's Chinese is not fluent.
（Incorrect: 王小年的中文是流利，格林的中文是不流利。）

Note: In the above sentences, 可以 is an auxiliary verb. See Lesson 5 in this grammar book for details on auxiliary verbs.

▶ II. Usage of Adjectives
(See Textbook I, Lessons 1, 2 and 3)

Selected examples from the textbook:

你是新學生嗎？(Lesson 1)

這個名字很好。(Lesson 1)

我才到紐約，英文不好。(Lesson 2)

1. As Predicates

In Chinese, adjectives may function as predicates. In such cases, no other verbs, such as 是, are needed at the same time. The adverb 很 is usually used before the adjective.

Affirmative sentence

Sentence structure:	S + A

Examples:

Wáng Xiǎonián de Zhōngwén hěn hǎo.

王小年的中文很好。

Xiaonian Wang's Chinese is very good.

(Incorrect: 王小年的中文是很好。)

Gé Lín de Zhōngwén míngzi hěn hǎo.

格林的中文名字很好。

Green's Chinese name is very good.

(Incorrect: 格林的中文名字是很好。)

Wáng Xiǎonián de Zhōngwén liúlì. Gé Lín de Zhōngwén bù liúlì.

王小年的中文流利，格林的中文不流利。

Xiaonian Wang's Chinese is fluent; Green's Chinese is not fluent.

(Incorrect: 王小年的中文是流利，格林的中文是不流利。)

Negative sentence

Sentence structure:	S ＋ 不 ＋ A

Examples:

Zhège cāntīng bù xiǎo.

这个餐厅不小。

This cafeteria is not small.

（Incorrect: 这个餐厅不是小。）

Xiǎo Wáng de mèimei bù hǎo.

小王的妹妹不好。

Little Wang's younger sister is not good.

（Incorrect: 小王的妹妹不是好。）

Interrogative sentence

Sentence structure: Or:	S ＋ A ＋ 吗 S ＋ A ＋ 不 ＋ A

Examples:

Nǐ de Zhōngwén hǎo ma?

你的中文好吗？

Is your Chinese good?

Nǐ de Zhōngwén hǎo bù hǎo?

你的中文好不好？

Is your Chinese good?

Note: In interrogative sentences, 很 is not used.

2. As Attributes or Modifiers

Adjectives may also function as attributes or modifiers. If the adjective is a one-syllable word, no 的 is necessary. However, if the adjective is a two-syllable word, or if the one-syllable adjective is modified by an adverb, a 的 should be added.

Negative sentence

Sentence structure:	S + 不 + A

Examples:

Zhège cāntīng bù xiǎo.

這個餐廳不小。

This cafeteria is not small.

(Incorrect: 這個餐廳不是小。)

Xiǎo Wáng de mèimei bù hǎo.

小王的妹妹不好。

Little Wang's younger sister is not good.

(Incorrect: 小王的妹妹不是好。)

Interrogative sentence

Sentence structure:	S + A + 嗎
Or:	S + A + 不 + A

Examples:

Nǐ de Zhōngwén hǎo ma?

你的中文好嗎？

Is your Chinese good?

Nǐ de Zhōngwén hǎo bù hǎo?

你的中文好不好？

Is your Chinese good?

Note: In interrogative sentences, 很 is not used.

2. As Attributes or Modifiers

Adjectives may also function as attributes or modifiers. If the adjective is a one-syllable word, no 的 is necessary. However, if the adjective is a two-syllable word, or if the one-syllable adjective is modified by an adverb, a 的 should be added.

Examples:

xīn cāntīng

新餐厅
（Not: 新的餐厅）

new cafeteria

hěn xiǎo de diànnǎo

很小的电脑
（Not: 很小电脑）

very small computer

liúlì de Zhōngwén

流利的中文
（Not: 流利中文）

fluent Chinese

▶ III. The Adverb 都
(See Textbook I, Lesson 2)

Selected examples from the textbook:

你哥哥和妹妹都上学吗？(Lesson 2)
他们不都上学。(Lesson 2)
妹妹跟我都在纽约大学学习。(Lesson 2)

In an affirmative sentence, the adverb 都 (dōu) means "both" or "all," and it should precede the predicate. But in a negative sentence, the meaning of 都 depends on the location of the word. If 都 precedes 不 (bù) or 没有 (méiyǒu), it means "not at all" or "none." If 都 appears after 不 or 没有, it means "some" or "not all." Note that the nouns preceding 都 should be plural in number.

Examples:

xīn cāntīng
新餐廳
(Not: 新的餐廳)
new cafeteria

hěn xiǎo de diànnǎo
很小的電腦
(Not: 很小電腦)
very small computer

liúlì de Zhōngwén
流利的中文
(Not: 流利中文)
fluent Chinese

▶ III. The Adverb 都
(See Textbook I, Lesson 2)

Selected examples from the textbook:

你哥哥和妹妹都上學嗎？(Lesson 2)
他們不都上學。(Lesson 2)
妹妹跟我都在紐約大學學習。(Lesson 2)

In an affirmative sentence, the adverb 都 (dōu) means "both" or "all," and it should precede the predicate. But in a negative sentence, the meaning of 都 depends on the location of the word. If 都 precedes 不 (bù) or 沒有 (méiyǒu), it means "not at all" or "none." If 都 appears after 不 or 沒有, it means "some" or "not all." Note that the nouns preceding 都 should be plural in number.

Affirmative sentence

Sentence structure:	S ＋ 都 ＋ V ＋ O

Examples:

Wǒ bàba hé wǒ māma dōu shì dàxué jiàoshòu.

我爸爸和我妈妈都是大学教授。

Both my father and my mother are college professors.

Tā de yéye, nǎinai hé gēge dōu shuō Zhōngwén.

他的爷爷、奶奶和哥哥都说中文。

His grandfather, grandmother and elder brother all speak Chinese.

Wǒ hé wǒ péngyou dōu shàng xué.

我和我朋友都上学。

My friend and I both go to school.

Note: If the subject is single in number but the speaker wishes to emphasize a plural object, s/he should reverse the word order by moving the plural object to the beginning of the sentence.

Examples:

Zhōngwén hé Yīngwén wǒ dōu xiǎng xué.

中文和英文我都想学。

I want to learn both Chinese and English.

（Incorrect: 我都想学中文和英文。）

Dìdi hé mèimei wǒ dōu yǒu.

弟弟和妹妹我都有。

I have both a younger brother and a younger sister.

（Incorrect: 我都有弟弟和妹妹。）

(In these examples, although 都 is placed after the single subject 我, 都 is not used to modify 我, but instead modifies the plural objects: 中文和英文 and 弟弟和妹妹.)

Affirmative sentence

Sentence structure:	S ＋ 都 ＋ V ＋ O

Examples:

Wǒ bàba hé wǒ māma dōu shì dàxué jiàoshòu.

我爸爸和我媽媽都是大學教授。

Both my father and my mother are college professors.

Tā de yéye, nǎinai hé gēge dōu shuō Zhōngwén.

他的爺爺、奶奶和哥哥都說中文。

His grandfather, grandmother and elder brother all speak Chinese.

Wǒ hé wǒ péngyou dōu shàng xué.

我和我朋友都上學。

My friend and I both go to school.

Note: If the subject is single in number but the speaker wishes to emphasize a plural object, s/he should reverse the word order by moving the plural object to the beginning of the sentence.

Examples:

Zhōngwén hé Yīngwén wǒ dōu xiǎng xué.

中文和英文我都想學。

I want to learn both Chinese and English.

(Incorrect: 我都想學中文和英文。)

Dìdi hé mèimei wǒ dōu yǒu.

弟弟和妹妹我都有。

I have both a younger brother and a younger sister.

(Incorrect: 我都有弟弟和妹妹。)

(In these examples, although 都 is placed after the single subject 我, 都 is not used to modify 我, but instead modifies the plural objects: 中文和英文 and 弟弟和妹妹.)

1. Total Negation (not at all, none)

Negative sentences

Sentence structure:	S ＋ 都 ＋ 不/没(有) ＋ V ＋ O

Examples:

Xiǎo Zhāng hé Xiǎo Wén dōu bù shì zhōngxué lǎoshī.

小张和小文都不是中学老师。

Neither Little Zhang nor Little Wen is a middle school teacher.

Wǒ bàba hé wǒ māma dōu méiyǒu diànnǎo.

我爸爸和我妈妈都没有电脑。

Neither my father nor my mother has a computer.

Tāmén dōu bù xiǎngjiā.

他们都不想家。

None of them are homesick.

2. Partial Negation (not all of..., some but not all)

Sentence structure:	S ＋ 不/没有 ＋ 都 ＋ V ＋ O

Examples:

Wǒmen bù dōu shì xīn yímín.

我们不都是新移民。

Not all of us are new immigrants.

Tā de péngyou bù dōu xué Yīngwén.

他的朋友不都学英文。

Not all of his friends study English.

Lǎoshī hé xuésheng méiyǒu dōu huílái.

老师和学生没有都回来。

Not all the teachers and students came back.

1. Total Negation (not at all, none)

Negative sentences

Sentence structure:	S + 都 + 不/沒(有) + V + O

Examples:

Xiǎo Zhāng hé Xiǎo Wén dōu bù shì zhōngxué lǎoshī.

小張和小文都不是中學老師。

Neither Little Zhang nor Little Wen is a middle school teacher.

Wǒ bàba hé wǒ māma dōu méiyǒu diànnǎo.

我爸爸和我媽媽都沒有電腦。

Neither my father nor my mother has a computer.

Tāmén dōu bù xiǎngjiā.

他們都不想家。

None of them are homesick.

2. Partial Negation (not all of..., some but not all)

Sentence structure:	S + 不/沒有 + 都 + V + O

Examples:

Wǒmen bù dōu shì xīn yímín.

我們不都是新移民。

Not all of us are new immigrants.

Tā de péngyou bù dōu xué Yīngwén.

他的朋友不都學英文。

Not all of his friends study English.

Lǎoshī hé xuésheng méiyǒu dōu huílái.

老師和學生沒有都回來。

Not all the teachers and students came back.

Interrogative sentence

Sentence structure:	S ＋ 都 ＋ V ＋ O ＋ 吗

Examples:

Question: Nǐ hé nǐ jiějie dōu shì yīshēng ma?

你和你姐姐都是医生吗？

Are you and your elder sister both doctors?

Answer: Wǒ hé wǒ jiějie dōu shì yīshēng.

我和我姐姐都是医生。

My elder sister and I are both doctors.

Question: Nǐmen dōu xué diànnǎo ma?

你们都学电脑吗？

Do all of you study computer science?

Answer: Wǒmen bù dōu xué diànnǎo.

我们不都学电脑。

Not all of us study computer science.

Question: Nǐ hé tā dōu qù shāngxuéyuàn ma?

你和他都去商学院吗？

Do you and he both go to business school?

Answer: Wǒ hé tā dōu bù qù shāngxuéyuàn.

我和他都不去商学院。

Neither he nor I goes to business school.

▶ IV. Sentences with 在
(See Textbook I, Lesson 2)

Selected examples from the textbook:

妹妹在商学院学会计学。(Lesson 2)
"ABC" 就是在美国生的中国人。(Lesson 2)
我的老家也在广东。(Lesson 2)

Interrogative sentence

Sentence structure:	S ＋ 都 ＋ V ＋ O ＋ 嗎

Examples:

Question: Nǐ hé nǐ jiějie dōu shì yīshēng ma?

你和你姐姐都是醫生嗎？

Are you and your elder sister both doctors?

Answer: Wǒ hé wǒ jiějie dōu shì yīshēng.

我和我姐姐都是醫生。

My elder sister and I are both doctors.

Question: Nǐmen dōu xué diànnǎo ma?

你們都學電腦嗎？

Do all of you study computer science?

Answer: Wǒmen bù dōu xué diànnǎo.

我們不都學電腦。

Not all of us study computer science.

Question: Nǐ hé tā dōu qù shāngxuéyuàn ma?

你和他都去商學院嗎？

Do you and he both go to business school?

Answer: Wǒ hé tā dōu bù qù shāngxuéyuàn.

我和他都不去商學院。

Neither he nor I goes to business school.

▶ IV. Sentences with 在
(See Textbook I, Lesson 2)

Selected examples from the textbook:

妹妹在商學院學會計學。(Lesson 2)

"ABC" 就是在美國生的中國人。(Lesson 2)

我的老家也在廣東。(Lesson 2)

The word 在 (zài) is usually used together with a noun to indicate the location of a person or object. When a 在 phrase (i.e., 在 ＋ place word) appears before an action verb, it indicates the location of an action, or where an action is carried out.

在 can have many meanings in English, such as "in," "at," "on," "under," "in front of," "behind," etc. Therefore, to determine the exact meaning of 在 in a sentence, one should examine the context carefully.

1. To signify the location of a person or an object, follow this pattern:

Affirmative sentence	S ＋ 在 ＋ PW

Examples:

Wǒ de lǎojiā zài Guǎngdōng.
我的老家在广东。
My hometown is in Guangdong (province).

Wǒ jiějie zài Zhōngguó.
我姐姐在中国。
My elder sister is in China.

2. To tell the location of an action, or where an action is carried out, follow this pattern:

S ＋ 在 ＋ PW ＋ V ＋ O

Examples:

Tā bàba zài jiā chī fàn.
他爸爸在家吃饭。
His father eats meals at home.

Wǒ zài jiā kànshū.
我在家看书。
I study at home.

The word 在 (zài) is usually used together with a noun to indicate the location of a person or object. When a 在 phrase (i.e., 在 ＋ place word) appears before an action verb, it indicates the location of an action, or where an action is carried out.

在 can have many meanings in English, such as "in," "at," "on," "under," "in front of," "behind," etc. Therefore, to determine the exact meaning of 在 in a sentence, one should examine the context carefully.

1. To signify the location of a person or an object, follow this pattern:

> **Affirmative sentence**   S ＋ 在 ＋ PW

Examples:

Wǒ de lǎojiā zài Guǎngdōng.

我的老家在廣東。

My hometown is in Guangdong (province).

Wǒ jiějie zài Zhōngguó.

我姐姐在中國。

My elder sister is in China.

2. To tell the location of an action, or where an action is carried out, follow this pattern:

> S ＋ 在 ＋ PW ＋ V ＋ O

Examples:

Tā bàba zài jiā chī fàn.

他爸爸在家吃飯。

His father eats meals at home.

Wǒ zài jiā kànshū.

我在家看書。

I study at home.

Note: In these examples, the prepositional phrases of place 在家 must appear before the action verbs 吃 and 看. It's incorrect to say 他爸爸吃饭在家 or 我看书在家.

Negative sentence

Sentence structure:	S ＋ 不/没 ＋ 在 ＋ PW (＋ V ＋ O)

Examples:

Gāo lǎoshī bù zài jiā.

高老师不在家。

Professor Gao is not at home.

Tā bù zài dàxué xuéxí Zhōngwén.

他不在大学学习中文。

He doesn't study Chinese at the college.

Tā bàba bù zài shāngxuéyuàn gōngzuò.

他爸爸不在商学院工作。

His father doesn't work at the business school.

Qùnián tā méi zài wǒ jiā xuéxí Zhōngwén.

去年他没在我家学习中文。

He didn't study Chinese in my house last year.

Interrogative sentence

Sentence structure:	S ＋ 在 ＋ PW (＋ V ＋ O) ＋ 吗

Examples:

Nǐ mèimei zài zhè jiā Zhōngguó cānguǎn ma?

你妹妹在这家中国餐馆吗？

Is your younger sister in this Chinese restaurant?

Tā zài Běijīng gōngzuò ma?

他在北京工作吗？

Does he work in Beijing?

Note: In these examples, the prepositional phrases of place 在家 must appear before the action verbs 吃 and 看. It's incorrect to say 他爸爸吃飯在家 or 我看書在家.

Negative sentence

Sentence structure:	S ＋ 不/沒 ＋ 在 ＋ PW (＋ V ＋ O)

Examples:

Gāo lǎoshī bù zài jiā.

高老師不在家。

Professor Gao is not at home.

Tā bù zài dàxué xuéxí Zhōngwén.

他不在大學學習中文。

He doesn't study Chinese at the college.

Tā bàba bù zài shāngxuéyuàn gōngzuò.

他爸爸不在商學院工作。

His father doesn't work at the business school.

Qùnián tā méi zài wǒ jiā xuéxí Zhōngwén.

去年他沒在我家學習中文。

He didn't study Chinese in my house last year.

Interrogative sentence

Sentence structure:	S ＋ 在 ＋ PW (＋ V ＋ O) ＋ 嗎

Examples:

Nǐ mèimei zài zhè jiā Zhōngguó cānguǎn ma?

你妹妹在這家中國餐館嗎？

Is your younger sister in this Chinese restaurant?

Tā zài Běijīng gōngzuò ma?

他在北京工作嗎？

Does he work in Beijing?

Nǐmen zài xuéxiào kànshū ma?

你们在学校看书吗？

Do you study (read books) at school?

Tā zài jiā chī Měiguó fàn ma?

他在家吃美国饭吗？

Does he eat American food at home?

3. 有 Versus 在

The word 有 can also be used to indicate existence, which denotes that there is something or somebody at a certain place, whereas 在 indicates that the thing or person in question is located somewhere. Usually in a 有 sentence, the noun is indefinite, while in a 在 sentence, the noun is definite.

Sentence structure:	PW ＋ 有 ＋ N (indefinite)
Or:	N (definite) ＋ 在 ＋ PW

Examples:

Cānguǎn lǐ yǒu rén.

餐馆里有人。

There are people in the restaurant.

Tā bàba, māma zài jiā.

她爸爸、妈妈在家。

Her father and mother are at home.

Shāngxuéyuàn lǐ yǒu diànnǎo.

商学院里有电脑。

There are computers in the business school.

Wǒ mèimei zài Běijīng.

我妹妹在北京。

My younger sister is in Beijing.

Nǐmen zài xuéxiào kànshū ma?

你們在學校看書嗎？

Do you study (read books) at school?

Tā zài jiā chī Měiguó fàn ma?

他在家吃美國飯嗎？

Does he eat American food at home?

3. 有 Versus 在

The word 有 can also be used to indicate existence, which denotes that there is something or somebody at a certain place, whereas 在 indicates that the thing or person in question is located somewhere. Usually in a 有 sentence, the noun is indefinite, while in a 在 sentence, the noun is definite.

Sentence structure:	PW ＋ 有 ＋ N (indefinite)
Or:	N (definite) ＋ 在 ＋ PW

Examples:

Cānguǎn lǐ yǒu rén.

餐館里有人。

There are people in the restaurant.

Tā bàba, māma zài jiā.

她爸爸、媽媽在家。

Her father and mother are at home.

Shāngxuéyuàn lǐ yǒu diànnǎo.

商學院里有電腦。

There are computers in the business school.

Wǒ mèimei zài Běijīng.

我妹妹在北京。

My younger sister is in Beijing.

▶ V. Ordinal Numbers
(See Textbook I, Lesson 2)

Selected example from the textbook:

我是第三代移民。 (Lesson 2)

Ordinal numbers are made by adding the word 第 (dì) before a cardinal number.

Examples:

dì qī gè xuésheng
第七个学生
the seventh student

dì wǔ zhāng zhǐ
第五张纸
the fifth sheet of paper

Dì sān gè rén de Zhōngwén shuō de hěn liúlì.
第三个人的中文说得很流利。
The third person speaks Chinese very fluently.

Dì yī wèi lǎoshī xìng Huáng.
第一位老师姓黄。
The first teacher's surname is Huang.

Jīntiān wǒmen yào xué dì sān kè.
今天我们要学第三课。
Today we are going to study Lesson 3.

Note: 第三课 (dì sān kè) is different from 三课 (sān kè). The former means "Lesson 3," while the latter means "three lessons (or three chapters)."

▶ VI. Questions with 好吗 or 对不对
(See Textbook I, Lesson 3)

Selected example from the textbook:

去酒吧玩儿，好吗？ (Lesson 3)

▶ V. Ordinal Numbers
(See Textbook I, Lesson 2)

Selected example from the textbook:

我是第三代移民。(Lesson 2)

Ordinal numbers are made by adding the word 第 (dì) before a cardinal number.

Examples:

dì qī gè xuésheng
第七個學生
the seventh student

dì wǔ zhāng zhǐ
第五張紙
the fifth sheet of paper

Dì sān gè rén de Zhōngwén shuō de hěn liúlì.
第三個人的中文說得很流利。
The third person speaks Chinese very fluently.

Dì yī wèi lǎoshī xìng Huáng.
第一位老師姓黃。
The first teacher's surname is Huang.

Jīntiān wǒmen yào xué dì sān kè.
今天我們要學第三課。
Today we are going to study Lesson 3.

Note: 第三課 (dì sān kè) is different from 三課 (sān kè). The former means "Lesson 3," while the latter means "three lessons (or three chapters)."

▶ VI. Questions with 好嗎 or 對不對
(See Textbook I, Lesson 3)

Selected example from the textbook:

去酒吧玩兒，好嗎？(Lesson 3)

Both 好吗 (hǎo ma, is it all right? how about it?) and 对不对 (duì bù duì, is that correct? is it right?) can be placed at the end of a sentence to form a question. In a 好吗 question, the questioner asks the listener's opinion about what the questioner has suggested. In a 对不对 question, the questioner wants to confirm with the listener whether the information the questioner has provided is true.

Note that a comma is usually needed before 好吗 and 对不对. In addition to 对不对, one can also use 对吗. Please note that 好吗 and 对不对 can never be put at the beginning of a sentence.

Examples:

Question: Wǒmen chī Zhōngguó fàn, hǎo ma?

我们吃中国饭，好吗？

Let's eat Chinese food, is that all right?

（Incorrect: 好吗，我们吃中国饭？）

Answers: Hǎo, wǒmen chī Zhōngguó fàn.

好，我们吃中国饭。

All right, let's eat Chinese food.

Bù hǎo, wǒmen bù chī Zhōngguó fàn.

不好，我们不吃中国饭。

No, let's not eat Chinese food.

Question: Nǐ gēge zài Niǔyuē, duì bù duì?

你哥哥在纽约，对不对 (or 你哥哥在纽约，对吗)？

Your elder brother is in New York, is that correct?

（Incorrect: 对不对，你哥哥在纽约？）

Answers: Duì, wǒ gēge zài Niǔyuē.

对，我哥哥在纽约。

Correct, my elder brother is in New York.

Bù duì, wǒ gēge bù zài Niǔyuē.

不对，我哥哥不在纽约。

No, my elder brother is not in New York.

Both 好嗎 (hǎo ma, is it all right? how about it?) and 對不對 (duì bù duì, is that correct? is it right?) can be placed at the end of a sentence to form a question. In a 好嗎 question, the questioner asks the listener's opinion about what the questioner has suggested. In a 對不對 question, the questioner wants to confirm with the listener whether the information the questioner has provided is true.

Note that a comma is usually needed before 好嗎 and 對不對. In addition to 對不對, one can also use 對嗎. Please note that 好嗎 and 對不對 can never be put at the beginning of a sentence.

Examples:

Question: Wǒmen chī Zhōngguó fàn, hǎo ma?

我們吃中國飯，好嗎？

Let's eat Chinese food, is that all right?

(Incorrect: 好嗎，我們吃中國飯？)

Answers: Hǎo, wǒmen chī Zhōngguó fàn.

好，我們吃中國飯。

All right, let's eat Chinese food.

Bù hǎo, wǒmen bù chī Zhōngguó fàn.

不好，我們不吃中國飯。

No, let's not eat Chinese food.

Question: Nǐ gēge zài Niǔyuē, duì bù duì?

你哥哥在紐約，對不對(or 你哥哥在紐約，對嗎)？

Your elder brother is in New York, is that correct?

(Incorrect: 對不對，你哥哥在紐約？)

Answers: Duì, wǒ gēge zài Niǔyuē.

對，我哥哥在紐約。

Correct, my elder brother is in New York.

Bù duì, wǒ gēge bù zài Niǔyuē.

不對，我哥哥不在紐約。

No, my elder brother is not in New York.

▶ 练习 Exercises

I. Change the following questions into A-not-A questions.

Example: 你学中文吗？ → 你学不学中文？

1. 王小年是第三代移民吗？
2. 你有兄弟姐妹吗？
3. 你吃饭了吗？
4. 你妹妹学会计学吗？
5. 你朋友有中文名字吗？

II. Translate the following phrases into Chinese.

1. fluent Chinese
2. very good computer
3. American teacher
4. Chinese students
5. your father
6. my friend's computer

III. Rearrange the following phrases to make correct sentences.

1. 都/你们/想家/不/我们/呢
2. 可是/他/北京/不/老家/的/在/说/他/中文
3. 饭/去/跟/你/他们/中国/餐馆/吗/吃
4. 人/都/华裔/二/三/人/个/第/个/和/第/是
5. 妹妹/你/跟/英文/你/不/都/学院/在/学

IV. Correct the errors, if there are any, in the following sentences.

1. 我都学习中文和英文。
2. 你的老乡帮助你在学校吗？
3. 美国留学生不在餐厅吃饭。
4. 七个人叫高大新。
5. 我朋友家有四张人。

▶ 練習 Exercises

. . . .

I. Change the following questions into A-not-A questions.

Example: 你學中文嗎？ → 你學不學中文？

1. 王小年是第三代移民嗎?
2. 你有兄弟姐妹嗎?
3. 你吃飯了嗎?
4. 你妹妹學會計學嗎?
5. 你朋友有中文名字嗎?

II. Translate the following phrases into Chinese.

1. fluent Chinese
2. very good computer
3. American teacher
4. Chinese students
5. your father
6. my friend's computer

III. Rearrange the following phrases to make correct sentences.

1. 都/你們/想家/不/我們/呢
2. 可是/他/北京/不/老家/的/在/說/他/中文
3. 飯/去/跟/你/他們/中國/餐館/嗎/吃
4. 人/都/華裔/二/三/人/個/第/個/和/第/是
5. 妹妹/你/跟/英文/你/不/都/學院/在/學

IV. Correct the errors, if there are any, in the following sentences.

1. 我都學習中文和英文。
2. 你的老鄉幫助你在學校嗎？
3. 美國留學生不在餐廳吃飯。
4. 七個人叫高大新。
5. 我朋友家有四張人。

6. 这位大学很好。

7. 他和他弟弟不都是医生。

8. 她姐姐有中国朋友，对不对吗？

V. Translate the following phrases into Chinese, and then make up sentences of your own using each of the phrases.

1. the first foreign student

2. the second university

3. the third-generation immigrant

4. the tenth computer

5. the fifth professor

6. the second doctor

VI. Read the following passage and answer the questions.

张开是一个华裔学生。他的英文说得很流利，可是他的中文说得不好，因为(yīnwèi, because)他是在美国生、美国长的。张开的爷爷、奶奶在北京，他们都是医生。张开的爸爸、妈妈都在美国，他们不都是大学教授。

今年(jīnnián, this year)张开要去北京，因为在北京他可以去大学跟老师学习中文，也可以请他的爷爷、奶奶帮助他学习中文。

1. Does Zhang Kai speak Chinese well? Why or why not?

2. Where are Zhang Kai's grandfather and grandmother?

3. Are both Zhang Kai's father and his mother college professors?

4. Is Zhang Kai going to Beijing this year? Why or why not?

5. Do Zhang Kai's grandparents know Chinese?

VII. Choose the right words to fill in the blanks, and then read the conversation aloud with a partner.

1. 对不对　2. 有没有　3. 很好　4. 吗　5. 好吗　6. 都　7. 不　8. 在

A: 你_____中文名字？

B: 我有，我叫张学文。

A: 这个名字_____。

B: 你和你的朋友_____有中文名字_____？

6. 這位大學很好。

7. 他和他弟弟不都是醫生。

8. 她姐姐有中國朋友，對不對嗎？

V. Translate the following phrases into Chinese, and then make up sentences of your own using each of the phrases.

1. the first foreign student

2. the second university

3. the third-generation immigrant

4. the tenth computer

5. the fifth professor

6. the second doctor

VI. Read the following passage and answer the questions.

張開是一個華裔學生。他的英文說得很流利，可是他的中文說得不好，因為(yīnwèi, because)他是在美國生、美國長的。張開的爺爺、奶奶在北京，他們都是醫生。張開的爸爸、媽媽都在美國，他們不都是大學教授。

今年(jīnnián, this year)張開要去北京，因為在北京他可以去大學跟老師學習中文，也可以請他的爺爺、奶奶幫助他學習中文。

1. Does Zhang Kai speak Chinese well? Why or why not?

2. Where are Zhang Kai's grandfather and grandmother?

3. Are both Zhang Kai's father and his mother college professors?

4. Is Zhang Kai going to Beijing this year? Why or why not?

5. Do Zhang Kai's grandparents know Chinese?

VII. Choose the right words to fill in the blanks, and then read the conversation aloud with a partner.

1. 對不對　2. 有沒有　3. 很好　4. 嗎　5. 好嗎　6. 都　7. 不　8. 在

A: 你_____中文名字？

B: 我有，我叫張學文。

A: 這個名字_____。

B: 你和你的朋友_____有中文名字_____？

A: 我们_____都有，我有，他没有。

B: 你的朋友_____哪儿？

A: 他在大学。

B: 大学里有很多留学生，_____？

A: 对。

B: 我们去看你的朋友，_____？

A: 好。

A: 我們＿＿＿＿＿都有，我有，他沒有。

B: 你的朋友＿＿＿＿＿哪兒？

A: 他在大學。

B: 大學里有很多留學生，＿＿＿＿＿？

A: 對。

B: 我們去看你的朋友，＿＿＿＿＿？

A: 好。

第三课
LESSON 3

▶ **I. Telling Time**

(See Textbook I, Lessons 3 and 7)

Selected examples from the textbook:

下午四点，怎么样？(Lesson 3)

美东时间当天晚10点可以到波士顿。(Lesson 7)

In Chinese, the words used to tell time include: 点钟 (diǎnzhōng, o'clock), 半 (bàn, half hour), 刻 (kè, quarter hour), and 分 (fēn, minute).

1. O'clock

When expressing a particular hour, the numeral comes first, followed by the word 点钟 (diǎnzhōng). 点钟 can be shortened to 点 (diǎn).

Examples:

sì diǎnzhōng (or sì diǎn)

4:00 四点钟 （or 四点）

jiǔ diǎnzhōng (or jiǔ diǎn)

9:00 九点钟 （or 九点）

2. Minutes

In Chinese, the hour comes first, then the numeral and the word 分 (fēn, minute). When expressing hours and minutes together, the word 钟 (zhōng) should be dropped. Also, in spoken Chinese, if the total minutes exceed 10, the word "分" can be omitted.

Examples:

shí diǎn èrshí fēn (or shí diǎn èrshí)

10:20 十点二十分 （or 十点二十）

(Incorrect: 十点钟二十分 or 十点钟二十)

第三課
LESSON 3

▶ I. Telling Time
(See Textbook I, Lessons 3 and 7)

Selected examples from the textbook:

下午四點，怎麼樣？(Lesson 3)

美東時間當天晚10點可以到波士頓。(Lesson 7)

In Chinese, the words used to tell time include: 點鐘 (diǎnzhōng, o'clock), 半 (bàn, half hour), 刻 (kè, quarter hour), and 分 (fēn, minute).

1. O'clock

When expressing a particular hour, the numeral comes first, followed by the word 點鐘 (diǎnzhōng). 點鐘 can be shortened to 點 (diǎn).

Examples:

sì diǎnzhōng (or sì diǎn)

4:00 四點鐘 (or 四點)

jiǔ diǎnzhōng (or jiǔ diǎn)

9:00 九點鐘 (or 九點)

2. Minutes

In Chinese, the hour comes first, then the numeral and the word 分 (fēn, minute). When expressing hours and minutes together, the word 鐘 (zhōng) should be dropped. Also, in spoken Chinese, if the total minutes exceed 10, the word "分" can be omitted.

Examples:

shí diǎn èrshí fēn (or shí diǎn èrshí)

10:20 十點二十分 (or 十點二十)

(Incorrect: 十點鐘二十分 or 十點鐘二十)

qī diǎn sìshíbā fēn (or qī diǎn sìshíbā)

7:48 七点四十八分 （or 七点四十八）

（Incorrect: 七点钟四十八分 or 七点钟四十八）

Note: The word 零 (líng, zero) is usually added if the total minutes are less than 10. For example: 2:01 should be 两点零一分 (liǎng diǎn líng yī fēn), and 7:05 should be 七点零五分 (qī diǎn líng wǔ fēn).

In addition, the word 差 (chà, to be short of, lack) can be used if the minutes are close to the next hour. For instance, 10:55 can be expressed in three ways: 十点五十五分 (shí diǎn wǔshíwǔ fēn), 十一点差五分 (shíyī diǎn chà wǔ fēn) or 差五分十一点 (chà wǔ fēn shíyī diǎn).

3. Half an Hour

To express half an hour, put the word 半 (bàn, half) after the hour.

Examples:

sān diǎn bàn (or sān diǎn sānshí fēn)

3:30 三点半 （or 三点三十分）

bā diǎn bàn (or bā diǎn sānshí fēn)

8:30 八点半 （or 八点三十分）

4. Quarters of an Hour

Quarters of an hour are formed by the numeral 一 (yī, 1) or 三 (sān, 3) and the word 刻 (kè, quarter).

Examples:

wǔ diǎn yī kè (or wǔ diǎn shíwǔ fēn)

5:15 五点一刻 （or 五点十五分）

jiǔ diǎn sān kè (or jiǔ diǎn sìshíwǔ fēn)

9:45 九点三刻 （or 九点四十五分）

Note: Just as in English, in Mandarin Chinese, such expressions as 两刻 (liǎng kè, two quarters) and 四刻 (sì kè, four quarters) do not exist.

qī diǎn sìshíbā fēn (or qī diǎn sìshíbā)

7:48 七點四十八分 (or 七點四十八)

(Incorrect: 七點鐘四十八分 or 七點鐘四十八)

Note: The word 零 (líng, zero) is usually added if the total minutes are less than 10. For example: 2:01 should be 兩點零一分 (liǎng diǎn líng yī fēn), and 7:05 should be 七點零五分 (qī diǎn líng wǔ fēn).

In addition, the word 差 (chà, to be short of, lack) can be used if the minutes are close to the next hour. For instance, 10:55 can be expressed in three ways: 十點五十五分 (shí diǎn wǔshíwǔ fēn), 十一點差五分 (shíyī diǎn chà wǔ fēn) or 差五分十一點 (chà wǔ fēn shíyī diǎn).

3. Half an Hour

To express half an hour, put the word 半 (bàn, half) after the hour.

Examples:

sān diǎn bàn (or sān diǎn sānshí fēn)

3:30 三點半 (or 三點三十分)

bā diǎn bàn (or bā diǎn sānshí fēn)

8:30 八點半 (or八點三十分)

4. Quarters of an Hour

Quarters of an hour are formed by the numeral 一 (yī, 1) or 三 (sān, 3) and the word 刻 (kè, quarter).

Examples:

wǔ diǎn yī kè (or wǔ diǎn shíwǔ fēn)

5:15 五點一刻 (or 五點十五分)

jiǔ diǎn sān kè (or jiǔ diǎn sìshíwǔ fēn)

9:45 九點三刻 (or 九點四十五分)

Note: Just as in English, in Mandarin Chinese, such expressions as 兩刻 (liǎng kè, two quarters) and 四刻 (sì kè, four quarters) do not exist.

5. Morning, Afternoon and Evening Time

Unlike English, the words 早上 (zǎoshang, early morning) or 上午 (shàngwǔ, morning), 下午 (xiàwǔ, afternoon), and 晚上 (wǎnshang, evening) precede the specific time of day.

Examples:

zǎoshang qī diǎn
7:00 a.m. 早上七点

xiàwǔ sì diǎn yī kè
4:15 p.m. 下午四点一刻

shàngwǔ jiǔ diǎn bàn
9:30 a.m. 上午九点半

wǎnshang shí diǎn
10:00 p.m. 晚上十点

▶ II. Years, Months, Dates and Weekdays
(See Textbook I, Lesson 7)

Selected examples from the textbook:

她叫Susan White，12月18日坐西北航空公司251航班从
夏威夷到纽约肯尼迪机场。(Lesson 7)

如果25号早上6点走，到旧金山转机，美东时间
当天晚10点可以到波士顿。(Lesson 7)

A. 请告诉我信用卡号码和到期时间。
B. 5234-5678-9876-5432，2009年11月5日。(Lesson 7)

1. Years

Years in Chinese are read one number at a time, followed by the word 年 (nián, year).

Examples:

yī jiǔ jiǔ bā nián
1998 一九九八年

èr líng líng sì nián
2004 二零零四年

yī liù qī sān nián
1673 一六七三年

yī líng wǔ yī nián
1051 一零五一年

2. Months

In Chinese, the months of the year are formed by a number and the word 月 (yuè, month). The twelve months of the year are as follows:

5. Morning, Afternoon and Evening Time

Unlike English, the words 早上 (zǎoshang, early morning) or 上午 (shàngwǔ, morning), 下午 (xiàwǔ, afternoon), and 晚上 (wǎnshang, evening) precede the specific time of day.

Examples:

zǎoshang qī diǎn
7:00 a.m. 早上七點

xiàwǔ sì diǎn yī kè
4:15 p.m. 下午四點一刻

shàngwǔ jiǔ diǎn bàn
9:30 a.m. 上午九點半

wǎnshang shí diǎn
10:00 p.m. 晚上十點

▶ II. Years, Months, Dates and Weekdays (See Textbook I, Lesson 7)

Selected examples from the textbook:

她叫Susan White,12月18日坐西北航空公司251航班從
夏威夷到紐約肯尼迪機場。 (Lesson 7)
如果25號早上6點走，到舊金山轉機，美東時間
當天晚10點可以到波士頓。 (Lesson 7)
A. 請告訴我信用卡號碼和到期時間。
B. 5234-5678-9876-5432，2009年11月5日。 (Lesson 7)

1. Years

Years in Chinese are read one number at a time, followed by the word 年 (nián, year).

Examples:

yī jiǔ jiǔ bā nián
1998 一九九八年

èr líng líng sì nián
2004 二零零四年

yī liù qī sān nián
1673 一六七三年

yī líng wǔ yī nián
1051 一零五一年

2. Months

In Chinese, the months of the year are formed by a number and the word 月 (yuè, month). The twelve months of the year are as follows:

yī yuè	qī yuè
一月 January	七月 July
èr yuè	bā yuè
二月 February	八月 August
sān yuè	jiǔ yuè
三月 March	九月 September
sì yuè	shí yuè
四月 April	十月 October
wǔ yuè	shíyī yuè
五月 May	十一月 November
liù yuè	shí'èr yuè
六月 June	十二月 December

3. Dates

Although both 号 (hào) and 日 (rì) mean "date" and are sometimes used interchangeably, the former appears more frequently in spoken Chinese while the latter is used mostly in written Chinese.

Examples:

sān yuè bā hào	wǔ yuè shí rì
March 8	May 10
三月八号 (spoken)	五月十日 (written)

4. Weekdays

In spoken Chinese, the days of the week are expressed with the words 星期 (xīngqī, week) or 礼拜 (lǐbài, week), followed by a number. In written Chinese, the word 周 (zhōu, week) is normally used. Note that Sunday is the only exception to these rules. Instead of saying 星期七, 礼拜七 or 周七, one should say 星期日, 星期天, or 礼拜日, 礼拜天.

As in English, Saturday and Sunday may be referred to together as 周末 (zhōumò, weekend).

The seven days of the week are as follows:

xīngqī yī (lǐbài yī) or zhōu yī

星期一 (礼拜一) or 周一 Monday

yī yuè
一月 January

qī yuè
七月 July

èr yuè
二月 February

bā yuè
八月 August

sān yuè
三月 March

jiǔ yuè
九月 September

sì yuè
四月 April

shí yuè
十月 October

wǔ yuè
五月 May

shíyī yuè
十一月 November

liù yuè
六月 June

shí'èr yuè
十二月 December

3. Dates

Although both 號 (hào) and 日 (rì) mean "date" and are sometimes used interchangeably, the former appears more frequently in spoken Chinese while the latter is used mostly in written Chinese.

Examples:

sān yuè bā hào
March 8
三月八號 (spoken)

wǔ yuè shí rì
May 10
五月十日 (written)

4. Weekdays

In spoken Chinese, the days of the week are expressed with the words 星期 (xīngqī, week) or 禮拜 (lǐbài, week), followed by a number. In written Chinese, the word 週 (zhōu, week) is normally used. Note that Sunday is the only exception to these rules. Instead of saying 星期七, 禮拜七 or 週七, one should say 星期日, 星期天, or 禮拜日, 禮拜天.

As in English, Saturday and Sunday may be referred to together as 週末 (zhōumò, weekend).

The seven days of the week are as follows:

xīngqī yī (lǐbài yī) or zhōu yī
星期一 (禮拜一) or 週一 Monday

xīngqī èr (lǐbài èr) or zhōu èr

星期二 (礼拜二) or 周二 Tuesday

xīngqī sān (lǐbài sān) or zhōu sān

星期三 (礼拜三) or 周三 Wednesday

xīngqī sì (lǐbài sì) or zhōu sì

星期四 (礼拜四) or 周四 Thursday

xīngqī wǔ (lǐbài wǔ) or zhōu wǔ

星期五 (礼拜五) or 周五 Friday

xīngqī liù (lǐbài liù) or zhōu liù

星期六 (礼拜六) or 周六 Saturday

xīngqī tiān or xīngqī rì (lǐbài tiān or lǐbài rì) or zhōu rì

星期天 or 星期日 (礼拜天 or 礼拜日) or 周日 Sunday

(Incorrect: 星期七, 礼拜七 or 周七)

5. Word Order of a Series of Time Units

In Chinese, multiple time units are placed in descending order, with the largest time unit first and the smallest last.

Examples:

xiàwǔ wǔ diǎn

下午五点

5:00 p.m.

xīngqī sān wǎnshang shíyī diǎn

星期三晚上十一点

11:00 p.m. on Wednesday

èr líng líng yī nián shí yuè liù rì xīngqī yī xiàwǔ sì diǎn

二零零一年十月六日星期一下午四点

4:00 p.m., Monday, October 6, 2001

xīngqī èr (lǐbài èr) or zhōu èr

星期二 (禮拜二) or 週二 Tuesday

xīngqī sān (lǐbài sān) or zhōu sān

星期三 (禮拜三) or 週三 Wednesday

xīngqī sì (lǐbài sì) or zhōu sì

星期四 (禮拜四) or 週四 Thursday

xīngqī wǔ (lǐbài wǔ) or zhōu wǔ

星期五 (禮拜五) or 週五 Friday

xīngqī liù (lǐbài liù) or zhōu liù

星期六 (禮拜六) or 週六 Saturday

xīngqī tiān or xīngqī rì (lǐbài tiān or lǐbài rì) or zhōu rì

星期天 or 星期日 (禮拜天 or 禮拜日) or 週日 Sunday

(Incorrect: 星期七, 禮拜七 or 週七)

5. Word Order of a Series of Time Units

In Chinese, multiple time units are placed in descending order, with the largest time unit first and the smallest last.

Examples:

xiàwǔ wǔ diǎn
下午五點
5:00 p.m.

xīngqī sān wǎnshang shíyī diǎn
星期三晚上十一點
11:00 p.m. on Wednesday

èr líng líng yī nián shí yuè liù rì xīngqī yī xiàwǔ sì diǎn
二零零一年十月六日星期一下午四點
4:00 p.m., Monday, October 6, 2001

yī jiǔ jiǔ qī nián wǔ yuè bā rì xīngqī sì shàngwǔ shí diǎn bàn

一九九七年五月八日星期四上午十点半

10:30 a.m., Thursday, May 8, 1997

▶ III. Time Words
(See Textbook I, Lessons 3 and 7)

Selected examples from the textbook:

下午四点，怎么样？(Lesson 3)

12月24号上午8点离开夏威夷……(Lesson 7)

In Chinese, time words are placed before or after the subject. Unlike English, they are not put at the end of a sentence.

Examples:

Zhège xīngqī sān xiàwǔ wǒ qù kàn diànyǐng.

这个星期三下午我去看电影（or 我这个星期三下午去看电影）。

I'm going to see a movie this Wednesday afternoon.

（Incorrect: 我去看电影这个星期三下午）

Bā yuè shí hào wǒmen bù shàngxué.

八月十号我们不上学（or 我们八月十号不上学）。

We won't go to school on August 10.

（Incorrect: 我们不上学八月十号）

Jīntiān shàngwǔ tā qù tǐyùguǎn.

今天上午他去体育馆（or 他今天上午去体育馆）。

He's going to the gymnasium this morning.

（Incorrect: 他去体育馆今天上午）

▶ IV. Numbers
(See Textbook I, Lessons 3, 6, and 7)

Selected examples from the textbook:

坐14路公共汽车, 在大新路下车。(Lesson 3)

那你可以坐地铁。先坐6号车到大中央车站，……(Lesson 6)

yī jiǔ jiǔ qī nián wǔ yuè bā rì xīngqī sì shàngwǔ shí diǎn bàn

一九九七年五月八日星期四上午十點半

10:30 a.m., Thursday, May 8, 1997

▶ III. Time Words
(See Textbook I, Lessons 3 and 7)

Selected examples from the textbook:

下午四點，怎麼樣？(Lesson 3)

12月24號上午8點离开夏威夷…… (Lesson 7)

In Chinese, time words are placed before or after the subject. Unlike English, they are not put at the end of a sentence.

Examples:

Zhège xīngqī sān xiàwǔ wǒ qù kàn diànyǐng.

這個星期三下午我去看電影 (or 我這個星期三下午去看電影)。

I'm going to see a movie this Wednesday afternoon.

(Incorrect: 我去看電影這個星期三下午)

Bā yuè shí hào wǒmen bù shàngxué.

八月十號我們不上學 (or 我們八月十號不上學)。

We won't go to school on August 10.

(Incorrect: 我們不上學八月十號)

Jīntiān shàngwǔ tā qù tǐyùguǎn.

今天上午他去體育館 (or 他今天上午去體育館)。

He's going to the gymnasium this morning.

(Incorrect: 他去體育館今天上午)

▶ IV. Numbers
(See Textbook I, Lessons 3, 6, and 7)

Selected examples from the textbook:

坐14路公共汽車,在大新路下車。(Lesson 3)

那你可以坐地鐵。先坐6號車到大中央車站，……(Lesson 6)

她叫Susan White，12月18日坐西北航空公司251航班从夏威夷到纽约肯尼迪机场。 (Lesson 7)

旅行社：好，请告诉我信用卡号码和到期时间。

苏珊爸爸：5234-5678-9876-5432，2009年11月5日。 (Lesson 7)

1. Telephone Numbers

Telephone numbers are read one digit at a time. For example, (212) 485-9976 is "èr yī èr sì bā wǔ jiǔ jiǔ qī liù."

2. Room Numbers

Room numbers are also expressed one digit at a time, followed by the word 房间 (fángjiān, room). The word 号 (hào) can be inserted between the number and 房间. For example: Room 315 is 三一五房间 (sān yī wǔ fángjiān) or 三一五号房间 (sān yī wǔ hào fángjiān). Note: In the telephone and room numbers, 一 (yī) can also be pronounced as "yāo."

3. Bus, Train and Subway Numbers

Although both the words 路 (lù) and 号 (hào) can be used to refer to bus routes, the former is most commonly used in Mainland China. For subway or train routes, however, only the word 号 is acceptable. For example: 三十路公共汽车 (sānshí lù gōnggòng qìchē) or 三十号公共汽车 (sānshí hào gōnggòng qìchē) means "#30 bus," and 七号地铁 (qī hào dìtiě) stands for "#7 train."

4. Sizes for Clothes and Shoes

Use the word 号 (hào) when expressing clothing and shoe sizes. In Chinese, "size 4 sportswear" is 四号的运动衣 (sì hào de yùndòng yī) and "size 10 sweater" is 十号的毛衣 (shí hào de máoyī).

▶ V. Money Expressions
(See Textbook I, Lesson 5)

Selected examples from the textbook:

牛奶一块七毛钱半加仑、面包一块八毛九一袋。 (Lesson 5)

我给售货员八十块，她只找了我三块两毛二分钱。 (Lesson 5)

The Chinese monetary units include 元 (yuán, dollar), 角 (jiǎo, dime), and 分 (fēn, cent). In spoken or colloquial Chinese, 块 (kuài, dollar) and 毛 (máo, dime) are commonly used.

她叫Susan White,12月18日坐西北航空公司251航班從夏威夷到紐約肯尼迪機場。(Lesson 7)
旅行社：好，請告訴我信用卡號碼和到期時間。
蘇珊爸爸：5234-5678-9876-5432，2009年11月5日。(Lesson 7)

1. Telephone Numbers

Telephone numbers are read one digit at a time. For example, (212) 485-9976 is "èr yī èr sì bā wǔ jiǔ jiǔ qī liù."

2. Room Numbers

Room numbers are also expressed one digit at a time, followed by the word 房間 (fángjiān, room). The word 號 (hào) can be inserted between the number and 房間. For example: Room 315 is 三一五房間 (sān yī wǔ fángjiān) or 三一五號房間 (sān yī wǔ hào fángjiān). Note: In the telephone and room numbers, 一 (yī) can also be pronounced as "yāo."

3. Bus, Train and Subway Numbers

Although both the words 路 (lù) and 號 (hào) can be used to refer to bus routes, the former is most commonly used in Mainland China. For subway or train routes, however, only the word 號 is acceptable. For example: 三十路公共汽車 (sānshí lù gōnggòng qìchē) or 三十號公共汽車 (sānshí hào gōnggòng qìchē) means "#30 bus," and 七號地鐵 (qī hào dìtiě) stands for "#7 train."

4. Sizes for Clothes and Shoes

Use the word 號 (hào) when expressing clothing and shoe sizes. In Chinese, "size 4 sportswear" is 四號的運動衣 (sì hào de yùndòng yī) and "size 10 sweater" is 十號的毛衣 (shí hào de máoyī).

▶ V. Money Expressions
(See Textbook I, Lesson 5)

Selected examples from the textbook:

牛奶一塊七毛錢半加侖、麵包一塊八毛九一袋。(Lesson 5)
我給售貨員八十塊，她只找了我三塊兩毛二分錢。(Lesson 5)

The Chinese monetary units include 元 (yuán, dollar), 角 (jiǎo, dime), and 分 (fēn, cent). In spoken or colloquial Chinese, 塊 (kuài, dollar) and 毛 (máo, dime) are commonly used.

When there are dollars only, the use of the word 钱 (qián, money) is optional. When cents are added to the amount, however, the word 钱 is omitted.

Examples:

sānshíwǔ yuán (qián) (or sānshíwǔ kuài [qián])

¥ 35.00 三十五元（钱）(or 三十五块钱)

sìshíbā yuán (qián) (or sìshíbā kuài [qián])

¥ 48.00 四十八元（钱）(or 四十八块钱)

wǔ yuán qī jiǎo (qián) (or wǔ kuài qī máo qián)

¥ 5.70 五元七角（钱）(or 五块七毛钱)
（Incorrect: 五元七十分 （钱） (or 五块七十分钱)

shí yuán líng liù fēn (qián) (or shí kuài líng liù fēn qián)

¥ 10.06 十元零六分（钱）(or 十块零六分钱)
（Incorrect: 十元六分钱 or 十块六分钱)

Note: In Chinese, for amounts over 10 cents, one must use the word 角 or 毛. For example, ¥3.84 should be read as 三元八角四分钱 (sān yuán bā jiǎo sì fēn qián) or 三块八毛四分钱 (sān kuài bā máo sì fēn qián). It is incorrect to say 三元八十四分钱 (sān yuán bāshísì fēn qián) or 三块八十四分钱 (sān kuài bāshísì fēn qián).

In spoken Chinese especially, it is common to omit the word 钱 and sometimes even the words 角 (or 毛) and 分 as well. For ¥7.80, for instance, instead of giving the complete expression of 七块八毛钱 (qī kuài bā máo qián) or 七元八角钱 (qī yuán bā jiǎo qián), one can simply say 七块八毛 (qī kuài bā máo) or 七块八 (qī kuài bā).

▶ VI. The Particle 呢
(See Textbook I, Lesson 2)

Selected examples from the textbook:

（我)妈妈是医生，爸爸是大学教授。你呢？(Lesson 2)
你爸爸妈妈都是做什么的呢？(Lesson 2)

The particle word 呢 (ne, how about) follows a noun or a pronoun to ask a short, informal question about a person or an object, when the full question is implied by the context.

When there are dollars only, the use of the word 錢 (qián, money) is optional. When cents are added to the amount, however, the word 錢 is omitted.

Examples:

sānshíwǔ yuán (qián) (or sānshíwǔ kuài [qián])
¥ 35.00 三十五元(錢) (or 三十五塊錢)

sìshíbā yuán (qián) (or sìshíbā kuài [qián])
¥ 48.00 四十八元(錢) (or 四十八塊錢)

wǔ yuán qī jiǎo (qián) (or wǔ kuài qī máo qián)
¥ 5.70 五元七角(錢) (or 五塊七毛錢)
(Incorrect: 五元七十分（錢） (or 五塊七十分錢)

shí yuán líng liù fēn (qián) (or shí kuài líng liù fēn qián)
¥ 10.06 十元零六分(錢) (or 十塊零六分錢)
(Incorrect: 十元六分錢 or 十塊六分錢)

Note: In Chinese, for amounts over 10 cents, one must use the word 角 or 毛. For example, ¥3.84 should be read as 三元八角四分錢 (sān yuán bā jiǎo sì fēn qián) or 三塊八毛四分錢 (sān kuài bā máo sì fēn qián). It is incorrect to say 三元八十四分錢 (sān yuán bāshísì fēn qián) or 三塊八十四分錢 (sān kuài bāshísì fēn qián).

In spoken Chinese especially, it is common to omit the word 錢 and sometimes even the words 角 (or 毛) and 分 as well. For ¥7.80, for instance, instead of giving the complete expression of 七塊八毛錢 (qī kuài bā máo qián) or 七元八角錢 (qī yuán bā jiǎo qián), one can simply say 七塊八毛 (qī kuài bā máo) or 七塊八 (qī kuài bā).

▶ VI. The Particle 呢
(See Textbook I, Lesson 2)

Selected examples from the textbook:

(我)媽媽是醫生，爸爸是大學教授。你呢？(Lesson 2)
你爸爸媽媽都是做什麼的呢？(Lesson 2)

The particle word 呢 (ne, how about) follows a noun or a pronoun to ask a short, informal question about a person or an object, when the full question is implied by the context.

Note that although the word 吗 is also a question particle, it is attached to the end of a complete sentence only.

Examples:

Question: Wáng Xiǎomèi qù xué tiàowǔ, nǐ ne?

王小妹去学跳舞，你呢？

Xiaomei Wang is going to learn how to dance, how about you?

(Incorrect: 王小妹去学跳舞，你吗？)

Answer: Wǒ yě qù xué tiàowǔ.

我也去学跳舞。

I'm going to learn how to dance, too.

Question: Sūshān bù qù Wáng Xiǎonián de shēngrì wǎnhuì, Yuēhàn ne?

苏珊不去王小年的生日晚会，约翰呢？

Susan is not going to Xiaonian Wang's birthday party, how about John?

(Incorrect: 苏珊不去王小年的生日晚会，约翰吗？)

Answer: Yuēhàn yě bù qù.

约翰也不去。

John is not going either.

呢 can be used at the end of a question to indicate uncertainty. Very often it functions to soften the tone of the question.

Examples:

Shísì lù chēzhàn zài nǎr ne?

14路车站在哪儿呢？

Where is #14 bus stop? (The speaker is not sure.)

Yuēhàn shì bù shì Měiguórén ne?

约翰是不是美国人呢？

Is John an American? (The speaker is not sure.)

Note that although the word 嗎 is also a question particle, it is attached to the end of a complete sentence only.

Examples:

Question: Wáng Xiǎomèi qù xué tiàowǔ, nǐ ne?

王小妹去學跳舞，你呢？

Xiaomei Wang is going to learn how to dance, how about you?

(Incorrect: 王小妹去學跳舞，你嗎？)

Answer: Wǒ yě qù xué tiàowǔ.

我也去學跳舞。

I'm going to learn how to dance, too.

Question: Sūshān bù qù Wáng Xiǎonián de shēngrì wǎnhuì, Yuēhàn ne?

蘇珊不去王小年的生日晚會，約翰呢？

Susan is not going to Xiaonian Wang's birthday party, how about John?

(Incorrect: 蘇珊不去王小年的生日晚會，約翰嗎？)

Answer: Yuēhàn yě bù qù.

約翰也不去。

John is not going either.

呢 can be used at the end of a question to indicate uncertainty. Very often it functions to soften the tone of the question.

Examples:

Shísì lù chēzhàn zài nǎr ne?

14路車站在哪兒呢？

Where is #14 bus stop? (The speaker is not sure.)

Yuēhàn shì bù shì Měiguórén ne?

約翰是不是美國人呢？

Is John an American? (The speaker is not sure.)

▶ 练习 **Exercises**

. . . .

I. Translate the following phrases into Chinese. If there are several possible ways of saying a phrase, provide as many possibilities as you can.

1. ¥9.86

2. ¥50.05

3. Bus #78

4. 2:03 p.m.

5. 10:58 a.m.

6. Monday, November 3, 2002

7. 4:45 p.m., Friday, October 11, 1998

8. (718) 392-5436

9. Room 645

II. Answer questions 1–3 affirmatively, and questions 4–6 negatively.

1. 这个星期一你去电影院吗？

2. 明天小王的爸爸出差吗？

3. 你和你弟弟都有八十块钱吗？

4. 六月十五号你坐公共汽车吗？

5. 他们今天晚上十二点睡觉吗？

6. 五月三号他妹妹去电影院吗？

III. Correct the errors, if there are any, in the following sentences.

1. 我和我朋友去玩这个星期天。

2. 他妈妈给他四十一块五十分钱。

3. 我们十一点钟二十分去看晚会。

4. 王教授今天下午四点两刻教学生英文。

5. 现在是八点三分差。

6. 这个星期七小张想去跳舞。

7. 那个美国大片不有意思。

▶ 練習 Exercises

··

I. Translate the following phrases into Chinese. If there are several possible ways of saying a phrase, provide as many possibilities as you can.

1. ￥9.86

2. ￥50.05

3. Bus #78

4. 2:03 p.m.

5. 10:58 a.m.

6. Monday, November 3, 2002

7. 4:45 p.m., Friday, October 11, 1998

8. (718) 392-5436

9. Room 645

II. Answer questions 1–3 affirmatively, and questions 4–6 negatively.

1. 這個星期一你去電影院嗎？

2. 明天小王的爸爸出差嗎？

3. 你和你弟弟都有八十塊錢嗎？

4. 六月十五號你坐公共汽車嗎？

5. 他們今天晚上十二點睡覺嗎？

6. 五月三號他妹妹去電影院嗎？

III. Correct the errors, if there are any, in the following sentences.

1. 我和我朋友去玩這個星期天。

2. 他媽媽給他四十一塊五十分錢。

3. 我們十一點鐘二十分去看晚會。

4. 王教授今天下午四點兩刻教學生英文。

5. 現在是八點三分差。

6. 這個星期七小張想去跳舞。

7. 那個美國大片不有意思。

IV. Rearrange the following phrases to make meaningful sentences, and then translate your sentences into English.

1. 上午／我／出／星期五／门／九点／想

2. 英文／毛／这／分／是／本／十八块／九／六／书／钱

3. 看／晚上／我／电影／十点／和／在／我爸爸／家／想

4. 英文／得／流利／说／你／中文／的／都／和／很

5. 这／十字／个／路口／没／红绿灯／有

V. With a partner, ask each other to state your telephone numbers, room numbers, etc.

VI. Rewrite the following sentences using 呢.

Example: 我没有吃饭。你吃饭了吗？ → 我没有吃饭，你呢？

1. 我喜欢看美国大片。他喜欢看美国大片吗？

2. 小高的工作很好。小王的工作好吗？

3. 苏珊不去体育馆。约翰去体育馆吗？

4. 这个电影院大。那个电影院大吗？

VII. Fill in the blanks with 吗 or 呢.

1. 今天上午我去体育馆。你_____？

2. 我喜欢看电影。你也喜欢看电影_____？

3. 小张不喝可乐。小谢_____？

4. 他和他弟弟明天都出差_____？

5. 这个人很有意思。那个人_____？

6. 我在电影院下车。你_____？

7. 王小新有一个美国朋友_____？

8. 星期五你去跳舞_____？

9. 苏珊有没有男朋友_____？

10. 那个美国留学生是谁_____？

IV. Rearrange the following phrases to make meaningful sentences, and then translate your sentences into English.

1. 上午/我/出/星期五/門/九點/想
2. 英文/毛/這/分/是/本/十八塊/九/六/書/錢
3. 看/晚上/我/電影/十點/和/在/我爸爸/家/想
4. 英文/得/流利/說/你/中文/的/都/和/很
5. 這/十字/個/路口/沒/紅綠燈/有

V. With a partner, ask each other to state your telephone numbers, room numbers, etc.

VI. Rewrite the following sentences using 呢.

Example: 我沒有吃飯。你吃飯了嗎？→ 我沒有吃飯，你呢？

1. 我喜歡看美國大片。他喜歡看美國大片嗎？
2. 小高的工作很好。小王的工作好嗎？
3. 蘇珊不去體育館。約翰去 體育館嗎？
4. 這個電影院大。那個電影院大嗎？

VII. Fill in the blanks with 嗎 or 呢.

1. 今天上午我去體育館。你_____？
2. 我喜歡看電影。你也喜歡看電影_____？
3. 小張不喝可樂。小謝_____？
4. 他和他弟弟明天都出差_____？
5. 這個人很有意思。那個人_____？
6. 我在電影院下車。你_____？
7. 王小新有一個美國朋友_____？
8. 星期五你去跳舞_____？
9. 蘇珊有沒有男朋友_____？
10. 那個美國留學生是誰_____？

VIII. Choose the right words to fill in the blanks, and then read the conversation aloud with a partner.

1.明天 2.吗 3.四点 4.下午 5.呢 6.吗 7. 两点 8.明天 9.2005年8月
10.1986年9月1号

A: 我＿＿＿＿＿＿＿下午＿＿＿＿＿＿＿去看美国大片。你去＿＿＿＿＿＿＿？

B: 我不去，我要去学校。

A: 你几点去学校？

B: 我＿＿＿＿＿＿＿去。你＿＿＿＿＿＿＿？

A: 我＿＿＿＿＿＿＿不去学校。你是＿＿＿＿＿＿＿上大学的，对不对？

B: 不，我是2006年9月1号上大学的。那天我跟你去了王小年的生日晚会。

A: 对，王小年的生日是＿＿＿＿＿＿＿。

B: 你可以跟王小年去看电影。

A: 你有他的电话 (diànhuà, telephone number)＿＿＿＿＿＿＿?

B: 我有，(212) 485-9976。

A: 太好了。

VIII. Choose the right words to fill in the blanks, and then read the conversation aloud with a partner.

1. 明天 2. 嗎 3. 四點 4. 下午 5. 呢 6. 嗎 7. 兩點 8. 明天 9. 2005年8月
10. 1986年9月1號

A: 我_____下午_____去看美國大片。你去_____?

B: 我不去，我要去學校。

A: 你幾點去學校?

B: 我_____去。你_____?

A: 我_____不去學校。你是_____上大學的，對不對?

B: 不，我是2006年9月1號上大學的。那天我跟你去了王小年的生日晚會。

A: 對，王小年的生日是_____。

B: 你可以跟王小年去看電影。

A: 你有他的電話(diànhuà, telephone number)_____?

B: 我有，(212) 485-9976。

A: 太好了。

第四课
LESSON 4

....

▶ I. Question Words
(See Textbook I, Lessons 1, 2 and 4)

Selected examples from the textbook:

你叫什么名字？(Lesson 1)

你的老家在哪儿？(Lesson 2)

你怎么会说中文？(Lesson 4)

In modern Chinese, the most frequently used question words are: 谁 (shéi, who or whom), 什么 (shénme, what), 哪 (nǎ, which), 哪儿 (nǎr, where), 几 (jǐ, how many, for a number under ten), 多少 (duōshǎo, how many or how much, for a number above ten), 怎么 (zěnme, how or how come), and 怎么样 (zěnmeyàng, how about).

When using a question word to ask a question, pay attention to the following two points: (1) a question word is placed where the questioner expects the answer, and so there is no need to reverse the word order of a sentence as in English; (2) question particles such as 吗 are not used at the same time.

Examples:

Question: Nǐ dǒng nǎ jù huà?

你懂哪句话？

Which sentence do you understand?

(Incorrect: 哪句话你懂？or 你懂哪句话吗？)

Answer: Wǒ dǒng zhè jù huà.

我懂这句话。

I understand this sentence.

第四課
LESSON 4

▶ **I. Question Words**
(See Textbook I, Lessons 1, 2 and 4)

Selected examples from the textbook:

你叫什麼名字？(Lesson 1)
你的老家在哪兒？(Lesson 2)
你怎麼會說中文？(Lesson 4)

In modern Chinese, the most frequently used question words are: 誰 (shéi, who or whom), 什麼 (shénme, what), 哪 (nǎ, which), 哪兒 (nǎr, where), 幾 (jǐ, how many, for a number under ten), 多少 (duōshǎo, how many or how much, for a number above ten), 怎麼 (zěnme, how or how come), and 怎麼樣 (zěnmeyàng, how about).

When using a question word to ask a question, pay attention to the following two points: (1) a question word is placed where the questioner expects the answer, and so there is no need to reverse the word order of a sentence as in English; (2) question particles such as 嗎 are not used at the same time.

Examples:

Question: Nǐ dǒng nǎ jù huà?
你懂哪句話？
Which sentence do you understand?
(Incorrect: 哪句話你懂? or 你懂哪句話嗎？)

Answer: Wǒ dǒng zhè jù huà.
我懂這句話。
I understand this sentence.

Question: Nǐ zài nǎr kàn Zhōngwén shū?

你在哪儿看中文书？

Where do you read Chinese books?

（Incorrect: 哪儿你在看中文书？or 你在哪儿看中文书吗？）

Answer: Wǒ zài jiā kàn Zhōngwén shū.

我在家看中文书。

I read Chinese books at home.

Question: Tā rènshí duōshǎo Hànzì?

他认识多少汉字？

How many Chinese characters does he know?

（Incorrect: 多少汉字他认识？or 他认识多少汉字吗？）

Answer: Tā rènshí jiǔbǎi gè Hànzì.

他认识九百个汉字。

He knows 900 Chinese characters.

Question: Nǐ bā diǎn kāishǐ xué shénme?

你八点开始学什么？

What will you begin to study at eight o'clock?

（Incorrect: 什么你八点开始学？or 你八点开始学什么吗？）

Answer: Wǒ bā diǎn kāishǐ xué pīnyīn.

我八点开始学拼音。

I'll begin studying pinyin at eight o'clock.

▶ II. Topic-Comment Sentences
(See Textbook I, Lesson 8)

Selected example from the textbook:

每份信件邮局都要登记，收件人要签字。(Lesson 8)

A topic-comment sentence is made by putting a topic at the beginning of a sentence and then commenting on it. Topic-comment sentences are different from the subject-predicate sentences introduced earlier in this book. A subject is usually an agent or doer of the action. But in a topic-comment sentence, the topic shows the focus of the sentence, not necessarily the subject of the sentence.

Question: Nǐ zài nǎr kàn Zhōngwén shū?

你在哪兒看中文書？

Where do you read Chinese books?

(Incorrect: 哪兒你在看中文書？ or 你在哪兒看中文書嗎？)

Answer: Wǒ zài jiā kàn Zhōngwén shū.

我在家看中文書。

I read Chinese books at home.

Question: Tā rènshí duōshǎo Hànzì?

他認識多少漢字？

How many Chinese characters does he know?

(Incorrect: 多少漢字他認識？ or 他認識多少漢字嗎？)

Answer: Tā rènshí jiǔbǎi gè Hànzì.

他認識九百個漢字。

He knows 900 Chinese characters.

Question: Nǐ bā diǎn kāishǐ xué shénme?

你八點開始學什麼？

What will you begin to study at eight o'clock?

(Incorrect: 什麼你八點開始學？ or 你八點開始學什麼嗎？)

Answer: Wǒ bā diǎn kāishǐ xué pīnyīn.

我八點開始學拼音。

I'll begin studying pinyin at eight o'clock.

▶ II. Topic-Comment Sentences
(See Textbook I, Lesson 8)

Selected example from the textbook:

每份信件郵局都要登記，收件人要簽字。 (Lesson 8)

A topic-comment sentence is made by putting a topic at the beginning of a sentence and then commenting on it. Topic-comment sentences are different from the subject-predicate sentences introduced earlier in this book. A subject is usually an agent or doer of the action. But in a topic-comment sentence, the topic shows the focus of the sentence, not necessarily the subject of the sentence.

Examples:

Zhōngwén diànyǐng tā juéde hěn yǒuyìsi.

中文电影他觉得很有意思。

Topic Comment

Chinese movies—he thinks they're very interesting. (He thinks that Chinese movies are very interesting).

Zhōngguó fàn wǒmen dōu xǐhuān.

中国饭我们都喜欢。

Topic Comment

Chinese food—we all like it. (We all like Chinese food).

Gēn Wáng lǎoshī xué Zhōngwén tèbié yǒuyìsi.

跟王老师学中文特别有意思。

Topic Comment

Learning Chinese with Professor Wang is really interesting. (It's really interesting to learn Chinese with Professor Wang).

▶ III. Pivotal Sentences
(See Textbook I, Lesson 3)

Selected example from the textbook:

王家生请张小妹去大华电影院看美国大片。(Lesson 3)

In this type of sentence, there are two verbs in the sentence, and the object (receiver) of the first verb is also the subject (actor) of the second verb.

Sentence structure:	S ＋ V1 ＋ NP (Pivot) ＋ V2
	↓　　　　　　↓
	Object (V1) / Subject (V2)

Examples:

Zhōngwén diànyǐng tā juéde hěn yǒuyìsi.

中文電影他覺得很有意思。

Topic Comment

Chinese movies—he thinks they're very interesting. (He thinks that Chinese movies are very interesting).

Zhōngguó fàn wǒmen dōu xǐhuān.

中國飯我們都喜歡。

Topic Comment

Chinese food—we all like it. (We all like Chinese food).

Gēn Wáng lǎoshī xué Zhōngwén tèbié yǒuyìsi.

跟王老師學中文特別有意思。

Topic Comment

Learning Chinese with Professor Wang is really interesting. (It's really interesting to learn Chinese with Professor Wang).

▶ III. Pivotal Sentences
(See Textbook I, Lesson 3)

Selected example from the textbook:

王家生請張小妹去大華電影院看美國大片。(Lesson 3)

In this type of sentence, there are two verbs in the sentence, and the object (receiver) of the first verb is also the subject (actor) of the second verb.

Sentence structure:	S + V1 + NP (Pivot) + V2
	↓ ↓
	Object (V1) / Subject (V2)

Examples:

Wáng Jiāshēng qǐng Zhāng Xiǎomèi kàn Měiguó dà piānr.

王家生请张小妹看美国大片儿。

Jiasheng Wang is inviting Xiaomei Zhang to see an "American Blockbuster" movie.

Yuēhàn jiào Sūshān zài jiā shuìjiào.

约翰叫苏珊在家睡觉。

John told Susan to sleep at home.

Lǎoshī jiào wǒ men fā zhǔn měi yī gè yīn hé shēngdiào.

老师叫我们发准每一个音和声调。

The teacher asked us to pronounce every sound and tone accurately.

Notes: 1. In general, verbs such as 请, 叫, 让 indicating request, command, etc., act as the first verb in a pivotal sentence.

2. The second verb indicates the purpose and result of the first verb. For example: in the sentence 王家生请张小妹看美国大片, "看美国大片" is the purpose of "请."

3. In the negative form of a pivotal sentence, the negative adverb 没有 or 不 is generally placed before the first verb. For example: 王家生没有请张小妹看美国大片。 It is incorrect to say: (王家生请张小妹没有看美国大片。)

▶ IV. The Particle 吧
(See Textbook I, Lesson 2, 3)

Selected examples from the textbook:

我们去吃中国饭吧。 (Lesson 2)

张小妹，我们明天去看电影吧。 (Lesson 3)

1. Statements with 吧

吧 (ba) can be used at the end of a statement to make a request or suggestion.

Sentence structure:	S ＋ V ＋ O ＋ 吧

Examples:

Wáng Jiāshēng qǐng Zhāng Xiǎomèi kàn Měiguó dà piānr.

王家生請張小妹看美國大片兒。

Jiasheng Wang is inviting Xiaomei Zhang to see an "American Blockbuster" movie.

Yuēhàn jiào Sūshān zài jiā shuìjiào.

約翰叫蘇珊在家睡覺。

John told Susan to sleep at home.

Lǎoshī jiào wǒ men fā zhǔn měi yī gè yīn hé shēngdiào.

老師叫我們發準每一個音和聲調。

The teacher asked us to pronounce every sound and tone accurately.

Notes: 1. In general, verbs such as 請, 叫, 讓 indicating request, command, etc., act as the first verb in a pivotal sentence.

2. The second verb indicates the purpose and result of the first verb. For example: in the sentence 王家生請張小妹看美國大片, "看美國大片" is the purpose of "請."

3. In the negative form of a pivotal sentence, the negative adverb 沒有 or 不 is generally placed before the first verb. For example: 王家生沒有請張小妹看美國大片。It is incorrect to say: (王家生請張小妹沒有看美國大片。)

▶ IV. The Particle 吧
(See Textbook I, Lesson 2, 3)

Selected examples from the textbook:

> 我們去吃中國飯吧。(Lesson 2)
> 張小妹，我們明天去看電影吧。(Lesson 3)

1. Statements with 吧

吧 (ba) can be used at the end of a statement to make a request or suggestion.

Sentence structure:	S + V + O + 吧

Examples:

Wǒmen qù wèn Cháng lǎoshī wèntí ba.

我们去问常老师问题吧。

Let's go to ask Professor Chang some questions.

Wǒmen qù tǐyùguǎn dǎqiú ba.

我们去体育馆打球吧。

Let's go to the gym.

(Wǒmen) shàng kè ba.

(我们)上课吧。

Let's begin class.

2. Questions with 吧

吧 (ba) can be added to the end of a descriptive statement to form a question. The 吧 question implies that, although the speaker can assume something to be a fact based on previous experience, s/he is not entirely sure if s/he is correct. The speaker is looking for confirmation from the listener. In a 吗 question, on the other hand, the questioner makes no assumption about the answer to the question.

Sentence structure:	S ＋ V ＋ O ＋ 吧

Examples:

Question: Yuēhàn huì shuō Zhōngwén ba?

约翰会说中文吧？

John can speak Chinese, I suppose?

(Compare: 约翰会说中文吗？ Can John speak Chinese?)

Answers: (Duì,) tā huì shuō Zhōngwén.

(对，)他会说中文。

(Yes,) John can speak Chinese.

(Bù duì,) tā bù huì shuō Zhōngwén.

(不对，)他不会说中文。 (No,) he can't speak Chinese.

Examples:

Wǒmen qù wèn Cháng lǎoshī wèntí ba.

我們去問常老師問題吧。

Let's go to ask Professor Chang some questions.

Wǒmen qù tǐyùguǎn dǎqiú ba.

我們去體育館打球吧。

Let's go to the gym.

(Wǒmen) shàng kè ba.

(我們)上課吧。

Let's begin class.

2. Questions with 吧

吧 (ba) can be added to the end of a descriptive statement to form a question. The 吧 question implies that, although the speaker can assume something to be a fact based on previous experience, s/he is not entirely sure if s/he is correct. The speaker is looking for confirmation from the listener. In a 嗎 question, on the other hand, the questioner makes no assumption about the answer to the question.

Sentence structure:	S ＋ V ＋ O ＋ 吧

Examples:

Question: Yuēhàn huì shuō Zhōngwén ba?

約翰會說中文吧?

John can speak Chinese, I suppose?

(Compare: 約翰會說中文嗎？ Can John speak Chinese?)

Answers: (Duì,) tā huì shuō Zhōngwén.

(對，) 他會說中文。

(Yes,) John can speak Chinese.

(Bù duì,) tā bù huì shuō Zhōngwén.

(不對，) 他不會說中文。 (No,) he can't speak Chinese.

Question: Zhōngwén de yǔyīn hé yǔfǎ hěn nán ba?

中文的语音和语法很难吧？

Chinese pronunciation and grammar are difficult, I suppose?

(Compare: 中文的语音和语法很难吗？

Are Chinese pronunciation and grammar difficult?)

Answers: (Duì,) Zhōngwén de yǔyīn hé yǔfǎ hěn nán.

（对，）中文的语音和语法很难。

(Yes), Chinese pronunciation and grammar are difficult.

(Bù duì,) Zhōngwén de yǔyīn hé yǔfǎ bù nán.

（不对，）中文的语音和语法不难。

(No), Chinese pronunciation and grammar are not difficult.

▶ V. Usage of 的
(See Textbook I, Lesson 1, 2, 3 and 4)

Selected examples from the textbook:

他是我的中国朋友，叫文国新。(Lesson 1)
在美国生的中国人。(Lesson 2)
我们还没到喝酒的年龄。(Lesson 3)

Some of the most frequently used functions of 的 (de) are as follows:

1. After a Noun or a Pronoun to Indicate a Possessive

Examples:

Tā de Zhōngwén hěn hǎo.

他的中文很好。

His Chinese is very good.

Nǐ de wèntí shì shénme?

你的问题是什么？

What's your question?

Sūshān de gēge, jiějie

苏珊的哥哥、姐姐

Susan's brother and sister

Question: Zhōngwén de yǔyīn hé yǔfǎ hěn nán ba?

中文的語音和語法很難吧?

Chinese pronunciation and grammar are difficult, I suppose?

(Compare: 中文的語音和語法很難嗎?

Are Chinese pronunciation and grammar difficult?)

Answers: (Duì,) Zhōngwén de yǔyīn hé yǔfǎ hěn nán.

(對,) 中文的語音和語法很難。

(Yes), Chinese pronunciation and grammar are difficult.

(Bù duì,) Zhōngwén de yǔyīn hé yǔfǎ bù nán.

(不對,) 中文的語音和語法不難。

(No), Chinese pronunciation and grammar are not difficult.

▶ V. Usage of 的
(See Textbook I, Lesson 1, 2, 3 and 4)

Selected examples from the textbook:

> 他是我的中國朋友,叫文國新。 (Lesson 1)
> 在美國生的中國人。 (Lesson 2)
> 我們還沒到喝酒的年齡。 (Lesson 3)

Some of the most frequently used functions of 的 (de) are as follows:

1. After a Noun or a Pronoun to Indicate a Possessive

Examples:

Tā de Zhōngwén hěn hǎo.

他的中文很好。

His Chinese is very good.

Nǐ de wèntí shì shénme?

你的問題是什麼?

What's your question?

Sūshān de gēge, jiějie

蘇珊的哥哥、姐姐

Susan's brother and sister

tā de péngyou

他的朋友

his friend

2. After an Adjective to Modify a Noun

Examples:

hěn zhǔn de fāyīn

很准的发音

very accurate pronunciation

hěn gāo de rén

很高的人

a very tall person

Nà liǎng gè qiú, hóng de shì wǒ de, lǜ de shì nǐ de.

那两个球，红的是我的，绿的是你的。 (After 的, the noun is omitted.)

Of the two balls, the red one is mine and the green one is yours.

3. After a Time Word, Measure Word, or Money Expression to Modify a Noun

Examples:

Míngtiān de diànyǐng zài Dàhuá Diànyǐngyuàn.

明天的电影在大华电影院。

Tommorow's movie is at Dahua Movie Theater.

Wǒ shàng xiàwǔ sì diǎn de kè.

我上下午四点的课。

I take the 4:00 o'clock afternoon class.

Wǒ chī le wǔ kuài qián de Zhōngguó fàn.

我吃了五块钱的中国饭。

I ate five dollars' worth of Chinese food.

Wǒ yào kāi sān gè xiǎoshí de huì.

我要开三个小时的会。

I will have three hours of meetings today.

tā de péngyou

他的朋友

his friend

2. After an Adjective to Modify a Noun

Examples:

hěn zhǔn de fāyīn

很準的發音

very accurate pronunciation

hěn gāo de rén

很高的人

a very tall person

Nà liǎng gè qiú, hóng de shì wǒ de, lǜ de shì nǐ de.

那兩個球，紅的是我的，綠的是你的。 (After 的, the noun is omitted.)

Of the two balls, the red one is mine and the green one is yours.

3. After a Time Word, Measure Word, or Money Expression to Modify a Noun

Examples:

Míngtiān de diànyǐng zài Dàhuá Diànyǐngyuàn.

明天的電影在大華電影院。

Tommorow's movie is at Dahua Movie Theater.

Wǒ shàng xiàwǔ sì diǎn de kè.

我上下午四點的課。

I take the 4:00 o'clock afternoon class.

Wǒ chī le wǔ kuài qián de Zhōngguó fàn.

我吃了五塊錢的中國飯。

I ate five dollars' worth of Chinese food.

Wǒ yào kāi sān gè xiǎoshí de huì.

我要開三個小時的會。

I will have three hours of meetings today.

4. After a Verb to Introduce a Relative Clause

Examples:

Zhè shì wǒ chāoxiě de Hànzì.

这是我抄写的汉字。

This is the Chinese character that I copied.

Gélín wèn de wèntí bù duō.

格林问的问题不多。

The questions that Green asked are not too many.

(Green did not ask too many questions.)

Wǒ qù kàn xīn dào de Zhōngguó diànyǐng.

我去看新到的中国电影。

I am going to see the newly arrived Chinese movie.

Diànnǎo dǎ de Hànzì hěn hǎo kàn.

电脑打的汉字很好看。

The characters typed on a computer look very nice.

Note: the word order in a Chinese sentence containing a relative clause (a verb or clause with 的 modifying a noun) is counter-intuitive to English-speaking learners. In English a relative clause comes after the noun it modifies: "the Wang Laoshi who just got back from a business trip"; "the Chinese who were born in the US." But in Chinese such modifiers go before the nouns they modify: "the just-got-back-from-business-trip de Wang Laoshi" (出差回来的王老师, Lesson 1); "the born-in-the-US de Chinese" (在美国出生的中国人, Lesson 2).

5. Omission of 的

的 is omitted when a name of a country is used to modify a noun. For example: 中国电影 (Zhōngguó diànyǐng, Chinese movies), 美国老师 (Měiguó lǎoshī, American teachers).

If there is a close relationship between two people, 的 can also be dropped. For example: 我爸爸 (wǒ bàba, my father), 你哥哥 (nǐ gēge, your elder brother). However, 的 remains when one is talking about the relationship between a person and an object or an animal. For example: 李小姐的汽车 (Lǐ xiǎojiě de qìchē, Miss Li's car), 我的球 (wǒ de qiú, my ball).

4. After a Verb to Introduce a Relative Clause

Examples:

Zhè shì wǒ chāoxiě de Hànzì.

這是我抄寫的漢字。

This is the Chinese character that I copied.

Gélín wèn de wèntí bù duō.

格林問的問題不多。

The questions that Green asked are not too many.

(Green did not ask too many questions.)

Wǒ qù kàn xīn dào de Zhōngguó diànyǐng.

我去看新到的中國電影。

I am going to see the newly arrived Chinese movie.

Diànnǎo dǎ de Hànzì hěn hǎo kàn.

電腦打的漢字很好看。

The characters typed on a computer look very nice.

Note: the word order in a Chinese sentence containing a relative clause (a verb or clause with 的 modifying a noun) is counter-intuitive to English-speaking learners. In English a relative clause comes after the noun it modifies: "the Wang Laoshi who just got back from a business trip"; "the Chinese who were born in the US." But in Chinese such modifiers go before the nouns they modify: "the just-got-back-from-business-trip de Wang Laoshi" (出差回來的王老師, Lesson 1); "the born-in-the-US de Chinese" (在美國出生的中國人, Lesson 2).

5. Omission of 的

的 is omitted when a name of a country is used to modify a noun. For example: 中國電影 (Zhōngguó diànyǐng, Chinese movies), 美國老師 (Měiguó lǎoshī, American teachers).

If there is a close relationship between two people, 的 can also be dropped. For example: 我爸爸 (wǒ bàba, my father), 你哥哥 (nǐ gēge, your elder brother). However, 的 remains when one is talking about the relationship between a person and an object or an animal. For example: 李小姐的汽車 (Lǐ xiǎojiě de qìchē, Miss Li's car), 我的球 (wǒ de qiú, my ball).

▶ VI. Alternative Questions with (是)······还是
(See Textbook I, Lesson 6)

Selected example from the textbook:

那要看你是要省钱还是要方便。 (Lesson 6)

The (是)······还是 (shì...háishì) pattern forms an alternative question. In this type of question, the questioner offers two options or "alternatives" for the listener to choose from. The first 是 can be omitted.

Sentence structure:	S ＋ (是) ＋ V1 ＋ 01 ＋ 还是 ＋ V2 ＋ 02

Examples:

Question: Nǐ juéde Zhōngwén yǔfǎ nán háishì fāyīn nán?

你觉得中文语法难还是发音难？

Do you think Chinese grammar is difficult or pronunciation (is difficult)?

Answer: Wǒ juéde fāyīn nán.

我觉得发音难。

I think pronunciation is difficult.

Question: Sūshān de nán péngyǒu shì Yuēhàn háishì Gélín?

苏珊的男朋友是约翰还是格林？

Is Susan's boyfriend John or Green?

Answer: Sūshān de nánpéngyǒu shì Yuēhàn.

苏珊的男朋友是约翰。

Susan's boyfriend is John.

Question: (Shì) nǐ gēn wǒ tiàowǔ háishì Xiǎo Wén gēn wǒ tiàowǔ?

（是）你跟我跳舞还是小文跟我跳舞？

Who is going to dance with me, you or Little Wen?

Answers: Xiǎo Wén gēn nǐ tiàowǔ.

小文跟你跳舞。

Little Wen is going to dance with you.

Wǒ hé Xiǎo Wén dōu gēn nǐ tiàowǔ.

我和小文都跟你跳舞。

Both Little Wen and I are going to dance with you.

▶ VI. Alternative Questions with (是)…… 還是

(See Textbook I, Lesson 6)

Selected example from the textbook:

那要看你是要省錢還是要方便。(Lesson 6)

The (是)…… 還是 (shì…háishì) pattern forms an alternative question. In this type of question, the questioner offers two options or "alternatives" for the listener to choose from. The first 是 can be omitted.

> **Sentence structure:**   S ＋ (是) ＋ V1 ＋ O1 ＋ 還是 ＋ V2 ＋ O2

Examples:

Question: Nǐ juéde Zhōngwén yǔfǎ nán háishì fāyīn nán?

你覺得中文語法難還是發音難？

Do you think Chinese grammar is difficult or pronunciation (is difficult)?

Answer: Wǒ juéde fāyīn nán.

我覺得發音難。

I think pronunciation is difficult.

Question: Sūshān de nán péngyǒu shì Yuēhàn háishì Gélín?

蘇珊的男朋友是約翰還是格林？

Is Susan's boyfriend John or Green?

Answer: Sūshān de nánpéngyǒu shì Yuēhàn.

蘇珊的男朋友是約翰。

Susan's boyfriend is John.

Question: (Shì) nǐ gēn wǒ tiàowǔ háishì Xiǎo Wén gēn wǒ tiàowǔ?

(是)你跟我跳舞還是小文跟我跳舞？

Who is going to dance with me, you or Little Wen?

Answers: Xiǎo Wén gēn nǐ tiàowǔ.

小文跟你跳舞。

Little Wen is going to dance with you.

Wǒ hé Xiǎo Wén dōu gēn nǐ tiàowǔ.

我和小文都跟你跳舞。

Both Little Wen and I are going to dance with you.

▶ 练习 **Exercises**

....

I. Answer the following questions.

1. 谁觉得会话比较容易?

2. 第几课有一点难?

3. 他明天在哪儿练中文发音?

4. 老师问谁问题?

5. 你哥哥什么时候睡觉?

6. 你觉得那家中餐馆怎么样?

II. Make questions from these statements, focusing on the underlined parts.

Examples: 他是美国留学生 → 谁是美国留学生?

我哥哥喜欢看英文电影 → 你哥哥喜欢看什么电影?

1. 王医生是第三代移民。

2. 第六位老师是北京人。

3. 星期天我想看英文电影。

4. 今天下午两点他练唱歌。

5. 明天晚上我想在家做作业。

6. 老师要我们抄写五十个汉字。

7. 我哥哥觉得输入拼音比较容易。

8. 他觉得写作特别有意思。

III. Complete the pivotal sentences by using the hints in parentheses.

1. 王小年＿＿＿＿＿＿＿＿＿＿＿＿＿＿＿＿＿＿＿＿＿＿＿＿＿＿＿＿＿。
   (invites the Chinese student to eat Chinese food.)

2. ＿＿＿＿＿＿＿＿＿＿＿＿＿＿＿＿＿叫王小年去他们开的中餐馆吃饭。
   (Xiaonian Wang's parents)

3. ＿＿＿＿＿＿＿＿＿＿＿＿＿＿＿＿＿＿＿请王家生看美国大片。
   (Jiasheng Wang's girlfriend)

4. 约翰叫苏珊＿＿＿＿＿＿＿＿＿＿＿＿＿＿＿＿＿＿＿＿＿＿＿＿＿＿。
   (wait for him at the school gate)

► 練習 Exercises

I. Answer the following questions.

1. 誰覺得會話比較容易？
2. 第幾課有一點難？
3. 他明天在哪兒練中文發音？
4. 老師問誰問題？
5. 你哥哥什麼時候睡覺？
6. 你覺得那家中餐館怎麼樣？

II. Make questions from these statements, focusing on the underlined parts.

Examples: 他是美國留學生 → 誰是美國留學生？
我哥哥喜歡看英文電影 → 你哥哥喜歡看什麼電影？

1. 王醫生是第三代移民。
2. 第六位老師是北京人。
3. 星期天我想看英文電影。
4. 今天下午兩點他練唱歌。
5. 明天晚上我想在家做作業。
6. 老師要我們抄寫五十個漢字。
7. 我哥哥覺得輸入拼音比較容易。
8. 他覺得寫作特別有意思。

III. Complete the pivotal sentences by using the hints in parentheses.

1. 王小年 _____ 。
   (invites the Chinese student to eat Chinese food.)

2. _____叫王小年去他們開的中餐館吃飯。
   (Xiaonian Wang's parents)

3. _____請王家生看美國大片。
   (Jiasheng Wang's girlfriend)

4. 約翰叫蘇珊_____ 。
   (wait for him at the school gate)

5. 老师叫我们_____。

    (ask him questions)

IV. Change the following sentences into topic-comment sentences.

Example: 我不喜欢看电影。→ 电影我不喜欢看。

1. 我们都有中文名字。
2. 我们还没到喝酒的年龄。
3. 格林觉得中文的语法不太难。
4. 我也练习抄写汉字。
5. 王小年说中文说得不流利。

V. Translate the following phrases into Chinese and then use them to make up your own sentences.

    1. tomorrow's movie

    2. one gallon of milk

    3. ten dollars cash

    4. my English teacher

    5. your mother's car

    6. the student who did the homework

    7. Professor Huang who teaches me Chinese

    8. the computer that he used

VI. Fill in the blanks with 的 where necessary.

星期一上午我和我_____妹妹想去超级市场买东西。我除了要买三加仑_____牛奶、十块钱_____奶酪以外，还要买一件蓝色_____西装。我_____妹妹想买一些便宜_____刀、叉，还想买一些减价_____日用品。下午三点，我们想去看一个中国_____电影，因为下午_____电影比较便宜_____。晚上，我们想去吃美国_____饭。

5. 老師叫我們_____。

(ask him questions)

IV. Change the following sentences into topic-comment sentences.

Example: 我不喜歡看電影。 → 電影我不喜歡看。

1. 我們都有中文名字。
2. 我們還沒到喝酒的年齡。
3. 格林覺得中文的語法不太難。
4. 我也練習抄寫漢字。
5. 王小年說中文說得不流利。

V. Translate the following phrases into Chinese and then use them to make up your own sentences.

1. tomorrow's movie

2. one gallon of milk

3. ten dollars cash

4. my English teacher

5. your mother's car

6. the student who did the homework

7. Professor Huang who teaches me Chinese

8. the computer that he used

VI. Fill in the blanks with 的 where necessary.

星期一上午我和我_____妹妹想去超級市場買東西。我除了要買三加侖_____牛奶、十塊錢_____乳酪以外，還要買一件藍色_____西裝。我_____妹妹想買一些便宜_____刀、叉，還想買一些減價_____日用品。下午三點，我們想去看一個中國_____電影，因為下午_____電影比較便宜_____。晚上，我們想去吃美國_____飯。

VII. Form questions with (是)······还是, and then provide answers using the phrases below.

Example: 学计算机/学会计学

Question: 你(是)学计算机还是学会计学?

Answer: 我学计算机(or 我学会计学)。

1. 练习发音/练习会话
2. 用拼音输入汉字/手写汉字
3. 去体育馆/去电影院
4. 问一个问题/问两个问题
5. 在家睡觉/去生日晚会

VIII. Choose the right words to fill in the blanks, and then read the conversation aloud with a partner.

1. 吧 2. 吧 3. 抄写汉字和会话 4. 叫 5. 哪 6. 是······还是 7. 什么

A: 你今天下午要练习会话_____?

B: _____我都要练习。

A: 你练习_____课的会话?

B: 老师_____我们练习第四课的会话。

A: 我们一起练习_____。

B: 好。今天老师教的语法你都懂了吗?

A: _____语法?_____"跟"_____"小王他们"?

B: 是"跟。"

A: 我懂,我可以帮助你。

B: 那太好了。

VII. Form questions with (是)……還是, and then provide answers using the phrases below.

Example: 學计算机/學會計學

Question: 你(是)學计算机還是學會計學？

Answer: 我學计算机(or 我學會計學)。

1. 練習發音/練習會話
2. 用拼音輸入漢字/手寫漢字
3. 去體育館/去電影院
4. 問一個問題/問兩個問題
5. 在家睡覺/去生日晚會

VIII. Choose the right words to fill in the blanks, and then read the conversation aloud with a partner.

1. 吧 2. 吧 3. 抄寫漢字和會話 4. 叫 5. 哪 6. 是……還是 7. 什麼

A: 你今天下午要練習會話_____？

B: _____我都要練習。

A: 你練習_____課的會話？

B: 老師_____我們練習第四課的會話。

A: 我們一起練習_____。

B: 好。今天老師教的語法你都懂了嗎

A: _____語法?_____"跟"_____"小王他們"？

B: 是"跟。"

A: 我懂，我可以幫助你。

B: 那太好了。

第五课
LESSON 5

▶ **I. The Particle 得**
(See Textbook I, Lessons 2, 4 and 9)

Selected examples from the textbook:

你的中文怎么说得不流利？ (Lesson 2)
我说得还不好…… (Lesson 4)
我肚子疼得厉害。 (Lesson 9)

1. As a Complement

The word 得 (de) may function in a number of different ways.

Unlike in English, in Chinese, to make a comment on an action or to indicate how an action is done, one needs a complement. Complements are postmodifying elements that show the duration, quantity, degree, result, direction or possibility of an action and the extent of a quality of a thing. With some types of complements, a 得 should be placed between a verb-object structure and an adjective. Note that in this type of sentence (which is called a "complement of degree"), the action verb should be repeated, unless the object has been mentioned previously. Alternatively, to avoid repeating the verb or to emphasize the object, one can put the object before or after the subject.

Affirmative sentence

Sentence structure:	S ＋ V ＋ O ＋ V ＋ 得 ＋ A
Or:	O ＋ S ＋ V ＋ 得 ＋ A
Or:	S ＋ O ＋ V ＋ 得 ＋ A

Examples:

Tā mǎi chī de dōngxi mǎi de hěn kuài.
他买吃的东西买得很快。
He bought food quickly.

第五課
LESSON 5

▶ I. The Particle 得
(See Textbook I, Lessons 2, 4 and 9)

Selected examples from the textbook:

你的中文怎麼說得不流利？(Lesson 2)

我說得還不好……(Lesson 4)

我肚子疼得厲害。(Lesson 9)

1. As a Complement

The word 得 (de) may function in a number of different ways.

Unlike in English, in Chinese, to make a comment on an action or to indicate how an action is done, one needs a complement. Complements are postmodifying elements that show the duration, quantity, degree, result, direction or possibility of an action and the extent of a quality of a thing. With some types of complements, a 得 should be placed between a verb-object structure and an adjective. Note that in this type of sentence (which is called a "complement of degree"), the action verb should be repeated, unless the object has been mentioned previously. Alternatively, to avoid repeating the verb or to emphasize the object, one can put the object before or after the subject.

Affirmative sentence

Sentence structure:	S ＋ V ＋ O ＋ V ＋ 得 ＋ A
Or:	O ＋ S ＋ V ＋ 得 ＋ A
Or:	S ＋ O ＋ V ＋ 得 ＋ A

Examples:

Tā mǎi chī de dōngxi mǎi de hěn kuài.

他買吃的東西買得很快。

He bought food quickly.

Or: Chī de dōngxi tā mǎi de hěn kuài.

吃的东西他买得很快。

He bought food quickly. (As for food, he bought it quickly.)

（Incorrect: 他买吃的东西很快。 Or 他买吃的东西得很快。）

Tā chīfàn chī de tèbié duō.

她吃饭吃得特别多。

She eats a lot.

Or: Fàn tā chī de tèbié màn.

饭她吃得特别慢。

She eats especially slowly.

（Incorrect: 她吃饭吃特别慢。 Or 她吃饭得特别慢。）

Negative sentence

Sentence structure:	S ＋ V ＋ O ＋ V ＋ 得 ＋ 不 ＋ A
Or:	O ＋ S ＋ V ＋ 得 ＋ 不 ＋ A
Or:	S ＋ O ＋ V ＋ 得 ＋ 不 ＋ A

Examples:

Jīntiān tā mǎi dōngxi mǎi de bù duō.

今天他买东西买得不多。

He did not buy many things today.

（Incorrect: 今天他不买东西买得多。 Or 今天他买东西不买得多。）

Tā shuō Zhōngwén shuō de bù liúlì.

他说中文说得不流利。

He doesn't speak Chinese fluently.

（Incorrect: 他不说中文说得流利。 Or 他说中文不说得流利。）

Or: Chī de dōngxi tā mǎi de hěn kuài.

吃的東西他買得很快。

He bought food quickly. (As for food, he bought it quickly.)

(Incorrect: 他買吃的東西很快。 Or 他買吃的東西得很快。)

Tā chīfàn chī de tèbié duō.

她吃飯吃得特別多。

She eats a lot.

Or: Fàn tā chī de tèbié màn.

飯她吃得特別慢。

She eats especially slowly.

(Incorrect: 她吃飯吃特別慢。 Or 她吃飯得特別慢。)

Negative sentence

Sentence structure:	S ＋ V ＋ O ＋ V ＋ 得 ＋ 不 ＋ A
Or:	O ＋ S ＋ V ＋ 得 ＋ 不 ＋ A
Or:	S ＋ O ＋ V ＋ 得 ＋ 不 ＋ A

Examples:

Jīntiān tā mǎi dōngxi mǎi de bù duō.

今天他買東西買得不多。

He did not buy many things today.

(Incorrect: 今天他不買東西買得多。 Or 今天他買東西不買得多。)

Tā shuō Zhōngwén shuō de bù liúlì.

他說中文說得不流利。

He doesn't speak Chinese fluently.

(Incorrect: 他不說中文說得流利。 Or 他說中文不說得流利。)

Interrogative sentence

Sentence structure:	S ＋ V ＋ O ＋ V ＋ 得 ＋ A ＋ 吗 /A not A
Or:	O ＋ S ＋ V ＋ 得 ＋ A ＋ 吗/A not A
Or:	S ＋ O ＋ V ＋ 得 ＋ A ＋ 吗/A not A

Examples:

Xīn xuésheng xué yǔfǎ xué de hǎo ma?

新学生学语法学得好吗？

Do the new students study grammar well?

Nǐ yīn fā de zhǔn ma?

你音发得准吗？

Do you pronounce (Chinese) accurately?

Nǐ xiànjīn dài de duō bù duō?

你现金带得多不多？

Did you bring much cash?

Note: If the object was mentioned previously or it was made clear to the listener, one can drop the object in a sentence, and in that case, the verb is not repeated. For example:

新学生学得好；or 她吃得特别多。

2. Adjective + 得很

When 得很 (dé hěn, very, extremely) follows an adjective, the "adjective + 得很" phrase indicates the extent or degree that the adjective has achieved or the consequence the adjective has led to. In such sentences, other adverbs such as 很, 特别 or 非常 should not be used.

Examples:

Zhèr de máoyī duō dé hěn.

这儿的毛衣多得很。

There are lots of sweaters here.

(Incorrect: 这儿的毛衣非常多得很。)

Interrogative sentence

Sentence structure:	S + V + O + V + 得 + A + 嗎 /A not A
Or:	O + S + V + 得 + A + 嗎/A not A
Or:	S + O + V + 得 + A + 嗎/A not A

Examples:

Xīn xuésheng xué yǔfǎ xué de hǎo ma?

新學生學語法學得好嗎？

Do the new students study grammar well?

Nǐ yīn fā de zhǔn ma?

你音發得准嗎？

Do you pronounce (Chinese) accurately?

Nǐ xiànjīn dài de duō bù duō?

你現金帶得多不多？

Did you bring much cash?

Note: If the object was mentioned previously or it was made clear to the listener, one can drop the object in a sentence, and in that case, the verb is not repeated. For example:

新學生學得好；or 她吃得特別多。

2. Adjective + 得很

When 得很 (dé hěn, very, extremely) follows an adjective, the "adjective + 得很" phrase indicates the extent or degree that the adjective has achieved or the consequence the adjective has led to. In such sentences, other adverbs such as 很, 特別 or 非常 should not be used.

Examples:

Zhèr de máoyī duō dé hěn.

這兒的毛衣多得很。

There are lots of sweaters here.

(Incorrect: 這兒的毛衣非常多得很。)

Kělè piányi dé hěn.

可乐便宜得很。

Cola is extremely cheap.

（Incorrect: 可乐很便宜得很。）

Nǐ de fāngfǎ hǎo dé hěn.

你的方法好得很。

Your method is very good.

（Incorrect: 你的方法特别好得很。）

▶ II. Auxiliary Verbs 能, 会, and 可以
(See Textbook I, Lessons 2, 4 and 9)

Selected examples from the textbook:

你可以教我学中文。(Lesson 2)

请问, 你会说中文吗？(Lesson 4)

张小妹生病了，今天不能来上课了。 (Lesson 9)

An auxiliary verb is placed before a main verb, and its function in a sentence is to "help" the main verb by expressing ability, capability, intention, likelihood, etc. In a negative sentence, the word 不 should precede the auxiliary verb rather than the main verb. In A-not-A type questions, the auxiliary verbs, not the main verbs, are changed to the question form.

There are many auxiliary verbs in Chinese. In this lesson we will introduce the most commonly used ones.

Affirmative sentence

Sentence structure:	S ＋ AV ＋ V ＋ O

Negative sentence

Sentence structure:	S ＋ 不 ＋ AV ＋ V ＋ O

Kělè piányi dé hěn.

可樂便宜得很。

Cola is extremely cheap.

(Incorrect: 可樂很便宜得很。)

Nǐ de fāngfǎ hǎo dé hěn.

你的方法好得很。

Your method is very good.

(Incorrect: 你的方法特別好得很。)

▶ II. Auxiliary Verbs 能，會，and 可以
(See Textbook I, Lessons 2, 4 and 9)

Selected examples from the textbook:

你可以教我學中文。(Lesson 2)

請問,你會說中文嗎？(Lesson 4)

張小妹生病了，今天不能來上課了。(Lesson 9)

An auxiliary verb is placed before a main verb, and its function in a sentence is to "help" the main verb by expressing ability, capability, intention, likelihood, etc. In a negative sentence, the word 不 should precede the auxiliary verb rather than the main verb. In A-not-A type questions, the auxiliary verbs, not the main verbs, are changed to the question form.

There are many auxiliary verbs in Chinese. In this lesson we will introduce the most commonly used ones.

Affirmative sentence

Sentence structure:	S + AV + V + O

Negative sentence

Sentence structure:	S + 不 + AV + V + O

Interrogative sentence

Sentence structure:	S ＋ AV ＋ V ＋ O ＋ 吗
Or:	S ＋ AV ＋ 不 ＋ AV ＋ V ＋ O

1. 能

As an auxiliary verb, 能 (néng) can mean "to be able to" or "to be capable of," and is usually translated as "can."

Examples:

Tā xīngqī wǔ néng qù chāojí shìchǎng.

他星期五能去超级市场。

He can go to the supermarket on Friday.

Wǒ bù néng zuò zhège gōngzuò.

我不能做这个工作。

I cannot do this job.

Question: Tā néng bù néng lái wǒmen xuéxiào?

她能不能来我们学校？

Can she come to our school?

Or: Tā néng lái wǒmen xuéxiào ma?

她能来我们学校吗？

Can she come to our school?

Answers: Tā néng lái wǒmen xuéxiào.

她能来我们学校。

She can come to our school.

Tā bù néng lái wǒmen xuéxiào.

她不能来我们学校。

She cannot come to our school.

The other meaning of 能 is "to permit" or "to be permitted to."

Interrogative sentence

Sentence structure:	S + AV + V + O + 嗎
Or:	S + AV + 不 + AV + V + O

1. 能

As an auxiliary verb, 能 (néng) can mean "to be able to" or "to be capable of," and is usually translated as "can."

Examples:

Tā xīngqī wǔ néng qù chāojí shìchǎng.

他星期五能去超級市場。

He can go to the supermarket on Friday.

Wǒ bù néng zuò zhège gōngzuò.

我不能做這個工作。

I cannot do this job.

Question: Tā néng bù néng lái wǒmen xuéxiào?

她能不能來我們學校？

Can she come to our school?

Or: Tā néng lái wǒmen xuéxiào ma?

她能來我們學校嗎？

Can she come to our school?

Answers: Tā néng lái wǒmen xuéxiào.

她能來我們學校。

She can come to our school.

Tā bù néng lái wǒmen xuéxiào.

她不能來我們學校。

She cannot come to our school.

The other meaning of 能 is "to permit" or "to be permitted to."

Examples:

Zhāng yīshēng shuō wǒ xiànzài bù néng hē niúnǎi.

张医生说我现在不能喝牛奶。

Doctor Zhang said that I'm not supposed to drink milk now.

Nǐ néng kāi wǒ de qìchē.

你能开我的汽车。

You are allowed to drive my car.

2. 会

As an auxiliary verb, 会 (huì) means "to be able to," "can," or "it's likely that."

Examples:

Míngtiān nǐ huì děng wǒ ma?

明天你会等我吗?

Are you able to wait for me tomorrow?

Shí diǎn le, tāmen jīntiān bù huì lái le.

十点了，他们今天不会来了。

It's already 10:00; it's not likely that they will come today.

3. 能 Versus 会

Both 能 and 会 can mean "to be able to" and they can sometimes be used interchangeably. But when expressing the idea of "having the learned skill to do something, 会 should be used.

Examples:

Sì niánjí de xuésheng dōu huì shuō Zhōngwén.

四年级的学生都会说中文。

The fourth-year students can all speak Chinese.

(Or: 四年级的学生都能说中文。)

Examples:

Zhāng yīshēng shuō wǒ xiànzài bù néng hē niúnǎi.

張醫生說我現在不能喝牛奶。

Doctor Zhang said that I'm not supposed to drink milk now.

Nǐ néng kāi wǒ de qìchē.

你能開我的汽車。

You are allowed to drive my car.

2. 會

As an auxiliary verb, 會 (huì) means "to be able to," "can," or "it's likely that."

Examples:

Míngtiān nǐ huì děng wǒ ma?

明天你會等我嗎？

Are you able to wait for me tomorrow?

Shí diǎn le, tāmen jīntiān bù huì lái le.

十點了，他們今天不會來了。

It's already 10:00; it's not likely that they will come today.

3. 能 Versus 會

Both 能 and 會 can mean "to be able to" and they can sometimes be used interchangeably. But when expressing the idea of "having the learned skill to do something, 會 should be used.

Examples:

Sì niánjí de xuésheng dōu huì shuō Zhōngwén.

四年級的學生都會說中文。

The fourth-year students can all speak Chinese.

(Or: 四年級的學生都能說中文。)

Wáng xiānsheng shí fēnzhōng néng xiě sānbǎi gè Hànzì.

王先生十分钟能写三百个汉字。

Mr. Wang can write 300 Chinese characters in 10 minutes.

（Incorrect: 王先生十分钟会写三百个汉字。）

能 generally indicates a person's ability to do something, or expresses possibility in terms of circumstances or capability, while 会 emphasizes possibility in terms of likelihood.

Examples:

Rúguǒ yǒu hǎo diànyǐng, wǒ huì gàosu nǐ.

如果有好电影，我会告诉你。

If there is a good movie, I'll let you know.

（Not: 如果有好电影，我能告诉你。）

4. 可以

可以 (kěyǐ) means "can" or "may."

Examples:

Xīngqī sì wǒ kěyǐ lái xuéxiào.

星期四我可以来学校。

I can come to school on Thursday.

Jīntiān tā bù máng, kěyǐ qù tǐyùguǎn.

她今天不忙，可以去体育馆。

She is not busy today; she can go to the gymnasium.

Like 能, 可以 can also indicate "permission."

Examples:

Question: Wǒmen kěyǐ zài diànyǐngyuàn lǐ chī dōngxi ma?

我们可以在电影院里吃东西吗？

Are we allowed to eat in the movie theatre?

Wáng xiānsheng shí fēnzhōng néng xiě sānbǎi gè Hànzì.

王先生十分鐘能寫三百個漢字。

Mr. Wang can write 300 Chinese characters in 10 minutes.

(Incorrect: 王先生十分鐘會寫三百個漢字。)

能 generally indicates a person's ability to do something, or expresses possibility in terms of circumstances or capability, while 會 emphasizes possibility in terms of likelihood.

Examples:

Rúguǒ yǒu hǎo diànyǐng, wǒ huì gàosu nǐ.

如果有好電影，我會告訴你。

If there is a good movie, I'll let you know.

(Not: 如果有好電影，我能告訴你。)

4. 可以

可以 (kěyǐ) means "can" or "may."

Examples:

Xīngqī sì wǒ kěyǐ lái xuéxiào.

星期四我可以來學校。

I can come to school on Thursday.

Jīntiān tā bù máng, kěyǐ qù tǐyùguǎn.

她今天不忙，可以去體育館。

She is not busy today; she can go to the gymnasium.

Like 能, 可以 can also indicate "permission."

Examples:

Question: Wǒmen kěyǐ zài diànyǐngyuàn lǐ chī dōngxi ma?

我們可以在電影院裏吃東西嗎？

Are we allowed to eat in the movie theatre?

Answers: Nǐmen kěyǐ zài diànyǐngyuàn lǐ chī dōngxi.

你们可以在电影院里吃东西。

You are allowed to eat in the movie theatre.

Duìbùqǐ, nǐmen bù kěyǐ zài diànyǐngyuàn lǐ chī dōngxi.

对不起，你们不可以在电影院里吃东西。

Sorry, you are not allowed to eat in the movie theatre.

▶ III. Auxiliary Verbs 要 and 想
(See Textbook I, Lessons 4 and 5)

Selected examples from the textbook:

下课以后要多练习。 (Lesson 4)
小姐，我想退这件衣服。 (Lesson 5)
我要买牛奶、面包、奶酪和可乐。 (Lesson 5)

1. 要

When 要 (yào) functions as an auxiliary verb, it can mean "want to" or "wish to."

Examples:

Tāmen yào mǎi kělè.

他们要买可乐。

They want to buy cola.

Question: Jīntiān nǐ yào qù mǎi dōngxi ma?

今天你要去买东西吗?

Do you want to go shopping today?

Answer: Jīntiān wǒ yào qù mǎi dōngxi.

今天我要去买东西。

I want to go shopping today.

Note: In Mainland China especially, when expressing the idea that one does not wish to do something, people usually use 不想 (bù xiǎng) instead of 不要 (bù yào).

Answers: Nǐmen kěyǐ zài diànyǐngyuàn lǐ chī dōngxi.

你們可以在電影院裏吃東西。

You are allowed to eat in the movie theatre.

Duìbùqǐ, nǐmen bù kěyǐ zài diànyǐngyuàn lǐ chī dōngxi.

對不起，你們不可以在電影院裏吃東西。

Sorry, you are not allowed to eat in the movie theatre.

▶ III. Auxiliary Verbs 要 and 想
(See Textbook I, Lessons 4 and 5)

Selected examples from the textbook:

下課以後要多練習。(Lesson 4)

小姐，我想退這件衣服。(Lesson 5)

我要買牛奶、麵包、奶酪和可樂。(Lesson 5)

1. 要

When 要 (yào) functions as an auxiliary verb, it can mean "want to" or "wish to."

Examples:

Tāmen yào mǎi kělè.

他們要買可樂。

They want to buy cola.

Question: Jīntiān nǐ yào qù mǎi dōngxi ma?

今天你要去買東西嗎？

Do you want to go shopping today?

Answer: Jīntiān wǒ yào qù mǎi dōngxi.

今天我要去買東西。

I want to go shopping today.

Note: In Mainland China especially, when expressing the idea that one does not wish to do something, people usually use 不想 (bù xiǎng) instead of 不要 (bù yào).

Examples:

Question: Míngtiān tā yào qù xué kāi qìchē ma?

明天他要去学开汽车吗？

Does he want to learn how to drive tomorrow?

Answers: Míngtiān tā yào qù xué kāi qìchē.

明天他要去学开汽车。

He wants to learn how to drive tomorrow.

Míngtiān tā bù xiǎng qù xué kāi qìchē.

明天他不想去学开汽车。

He does not want to learn how to drive tomorrow.

（Not: 明天他不要去学开汽车。）

The auxiliary verb 要 can also mean "must," "should," or "it is necessary that."

Examples:

Shàng kè yǐqián nǐ yào liànxí.

上课以前你要练习。

You should practice before going to a class.

Kāi qìchē de shíhou, nǐ bù yào hē jiǔ.

开汽车的时候，你不要喝酒。

You should not drink wine when driving a car.

Zhè jiàn yùndòngyī de yánsè bù hǎo kàn, nǐ bù yào mǎi.

这件运动衣的颜色不好看，你不要买。

The color of this sportswear is ugly; you should not buy it.

The auxiliary verb 要 can also mean that some planned action will indeed happen.

Examples:

Míngtiān wǒmen yào kǎoshì.

明天我们要考试。

We will have a test tomorrow (as planned).

Jīntiān wǒ yào mǎi miànbāo.

今天我要买面包。

I should buy some bread today (as planned).

Examples:

Question: Míngtiān tā yào qù xué kāi qìchē ma?

明天他要去學開汽車嗎？

Does he want to learn how to drive tomorrow?

Answers: Míngtiān tā yào qù xué kāi qìchē.

明天他要去學開汽車。

He wants to learn how to drive tomorrow.

Míngtiān tā bù xiǎng qù xué kāi qìchē.

明天他不想去學開汽車。

He does not want to learn how to drive tomorrow.

(Not: 明天他不要去學開汽車。)

The auxiliary verb 要 can also mean "must," "should," or "it is necessary that."

Examples:

Shàng kè yǐqián nǐ yào liànxí.

上課以前你要練習。

You should practice before going to a class.

Kāi qìchē de shíhou, nǐ bù yào hē jiǔ.

開汽車的時候，你不要喝酒。

You should not drink wine when driving a car.

Zhè jiàn yùndòngyī de yánsè bù hǎo kàn, nǐ bù yào mǎi.

這件運動衣的顏色不好看，你不要買。

The color of this sportswear is ugly; you should not buy it.

The auxiliary verb 要 can also mean that some planned action will indeed happen.

Examples:

Míngtiān wǒmen yào kǎoshì.

明天我們要考試。

We will have a test tomorrow (as planned).

Jīntiān wǒ yào mǎi miànbāo.

今天我要買麵包。

I should buy some bread today (as planned).

2. 想

As an auxiliary verb, 想 (xiǎng) means "hope to," "want to," or "would like to."

Examples:

Huáng xiānsheng xiǎng qù Guǎngdōng kàn péngyou.

黄先生想去广东看朋友。

Mr. Huang would like to go to Guangdong to see his friends.

Question: Nǐ xiǎng bù xiǎng qù Běijīng?

你想不想去北京？

Do you want to go to Beijing?

Answer: Wǒ xiǎng qù Běijīng.

我想去北京。

I want to go to Beijing.

Question: Nǐ xiǎng bù xiǎng hē niúnǎi?

你想不想喝牛奶？

Do you want to drink milk?

Answer: Wǒ bù xiǎng hē niúnǎi.

我不想喝牛奶。

I don't want to drink milk.

Note: both 要 and 想 mean "want" or "intend to," but 想 can be modified by an adverb such as 很, 非常, 特别 etc., while 要 cannot be so modified: 他<u>很想</u>学中文 (Incorrect: 他<u>很要</u>学中文).

▶ IV. Auxiliary Verbs 得 and 应该
(See Textbook I, Lessons 7 and 9)

Selected examples from the textbook:

他得把12月18日的票改到25日。 (Lesson 7)
要是学生和教师生了病，可以直接去看，不用预约。 (Lesson 9)

2. 想

As an auxiliary verb, 想 (xiǎng) means "hope to," "want to," or "would like to."

Examples:

Huáng xiānsheng xiǎng qù Guǎngdōng kàn péngyou.

黃先生想去廣東看朋友。

Mr. Huang would like to go to Guangdong to see his friends.

Question: Nǐ xiǎng bù xiǎng qù Běijīng?

你想不想去北京？

Do you want to go to Beijing?

Answer: Wǒ xiǎng qù Běijīng.

我想去北京。

I want to go to Beijing.

Question: Nǐ xiǎng bù xiǎng hē niúnǎi?

你想不想喝牛奶？

Do you want to drink milk?

Answer: Wǒ bù xiǎng hē niúnǎi.

我不想喝牛奶。

I don't want to drink milk.

Note: both 要 and 想 mean "want" or "intend to," but 想 can be modified by an adverb such as 很, 非常, 特別 etc., while 要 cannot be so modified: 他很想學中文 (Incorrect: 他很要學中文).

▶ IV. Auxiliary Verbs 得 and 應該
(See Textbook I, Lessons 7 and 9)

Selected examples from the textbook:

他得把12月18日的票改到25日。 (Lesson 7)

要是學生和教師生了病，可以直接去看，不用預約。 (Lesson 9)

1. 得

When functioning as an auxiliary verb, 得 is pronounced "děi" and means "have to" or "must."

Examples:

Xiànzài wǒ děi qù gōngzuò.

现在我得去工作。

I have to go to work now.

Xuésheng dōu děi shàngkè.

学生都得上课。

Students all have to go to class.

Note: Unlike the other auxiliary verbs, the negative form of 得 is always 不用 (bù yòng, don't have to) rather than 不得. Therefore, in an interrogative sentence, one should not use the A-not-A (here, 得不得) question pattern.

Examples:

Question: Míngtiān tāmen děi mǎi rìyòngpǐn ma?

明天他们得买日用品吗?

Do they have to buy daily necessities tomorrow?

(Incorrect: 明天他们得不得买日用品?)

Answers: Míngtiān tāmen děi mǎi rìyòngpǐn.

明天他们得买日用品。

They must buy daily necessities tomorrow.

Míngtiān tāmen bù yòng mǎi rìyòngpǐn.

明天他们不用买日用品。

They don't need to buy daily necessities tomorrow.

(Incorrect: 明天他们不得买日用品。)

2. 应该

应该 (yīnggāi) means "should" or "must."

1. 得

When functioning as an auxiliary verb, 得 is pronounced "děi" and means "have to" or "must."

Examples:

> Xiànzài wǒ děi qù gōngzuò.
> 現在我得去工作。
> I have to go to work now.

> Xuésheng dōu děi shàngkè.
> 學生都得上課。
> Students all have to go to class.

Note: Unlike the other auxiliary verbs, the negative form of 得 is always 不用 (bù yòng, don't have to) rather than 不得. Therefore, in an interrogative sentence, one should not use the A-not-A (here, 得不得) question pattern.

Examples:

> Question: Míngtiān tāmen děi mǎi rìyòngpǐn ma?
> 明天他們得買日用品嗎？
> Do they have to buy daily necessities tomorrow?
> (Incorrect: 明天他們得不得買日用品？)

> Answers: Míngtiān tāmen děi mǎi rìyòngpǐn.
> 明天他們得買日用品。
> They must buy daily necessities tomorrow.

> Míngtiān tāmen bù yòng mǎi rìyòngpǐn.
> 明天他們不用買日用品。
> They don't need to buy daily necessities tomorrow.
> (Incorrect: 明天他們不得買日用品。)

2. 應該

應該 (yīnggāi) means "should" or "must."

Examples:

Huáng Huá jīntiān méiyǒu lái shàngkè, wǒmen yīnggāi qù kànkan tā.

黄华今天没有来上课，我们应该去看看她。

Hua Huang did not come to class today; we should go see her.

Nǐ gěi wǒ mǎi le zhème duō dōngxī, wǒ yìnggāi gěi nǐ qián.

你给我买了这么多东西，我应该给你钱。

You bought so many things for me, I should pay you.

Note: Some auxiliary verbs, such as 要, 会 and 想 may also function as main verbs. For example: 我想我妈妈 (I miss my mother). 他要钱 (He wants money). 王小年会中文 (Xiaonian Wang knows Chinese). In these sentences, 想, 要 and 会 are the main verbs, not auxiliary verbs, and they don't need other main verbs.

▶ V. Imperative Sentences
(See Textbook I, Lessons 1)

Selected example from the textbook:

快去餐厅吃饭吧，再见。 (Lesson 1)

Like in English, in Chinese, imperative sentences are used when demanding or expecting other people to do or not do something. The subject is often omitted in an imperative sentence. In a negative sentence, add 不要 (bù yào, do not) or 别 (bié, do not) before the action verb.

Examples:

Qǐng zuò!

请坐！

Please sit down!

Kāishǐ shàngkè!

开始上课！

Start class!

Kuài qù cāntīng chīfàn ba.

快去餐厅吃饭吧。

Hurry up to the cafeteria and eat.

Examples:

Huáng Huá jīntiān méiyǒu lái shàngkè, wǒmen yīnggāi qù kànkan tā.

黃華今天沒有來上課，我們應該去看看她。

Hua Huang did not come to class today; we should go see her.

Nǐ gěi wǒ mǎi le zhème duō dōngxī, wǒ yìnggāi gěi nǐ qián.

你給我買了這麼多東西，我應該給你錢。

You bought so many things for me, I should pay you.

Note: Some auxiliary verbs, such as 要, 會 and 想 may also function as main verbs. For example: 我想我媽媽 (I miss my mother). 他要錢 (He wants money). 王小年會中文 (Xiaonian Wang knows Chinese). In these sentences, 想, 要 and 會 are the main verbs, not auxiliary verbs, and they don't need other main verbs.

▶ V. Imperative Sentences
(See Textbook I, Lessons 1)

Selected example from the textbook:

快去餐廳吃飯吧，再見。(Lesson 1)

Like in English, in Chinese, imperative sentences are used when demanding or expecting other people to do or not do something. The subject is often omitted in an imperative sentence. In a negative sentence, add 不要 (bù yào, do not) or 別 (bié, do not) before the action verb.

Examples:

Qǐng zuò!

請坐!

Please sit down!

Kāishǐ shàngkè!

開始上課!

Start class!

Kuài qù cāntīng chīfàn ba.

快去餐廳吃飯吧。

Hurry up to the cafeteria and eat.

▶ 练习 Exercises

I. Fill in the blanks with 的 or 得.

1. 黄小姐写_____字是 " 人。"
2. 星期天我弟弟睡觉睡_____真多。
3. 我不喜欢看一九八一年_____电影。
4. 你觉得我_____杯子怎么样？
5. 超市_____用的东西多_____很。
6. 汉字我写_____很快。
7. 对不起，这是我_____钱，不是你_____。
8. 他用刀叉用_____很好。

II. Correct the errors, if there are any, in the following sentences.

1. 小王学语法很快，但是写汉字很慢。
2. 这个超市面包很好。
3. 他只喝牛奶，不喝别。
4. 退衣服是很容易。
5. 我们想下车在体育馆。
6. 这个电脑是棒。
7. 那件很新衣服不是我哥哥的。

III. Translate the following sentences into Chinese.

1. Soap is not on sale today, I guess?
2. Which suit would you like to buy, the black one or the yellow one?
3. The plastic cup that I used was very big.
4. My friend didn't see this week's movie.
5. This sweater is very expensive, I suppose?
6. The blue car is my teacher's.
7. Who wants to see that American movie, you or he?

▶ 練習 Exercises

I. Fill in the blanks with 的 or 得.

1. 黃小姐寫_____字是 "人。"
2. 星期天我弟弟睡覺睡_____真多。
3. 我不喜歡看一九八一年_____電影。
4. 你覺得我_____杯子怎麼樣？
5. 超市_____用的东西多_____很。
6. 漢字我寫_____很快。
7. 對不起，這是我_____錢，不是你_____。
8. 他用刀叉用_____很好。

II. Correct the errors, if there are any, in the following sentences.

1. 小王學語法很快，但是寫漢字很慢。
2. 這個超市麵包很好。
3. 他只喝牛奶，不喝別。
4. 退衣服是很容易。
5. 我們想下車在體育館。
6. 這個電腦是棒。
7. 那件很新衣服不是我哥哥的。

III. Translate the following sentences into Chinese.

1. Soap is not on sale today, I guess?
2. Which suit would you like to buy, the black one or the yellow one?
3. The plastic cup that I used was very big.
4. My friend didn't see this week's movie.
5. This sweater is very expensive, I suppose?
6. The blue car is my teacher's.
7. Who wants to see that American movie, you or he?

IV. Underline the auxiliary verb of each sentence, then change the sentences into questions. (Use the A-not-A pattern to ask questions for the first five sentences, and use 吗 to ask questions for the last five sentences.)

1. 牛奶不能退。
2. 明天我能去王小年的生日晚会。
3. 他买了很多吃的东西，不会跟我们去超市。
4. 我会跳中国舞，格林不会。
5. 我明天可以去问高老师问题。
6. 我要喝牛奶，不想喝可乐。
7. 你要发准每一个音。
8. 我想去超市买日用品。
9. 两点了，我得上课了。
10. 你不应该去酒吧，你还没到喝酒的年龄。

V. Fill in the blanks with the appropriate auxiliary verbs. (You can have more than one answer.)

1. 我今天有时间，＿＿＿＿跟你去超市买东西。
2. 这个汉字我不认识。你＿＿＿＿教我吗？
3. 那个电脑没有人用。你＿＿＿＿用。
4. 对不起，你不＿＿＿＿在电影院里唱歌。
5. 学生都＿＿＿＿学习。
6. 下个星期黄老师＿＿＿＿给我们上 课。
7. 要是你有时间，你＿＿＿＿到哪儿去玩儿？
8. 今天下午我＿＿＿＿去超市退我买的东西。
9. 明天晚上他不＿＿＿＿练习阅读。

VI. You went shopping yesterday. Write an essay in Chinese, describing what you bought and how much money you spent. Try to use as many new grammatical patterns from Lessons 1–5 as you can.

IV. Underline the auxiliary verb of each sentence, then change the sentences into questions. (Use the A-not-A pattern to ask questions for the first five sentences, and use 嗎 to ask questions for the last five sentences.)

1. 牛奶不能退。
2. 明天我能去王小年的生日晚會。
3. 他買了很多吃的東西，不會跟我們去超市。
4. 我會跳中國舞，格林不會。
5. 我明天可以去問高老師問題。
6. 我要喝牛奶，不想喝可樂。
7. 你要發準每一個音。
8. 我想去超市買日用品。
9. 兩點了，我得上課了。
10. 你不應該去酒吧，你還沒到喝酒的年齡。

V. Fill in the blanks with the appropriate auxiliary verbs. (You can have more than one answer.)

1. 我今天有時間，＿＿＿＿＿＿跟你去超市買東西。
2. 這個漢字我不認識。你＿＿＿＿＿＿教我嗎？
3. 那個電腦沒有人用。你＿＿＿＿＿＿用。
4. 對不起，你不＿＿＿＿＿＿在電影院裏唱歌。
5. 學生都＿＿＿＿＿＿學習。
6. 下個星期黃老師＿＿＿＿＿＿給我們上課。
7. 要是你有時間，你＿＿＿＿＿＿到哪兒去玩兒？
8. 今天下午我＿＿＿＿＿＿去超市退我買的東西。
9. 明天晚上他不＿＿＿＿＿＿練習閱讀。

VI. You went shopping yesterday. Write an essay in Chinese, describing what you bought and how much money you spent. Try to use as many new grammatical patterns from Lessons 1–5 as you can.

VII. Choose the right words to fill in the blanks, and then read the conversation aloud with a partner.

1. 得很快   2. 得   3. 得   4. 想   5. 能   6. 能   7. 会   8. 可以   9. 应该   10. 应该
11. 得   12. 要

A: 我＿＿＿＿＿去超市买东西，你去不去？

B: 我不＿＿＿＿＿去，我＿＿＿＿＿写中文作业。

A: 你用电脑就做＿＿＿＿＿快了。

B: 可是我不＿＿＿＿＿用电脑。你＿＿＿＿＿教我吗？

A: 今天我＿＿＿＿＿去超市，明天下午我＿＿＿＿＿教你。

B: 好，谢谢。你去超市买什么？

A: 我＿＿＿＿＿买纸杯和餐巾纸，还有刀、叉。

B: 那你＿＿＿＿＿去"一块钱"商店买，那儿的东西很便宜。

A: 你说的对，这些东西用＿＿＿＿＿，＿＿＿＿＿买便宜的。我走了，再见。

B: 快去吧，再见。

VII. Choose the right words to fill in the blanks, and then read the conversation aloud with a partner.

1.得很快　2.得　3.得　4.想　5.能　6.能　7.會　8.可以　9.應該　10.應該
11.得　12.要

A: 我_____去超市買東西，你去不去?

B: 我不_____去，我_____寫中文作業。

A: 你用電腦就做_____快了。

B: 可是我不_____用電腦。你_____教我嗎?

A: 今天我_____去超市，明天下午我_____教你。

B: 好，謝謝。你去超市買什麼?

A: 我_____買紙杯和餐巾紙，還有刀、叉。

B: 那你_____去"一塊錢"商店買，那兒的東西很便宜。

A: 你說的對，這些東西用_____，_____買便宜的。我走了，再見。

B: 快去吧，再見。

第六课
LESSON 6

▶ I. The Particle 了
(See Textbook I, Lessons 1, 2, 4, 7 and 9.)

As mentioned in the "Brief Introduction to Chinese Grammar" at the beginning of this book, Chinese verb forms are never inflected. A verb itself doesn't indicate the time of the action or state expressed by the verb.

The particle 了 (le) after an action verb can denote an action or event that was completed in the past.

However, 了 is by no means equivalent to the past tense in English. 了 can also signify an action or event that will be completed in the future. Besides, 了 can introduce a change of a status or a new situation.

1. Past Actions or Events with 了

Selected examples from the textbook:

> 你吃饭了吗？ (Lesson 1)
> 爸爸、妈妈开了一家中餐馆。 (Lesson 2)
> 我在中国学了一年中文。 (Lesson 4)
> 爸爸妈妈已经给她买了12月18日的飞机票。 (Lesson 7)
> 化验结果来了。 (Lesson 9)
> 我饿了，吃了些冰箱里的剩菜。 (Lesson 9)
> 张小妹生病了。 (Lesson 9)

To express the idea that an action or event was completed in the past, use this pattern:

Affirmative sentence	S + V + 了 + O

Examples:

Shànggè xīngqī yī wǒ qù le Kěnnídí jīchǎng.
上个星期一我去了肯尼迪机场。
I went to JFK Airport last Monday.

第六課
LESSON 6

▶ I. The Particle 了
(See Textbook I, Lessons 1, 2, 4, 7 and 9.)

As mentioned in the "Brief Introduction to Chinese Grammar" at the beginning of this book, Chinese verb forms are never inflected. A verb itself doesn't indicate the time of the action or state expressed by the verb.

The particle 了 (le) after an action verb can denote an action or event that was completed in the past.

However, 了 is by no means equivalent to the past tense in English. 了 can also signify an action or event that will be completed in the future. Besides, 了 can introduce a change of a status or a new situation.

1. Past Actions or Events with 了

Selected examples from the textbook:

你吃飯了嗎？(Lesson 1)
爸爸、媽媽開了一家中餐館。(Lesson 2)
我在中國學了一年中文。(Lesson 4)
爸爸媽媽已經給她買了12月18日的飛機票。(Lesson 7)
化驗結果來了。(Lesson 9)
我餓了，吃了些冰箱裏的剩菜。(Lesson 9)
張小妹生病了。(Lesson 9)

To express the idea that an action or event was completed in the past, use this pattern:

Affirmative sentence	S + V + 了 + O

Examples:

Shànggè xīngqī yī wǒ qù le Kěnnídí jīchǎng.

上個星期一我去了肯尼迪機場。

I went to JFK Airport last Monday.

Xiè jiàoshòu mǎi le liǎng zhāng diànyǐng piào.

谢教授买了两张电影票。

Professor Xie bought two movie tickets.

Tā jīntiān zǎoshàng huàn le yīxiē Měiyuán.

她今天早上换了一些美元。

She exchanged some US dollars this morning.

Note: The following pattern is used less frequently, but can also indicate a past action or event:

$$\boxed{S + V + 0 + 了}$$

Examples:

Nǐ chīfàn le ma?

你吃饭了吗？

Did you eat?

Zuótiān wǒ māma hē niúnǎi le.

昨天我妈妈喝牛奶了。

My mother drank (some) milk yesterday.

Tā gàosù wǒ tā de míngzi le.

他告诉我他的名字了。

He told me his name.

To express the idea that an action or event did not take place in the past, add 没有 (méiyǒu) or 没 (méi) before the verb. Note that no 了 is needed in this case.

Negative sentence

$$\boxed{\textbf{Sentence structure:} \quad S + 没(有) + V + 0}$$

Examples:

Jiǔyuè wǒ péngyou méi (yǒu) qù Kěnnídí jīchǎng.

九月我朋友没(有)去肯尼迪机场。

My friend didn't go to JFK Airport in September.

(Incorrect: 九月我朋友没(有)去了肯尼迪机场。)

Xiè jiàoshòu mǎi le liǎng zhāng diànyǐng piào.

謝教授買了兩張電影票。

Professor Xie bought two movie tickets.

Tā jīntiān zǎoshàng huàn le yīxiē Měiyuán.

她今天早上換了一些美元。

She exchanged some US dollars this morning.

Note: The following pattern is used less frequently, but can also indicate a past action or event:

$$\boxed{S + V + O + 了}$$

Examples:

Nǐ chīfàn le ma?

你吃飯了嗎？

Did you eat?

Zuótiān wǒ māma hē niúnǎi le.

昨天我媽媽喝牛奶了。

My mother drank (some) milk yesterday.

Tā gàosù wǒ tā de míngzi le.

他告訴我他的名字了。

He told me his name.

To express the idea that an action or event did not take place in the past, add 沒有 (méiyǒu) or 沒 (méi) before the verb. Note that no 了 is needed in this case.

Negative sentence

$$\boxed{\textbf{Sentence structure:} \quad S + 沒(有) + V + O}$$

Examples:

Jiǔyuè wǒ péngyou méi (yǒu) qù Kěnnídí jīchǎng.

九月我朋友沒(有)去肯尼迪機場。

My friend didn't go to JFK Airport in September.

(Incorrect: 九月我朋友沒(有)去了肯尼迪機場。)

Wǒ zài Zhōngguó méiyǒu zuò dìtiě.

我在中国没有坐地铁。

I did not take the subway while in China.

（Incorrect: 我在中国没有坐地铁了。）

Note: To express the idea that a planned action has not taken place yet, insert the word 还 (hái, still, yet) between the subject and the verb.

Sentence structure:　　　S ＋ 还 ＋ 没（有）＋ V ＋ O

Example:

Wǒ hái méiyǒu qù tā jiā.

我还没有去他家。

I have not been to his house yet. (But I am planning to go.)

Compare:

Wǒ méiyǒu qù tā jiā.

我没有去他家。

I did not go to his house. (I didn't go at all in the past.)

To ask if an action or event took place in the past, any of the four patterns below may be used:

Interrogative sentence:	S ＋ V ＋ 了 ＋ O ＋ 吗
Or:	S ＋ V ＋ O ＋ 了 ＋ 吗
Or:	S ＋ V ＋ O ＋ 了 ＋ 没有
Or:	S ＋ V ＋ 了 ＋ O ＋ 没有

Example:

Question: Nà gè shòuhuòyuán zhǎo nǐ qián le ma?

那个售货员找你钱了吗？

Did that cashier give you the change?

Answers: Zhǎo le, tā zhǎo wǒ qián le.

找了，他找我钱了。

Yes, he gave me the change.

Wǒ zài Zhōngguó méiyǒu zuò dìtiě.

我在中國沒有坐地鐵。

I did not take the subway while in China.

(Incorrect: 我在中國沒有坐地鐵了。)

Note: To express the idea that a planned action has not taken place yet, insert the word 還 (hái, still, yet) between the subject and the verb.

Sentence structure: S ＋ 還 ＋ 沒(有) ＋ V ＋ O

Example:

Wǒ hái méiyǒu qù tā jiā.

我還沒有去他家。

I have not been to his house yet. (But I am planning to go.)

*Compare:

Wǒ méiyǒu qù tā jiā.

我沒有去他家。

I did not go to his house. (I didn't go at all in the past.)

To ask if an action or event took place in the past, any of the four patterns below may be used:

Interrogative sentence	S ＋ V ＋ 了 ＋ O ＋ 嗎
Or:	S ＋ V ＋ O ＋ 了 ＋ 嗎
Or:	S ＋ V ＋ O ＋ 了 ＋ 沒有
Or:	S ＋ V ＋ 了 ＋ O ＋ 沒有

Example:

Question: Nà gè shòuhuòyuán zhǎo nǐ qián le ma?

那個售貨員找你錢了嗎？

Did that cashier give you the change?

Answers: Zhǎo le, tā zhǎo wǒ qián le.

找了，他找我錢了。

Yes, he gave me the change.

Méi (yǒu), tā méi (yǒu) zhǎo wǒ qián.

没(有)，他没(有)找我钱。

No, he didn't give me any change.

Hái méi (yǒu), tā hái méi (yǒu) zhǎo wǒ qián.

还没(有)，他还没(有)找我钱。

Not yet, he hasn't given me the change yet.

Question: Tā hē le jiǔ méiyǒu?

他喝了酒没有？

Did he drink any alcohol?

Answers: Hē le, tā hē le jiǔ.

喝了，他喝了酒。

Yes, he did drink (some) alcohol.

Méi (yǒu), tā méi (yǒu) hē jiǔ.

没(有)，他没(有)喝酒。

No, he didn't drink (any) alcohol.

Hái méi (yǒu), tā hái méi (yǒu) hē jiǔ.

还没(有)，他还没(有)喝酒。

Not yet, he hasn't drunk (any) alcohol yet.

Note: There are functional differences between S + V + 了 + O and S + V + O + 了. In the former, the focus of the message is on O, whereas in the latter, the focus is on VO. For example: 吃饭以后他去了机场（他没去超市）；吃饭以后他去机场了（他没去超市买东西 or 没去电影院看电影）。

2. Future Actions or Events with 了

Selected example from the textbook:

等会儿下了课我陪她去学校医院看看。 (Lesson 9)

了 can be used in a non-past sentence to suggest that, in the future, something else will take place after an action or event has been completed.

Méi (yǒu), tā méi (yǒu) zhǎo wǒ qián.

沒(有)，他沒(有)找我錢。

No, he didn't give me any change.

Hái méi (yǒu), tā hái méi (yǒu) zhǎo wǒ qián.

還沒(有)，他還沒(有)找我錢。

Not yet, he hasn't given me the change yet.

Question: Tā hē le jiǔ méiyǒu?

他喝了酒沒有？

Did he drink any alcohol?

Answers: Hē le, tā hē le jiǔ.

喝了，他喝了酒。

Yes, he did drink (some) alcohol.

Méi (yǒu), tā méi (yǒu) hē jiǔ.

沒(有)，他沒(有)喝酒。

No, he didn't drink (any) alcohol.

Hái méi (yǒu), tā hái méi (yǒu) hē jiǔ.

還沒(有)，他還沒(有)喝酒。

Not yet, he hasn't drunk (any) alcohol yet.

Note: There are functional differences between S + V + 了 + O and S + V + O + 了. In the former, the focus of the message is on O, whereas in the latter, the focus is on VO. For example: 吃飯以後他去了機場（他沒去超市）；吃飯以後他去機場了（他沒去超市買東西 or 沒去電影院看電影）。

2. Future Actions or Events with 了

Selected examples from the textbook:

等會兒下了課我陪她去學校醫院看看。(Lesson 9)

了 can be used in a non-past sentence to suggest that, in the future, something else will take place after an action or event has been completed.

| Sentence structure: | S ＋ V1 ＋ 了 ＋ 01 ＋ （就） ＋ V2 ＋ 02 |

Examples:

Wǒ mǎi le miànbāo mǎshàng jiù huílái.

我买了面包马上就回来。

After I buy the bread I'll come right back (I have neither bought the bread nor come back yet).

Tā chī le wǎnfàn (jiù) qù chāojí shìchǎng.

她吃了晚饭（就）去超级市场。

She'll go to the supermarket after eating dinner (she has neither eaten dinner nor been to the supermarket yet).

Note: If both of the action verbs are followed by a 了, it means that the actions were both completed in the past.

Compare the differences in the following sentences:

Future: Xiǎo Wáng xiǎng ná le xiànjīn jiù zǒu.

小王想拿了现金就走。

Little Wang wants to leave right after he takes the cash (he has neither taken the cash nor left yet).

Past: Xiǎo Wáng ná le xiànjīn jiù zǒu le.

小王拿了现金就走了。

Little Wang left right after he took the cash (he left and took the cash as well).

Note: as a completion marker, 了 is used only with verbs that can be completed. Verbs expressing stative or psychological states, such as 是, 有, 在, 觉得, 喜欢, etc. do not take 了 even if the speaker is describing a past action or event. Verbs that take auxiliary verbs before them do not take 了.

Examples:

Yī jiǔ jiǔ qī nián tā zài Bōshìdùn.

一九九七年他在波士顿。

He was in Boston in 1997.

（Incorrect: 一九九七年他在了波士顿。）

| Sentence structure: | S + V1 + 了 + O1 + (就) + V2 + O2 |

Examples:

Wǒ mǎi le miànbāo mǎshàng jiù huílái.

我買了麵包馬上就回來。

After I buy the bread I'll come right back (I have neither bought the bread nor come back yet).

Tā chī le wǎnfàn (jiù) qù chāojí shìchǎng.

她吃了晚飯(就)去超級市場。

She'll go to the supermarket after eating dinner (she has neither eaten dinner nor been to the supermarket yet).

Note: If both of the action verbs are followed by a 了, it means that the actions were both completed in the past.

Compare the differences in the following sentences:

Future: Xiǎo Wáng xiǎng ná le xiànjīn jiù zǒu.

小王想拿了現金就走。

Little Wang wants to leave right after he takes the cash (he has neither taken the cash nor left yet).

Past: Xiǎo Wáng ná le xiànjīn jiù zǒu le.

小王拿了現金就走了。

Little Wang left right after he took the cash (he left and took the cash as well).

Note: as a completion marker, 了 is used only with verbs that can be completed. Verbs expressing stative or psychological states, such as 是, 有, 在, 覺得, 喜歡, etc. do not take 了 even if the speaker is describing a past action or event. Verbs that take auxiliary verbs before them do not take 了.

Examples:

Yī jiǔ jiǔ qī nián tā zài Bōshìdùn.

一九九七年他在波士頓。

He was in Boston in 1997.

(Incorrect: 一九九七年他在了波士頓。)

Wén xiǎojie yǐqián shì dàxuésheng.

文小姐以前是大学生。

Miss Wen used to be a college student.

（Incorrect: 文小姐以前是了大学生。）

Tā zuótiān shuō tā kěyǐ zuò dìtiě qù Kěnnídí jīchǎng.

他昨天说他可以坐地铁去肯尼迪机场。

Yesterday he said that he could take the subway to JFK Airport.

（Incorrect: 他昨天说他可以坐了地铁去肯尼迪机场。）

3. Change of Status or New Situation with 了

Selected examples from the textbook:

> 我有中文名字了　(Lesson 1)
> 怎么可乐比上星期贵了？(Lesson 5)
> 高老师，张小妹生病了。(Lesson 9)
> 她现在烧已经退了。(Lesson 9)

When placed at the end of a sentence or in the middle of a sentence at a pause, 了 suggests a change of status or a new situation, especially in comparison with a previous state or situation.

Examples:

Máo xiānsheng de qìchē huàn le.

毛先生的汽车换了。

Mr. Mao has changed his car.(He now has a new car).

Tài wǎn le, wǒ jīntiān bù qù mǎi dōngxi le.

太晚了，我今天不去买东西了。

It's too late, I won't go shopping today. (I wanted to go shopping before, but now I've changed my mind.)

Wǒ yǒu Zhōngwén míngzì le.

我有中文名字了。

Now I have a Chinese name. (I didn't have one before.)

Wén xiǎojie yǐqián shì dàxuéshēng.

文小姐以前是大學生。

Miss Wen used to be a college student.

(Incorrect: 文小姐以前是了大學生。)

Tā zuótiān shuō tā kěyǐ zuò dìtiě qù Kěnnídí jīchǎng.

他昨天說他可以坐地鐵去肯尼迪機場。

Yesterday he said that he could take the subway to JFK Airport.

(Incorrect: 他昨天說他可以坐了地鐵去肯尼迪機場。)

3. Change of Status or New Situation with 了

Selected examples from the textbook:

我有中文名字了 (Lesson 1)
怎麼可樂比上星期貴了？ (Lesson 5)
高老師，張小妹生病了。 (Lesson 9)
她現在燒已經退了。 (Lesson 9)

When placed at the end of a sentence or in the middle of a sentence at a pause, 了 suggests a change of status or a new situation, especially in comparison with a previous state or situation.

Examples:

Máo xiānsheng de qìchē huàn le.

毛先生的汽車換了。

Mr. Mao has changed his car.(He now has a new car).

Tài wǎn le, wǒ jīntiān bù qù mǎi dōngxi le.

太晚了，我今天不去買東西了。

It's too late, I won't go shopping today. (I wanted to go shopping before, but now I've changed my mind.)

Wǒ yǒu Zhōngwén míngzì le.

我有中文名字了。

Now I have a Chinese name. (I didn't have one before.)

Jīntiān kělè guì le.

今天可乐贵了。

Cola is expensive today. (Cola was cheaper before today.)

▶ II. Rhetorical Questions
(See Textbook I, Lesson 10)

Selected example from the textbook:

（天气预报）准什么呀？ (Lesson 10)

Like in English, in Chinese rhetorical questions are asked for the sake of reinforcing the effect or impression on the listener. In most cases, the questioner does not necessarily expect an answer from the listener.

Examples:

Wǒ zěnme zhīdào Dàzhōngyāng Chēzhàn?

我怎么知道大中央车站？

How could I know Grand Central Station? (I don't know it.)

Nǐ qù mǎi cānjīnzhǐ, bù xíng ma?

你去买餐巾纸, 不行吗？

Can't you go buy some napkins? (It should not be a problem for you to go.)

Zhège Hànzì wǒmen zuótiān bù shì xué le ma?

这个汉字我们昨天不是学了吗？

Didn't we learn this Chinese character yesterday? (We don't need to learn it again.)

Nǐmen dào hē jiǔ de niánlíng le ma?

你们到喝酒的年龄了吗？

Have you reached the legal drinking age? (You are under the drinking age, so you should not drink.)

▶ III. The Particle 地

The particle word 地 (de) is preceded by a two-syllable adjective, an adverb, or a phrase, rather than by a noun or pronoun. The 地 phrase functions as an adverbial, suggesting with what kind of manner or attitude an action was or should be performed.

Jīntiān kělè guì le.

今天可樂貴了。

Cola is expensive today. (Cola was cheaper before today.)

▶ II. Rhetorical Questions
(See Textbook I, Lesson 10)

Selected example from the textbook:

(天氣預報)准什麼呀？(Lesson 10)

Like in English, in Chinese rhetorical questions are asked for the sake of reinforcing the effect or impression on the listener. In most cases, the questioner does not necessarily expect an answer from the listener.

Examples:

Wǒ zěnme zhīdào Dàzhōngyāng Chēzhàn?

我怎麼知道大中央車站？

How could I know Grand Central Station? (I don't know it.)

Nǐ qù mǎi cānjīnzhǐ, bù xíng ma?

你去買餐巾紙,不行嗎？

Can't you go buy some napkins? (It should not be a problem for you to go.)

Zhège Hànzì wǒmen zuótiān bù shì xué le ma?

這個漢字我們昨天不是學了嗎？

Didn't we learn this Chinese character yesterday? (We don't need to learn it again.)

Nǐmen dào hē jiǔ de niánlíng le ma?

你們到喝酒的年齡了嗎？

Have you reached the legal drinking age? (You are under the drinking age, so you should not drink.)

▶ III. The Particle 地

The particle word 地 (de) is preceded by a two-syllable adjective, an adverb, or a phrase, rather than by a noun or pronoun. The 地 phrase functions as an adverbial, suggesting with what kind of manner or attitude an action was or should be performed.

Examples:

Lǎoshī hěn kuài de wèn le xuésheng yīxiē wèntí.

老师很快地问了学生一些问题。

The teacher quickly asked the students some questions.

（Incorrect: 老师快地问了学生一些问题。）

Tā gāoxìng de gàosu wǒ: "wǒ zuótiān mǎi le yí liàng xīn chē."

他高兴（gāoxìng, happy）地告诉我："我昨天买了一辆新车。"

He told me happily: "I bought a new car yesterday."

Note: We have learned three structural particles, 的 (Grammar Book Lesson 4), 得 (Grammar Book Lesson 5) and 地 (Grammar Book Lesson 6). All three structural particles are pronounced as "de," but written differently and used differently. Generally, 的 is used before a noun, 地 is used before a verb, and 得 is used after a verb.

Examples:

的

lǎoshī de diànnǎo

老师的电脑

the teacher's computer

Běijīng de dìtiě

北京的地铁

the subway in Beijing

liúlì de fāyīn

流利的发音

fluent pronunciation

wǒ zuótiān zuò de gōnggòng qìchē

我昨天坐的公共汽车

the bus that I took yesterday

Examples:

Lǎoshī hěn kuài de wèn le xuésheng yīxiē wèntí.

老師很快地問了學生一些問題。

The teacher quickly asked the students some questions.

(Incorrect: 老師快地問了學生一些問題。)

Tā gāoxìng de gàosu wǒ: "wǒ zuótiān mǎi le yí liàng xīn chē."

他高興(gāoxìng, happy)地告訴我： "我昨天買了一輛新車。"

He told me happily: "I bought a new car yesterday."

Note: We have learned three structural particles, 的 (Grammar Book Lesson 4), 得 (Grammar Book Lesson 5) and 地 (Grammar Book Lesson 6). All three structural particles are pronounced as "de," but written differently and used differently. Generally, 的 is used before a noun, 地 is used before a verb, and 得 is used after a verb.

Examples:

的

lǎoshī de diànnǎo

老師的電腦

the teacher's computer

Běijīng de dìtiě

北京的地鐵

the subway in Beijing

liúlì de fāyīn

流利的發音

fluent pronunciation

wǒ zuótiān zuò de gōnggòng qìchē

我昨天坐的公共汽車

the bus that I took yesterday

地

Sūshān ānquán de dào jiā le.

苏珊安全地到家了。

Susan safely arrived home.

Lǎoshī kèqì de xièxie wǒ.

老师客气地谢谢我。

The teacher politely thanked me.

得

tiào de gāo

跳得高

jump high

zǒu de kuài

走得快

walk quickly

Gélín fāyīn fā de zhǔn.

格林发音发得准。

Green pronounces [Chinese] accurately.

Wáng Xiǎonián mǎi dōngxi mǎi de duō.

王小年买东西买得多。

Xiaonian Wang bought a lot of things.

▶ IV. Sentences with 是⋯⋯的
(See Textbook I, Lesson 2)

Selected example from the textbook:

我的爷爷、 奶奶是从中国广东来美国的。 (Lesson 2)

The 是⋯⋯的 (shì...de, it is...that) pattern is used to emphasize the time when, the place where, or the manner in which an action or event happened in the past. Note that in a 是⋯⋯的 sentence, 了 should be omitted.

地

Sūshān ānquán de dào jiā le.

蘇珊安全地到家了。

Susan safely arrived home.

Lǎoshī kèqì de xièxie wǒ.

老師客氣地謝謝我。

The teacher politely thanked me.

得

tiào de gāo

跳得高

jump high

zǒu de kuài

走得快

walk quickly

Gélín fāyīn fā de zhǔn.

格林發音發得準。

Green pronounces [Chinese] accurately.

Wáng Xiǎonián mǎi dōngxi mǎi de duō.

王小年買東西買得多。

Xiaonian Wang bought a lot of things.

▶ IV. Sentences with 是……的
(See Textbook I, Lesson 2)

Selected example from the textbook:

> 我的爺爺、奶奶是從中國廣東來美國的。 (Lesson 2)

The 是……的 (shì...de, it is...that) pattern is used to emphasize the time when, the place where, or the manner in which an action or event happened in the past. Note that in a 是……的 sentence, 了 should be omitted.

Affirmative sentence

Sentence structure:

$$S + 是 + \begin{matrix} \text{Time} \\ \text{Place} \\ \text{Manner} \end{matrix} + V + O + 的$$

Or:

$$S + 是 + \begin{matrix} \text{Time} \\ \text{Place} \\ \text{Manner} \end{matrix} + V + 的 + O$$

Examples:

Tāmen shì shànggè xīngqī huíjiā de.

他们是上个星期回家的。

It was last week that they went home.

（Incorrect: 他们是上个星期回家了的。）

Wǒ shì zuò dìtiě qù de Zhōngguóchéng.

我是坐地铁去的中国城。

It was by subway that I went to Chinatown.

（Incorrect: 我是坐地铁去了的中国城。）

Huáng jiàoshòu shì zài chāoshì mǎi de xǐfàyè.

黄教授是在超市买的洗发液。

It was at the supermarket that Professor Huang bought the shampoo.

Lǐ xiǎojie shì gēn wǒ yīqǐ qù de Shídài Guǎngchǎng.

李小姐是跟我一起去的时代广场。

It was with me that Miss Li went to Times Square.

Note: The 是⋯⋯的 pattern can also emphasize the person who completed an action.

Affirmative sentence

Sentence structure:

$$S + 是 + \text{Place} + V + O + 的$$

with Time / Manner positioned with Place

Time
S + 是 + Place + V + O + 的
Manner

Or:

Time
S + 是 + Place + V + 的 + O
Manner

Examples:

Tāmen shì shànggè xīngqī huíjiā de.

他們是上個星期回家的。

It was last week that they went home.

(Incorrect: 他們是上個星期回家了的。)

Wǒ shì zuò dìtiě qù de Zhōngguóchéng.

我是坐地鐵去的中國城。

It was by subway that I went to Chinatown.

(Incorrect: 我是坐地鐵去了的中國城。)

Huáng jiàoshòu shì zài chāoshì mǎi de xǐfàyè.

黃教授是在超市買的洗髮液。

It was at the supermarket that Professor Huang bought the shampoo.

Lǐ xiǎojie shì gēn wǒ yīqǐ qù de Shídài Guǎngchǎng.

李小姐是跟我一起去的時代廣場。

It was with me that Miss Li went to Times Square.

Note: The 是……的 pattern can also emphasize the person who completed an action.

Example:

Shì Yuēhàn jiào wǒ dǎ dī de.

是约翰叫我打的的。

It was John who told me to take a taxi.

Negative sentence

Sentence structure:

$$\text{S} + 不是 + \begin{array}{c}\text{Time}\\\text{Place}\\\text{Manner}\end{array} + \text{V} + 0 + 的$$

Or:

$$\text{S} + 不是 + \begin{array}{c}\text{Time}\\\text{Place}\\\text{Manner}\end{array} + \text{V} + 的 + 0$$

Examples:

Nǐ bù shì bā diǎn zhōng lái de.

你不是八点钟来的。

You didn't come at eight o'clock. (You came at a different time.)

Tā bù shì zài Měiguó chūshēng de.

他不是在美国出生的。

He was not born in the United States. (He was born elsewhere.)

Example:

Shì Yuēhàn jiào wǒ dǎ dī de.

是約翰叫我打的的。

It was John who told me to take a taxi.

Negative sentence

Sentence structure:

$$S + 不是 + \begin{matrix} \text{Time} \\ \text{Place} \\ \text{Manner} \end{matrix} + V + O + 的$$

Or:

$$S + 不是 + \begin{matrix} \text{Time} \\ \text{Place} \\ \text{Manner} \end{matrix} + V + 的 + O$$

Examples:

Nǐ bù shì bā diǎn zhōng lái de.

你不是八點鐘來的。

You didn't come at eight o'clock. (You came at a different time.)

Tā bù shì zài Měiguó chūshēng de.

他不是在美國出生的。

He was not born in the United States. (He was born elsewhere.)

Interrogative sentence

```
Sentence structure:

                    Time
S ＋ 是 ＋ Place ＋ V ＋ O ＋ 的 ＋ 吗
                    Manner

Or:

                    Time
S ＋ 是 ＋ Place ＋ V ＋ 的 ＋ O ＋ 吗
                    Manner
```

Examples:

Question: Xiǎo Bái shì gēn nǐ yīqǐ qù de Zhōngguó ma?

小白是跟你一起去的中国吗？

Was it with you that Little Bai went to China?

Answers: Shì, Xiǎo Bái shì gēn wǒ yīqǐ qù de Zhōngguó.

是，小白是跟我一起去的中国。

Yes, it was with me that Little Bai went to China.

Bù shì, Xiǎo Bái bù shì gēn wǒ yīqǐ qù de Zhōngguó.

不是，小白不是跟我一起去的中国。

No, Little Bai didn't go to China with me. (Little Bai went to China with someone else.)

Note: 是 precedes the word representing the time, place or manner to be emphasized, and 的 is usually at the end of the sentence. When a V-O phrase is emphasized by 是……的, 的 can be placed either before the object (O) or at the end of the sentence. In an affirmative sentence with a subject, 是 can be omitted. For example: 他们（是）上个星期回家的。王小姐（是）跟我一起去的时代广场。

Interrogative sentence

Sentence structure:

Time

S ＋ 是 ＋ Place ＋ V ＋ O ＋ 的 ＋ 嗎

Manner

Or:

Time

S ＋ 是 ＋ Place ＋ V ＋ 的 ＋ O ＋ 嗎

Manner

Examples:

Question: Xiǎo Bái shì gēn nǐ yīqǐ qù de Zhōngguó ma?

小白是跟你一起去的中國嗎？

Was it with you that Little Bai went to China?

Answers: Shì, Xiǎo Bái shì gēn wǒ yīqǐ qù de Zhōngguó.

是，小白是跟我一起去的中國。

Yes, it was with me that Little Bai went to China.

Bù shì, Xiǎo Bái bù shì gēn wǒ yīqǐ qù de Zhōngguó.

不是，小白不是跟我一起去的中國。

No, Little Bai didn't go to China with me. (Little Bai went to China with someone else.)

Note: 是 precedes the word representing the time, place or manner to be emphasized, and 的 is usually at the end of the sentence. When a V-O phrase is emphasized by 是……的, 的 can be placed either before the object (O) or at the end of the sentence. In an affirmative sentence with a subject, 是 can be omitted. For example: 他們(是)上個星期回家的。王小姐(是)跟我一起去的時代廣場。

▶ V. The Conjunction 因为……所以
(See Textbook I, Lesson 7)

Selected example from the textbook:

因为苏珊要去夏威夷，（所以）她爸爸只好给她改飞机票。 (Lesson 7)

The pair of conjunctions 因为……所以 (yīnwèi... suǒyǐ, because...therefore) is used to introduce a cause or reason and a result. In most cases, both 因为 and 所以 are used. However, it is possible to omit either 因为 or 所以.

Examples:

Yīnwèi zhège kōngtiáo bù cuò, suǒyǐ wǒ xiǎng mǎi.
因为这个空调不错，所以我想买。

Or: Zhège kōngtiáo bù cuò, suǒyǐ wǒ xiǎng mǎi.
这个空调不错，所以我想买。

Or: Wǒ xiǎng mǎi zhège kōngtiáo, yīnwèi (zhège kōngtiáo) bù cuò.
我想买这个空调，因为(这个空调)不错。

I want to buy this air conditioner because it's pretty good.
(Incorrect: 所以我想买这个空调，因为(这个空调)不错。)

Yīnwèi dǎdī fāngbiàn, suǒyǐ wǒmen juédìng dǎdī qù.
因为打的方便，所以我们决定打的去。

Or: Dǎdī fāngbiàn, suǒyǐ wǒmen juédìng dǎdī qù.
打的方便，所以我们决定打的去。

Or: Wǒmen juédìng dǎdī qù, yīnwèi dǎdī fāngbiàn.
我们决定打的去，因为打的方便。

We decided to go by taxi because taking a taxi is convenient.
(Incorrect: 所以我们打的去，因为打的方便。)

Note: 因为 can be used alone in both the first and second clauses, but 所以 can only be used alone at the beginning of the second clause. It cannot be placed after the subject. It is right to say: "打的方便，所以我们决定打的去。" But it is incorrect to say: "打的方便，我们所以决定打的去。"

▶ V. The Conjunction 因爲······所以

(See Textbook I, Lesson 7)

Selected example from the textbook:

因爲蘇珊要去夏威夷，(所以)她爸爸只好給她改飛機票。 (Lesson 7)

The pair of conjunctions 因爲······所以 (yīnwèi... suǒyǐ, because...therefore) is used to introduce a cause or reason and a result. In most cases, both 因爲 and 所以 are used. However, it is possible to omit either 因爲 or 所以.

Examples:

Yīnwèi zhège kōngtiáo bù cuò, suǒyǐ wǒ xiǎng mǎi.
因爲這個空調不錯，所以我想買。

Or: Zhège kōngtiáo bù cuò, suǒyǐ wǒ xiǎng mǎi.
這個空調不錯，所以我想買。

Or: Wǒ xiǎng mǎi zhège kōngtiáo, yīnwèi (zhège kōngtiáo) bù cuò.
我想買這個空調，因爲(這個空調)不錯。

I want to buy this air conditioner because it's pretty good.
(Incorrect: 所以我想買這個空調，因爲(這個空調)不錯。)

Yīnwèi dǎdī fāngbiàn, suǒyǐ wǒmen juédìng dǎdī qù.
因爲打的方便，所以我們決定打的去。

Or: Dǎdī fāngbiàn, suǒyǐ wǒmen juédìng dǎdī qù.
打的方便，所以我們決定打的去。

Or: Wǒmen juédìng dǎdī qù, yīnwèi dǎdī fāngbiàn.
我們決定打的去，因爲打的方便。

We decided to go by taxi because taking a taxi is convenient.
(Incorrect: 所以我們打的去，因爲打的方便。)

Note: 因爲 can be used alone in both the first and second clauses, but 所以 can only be used alone at the beginning of the second clause. It cannot be placed after the subject. It is right to say: "打的方便，所以我們決定打的去。" But it is incorrect to say: "打的方便，我們所以決定打的去。"

▶ 练习 Exercises

I. Fill in the blanks with 的, 得, **or** 地.

1. 妹妹一共买了二十块钱_____东西。

2. 我想快快_____去时代广场。

3. 我们_____新老师发音发_____特别准。

4. 这件衣服_____颜色很好看。

5. 妈妈叫我慢慢_____吃东西。

6. 平时他喝牛奶喝_____比较快。

7. 这件衣服_____大小 (dàxiǎo, size) 不合适。

8. 对不起，我不知道小黄_____电话号码。

9. 因为买机票_____人很多，所以我只好早早 (zǎozǎo, early) _____
   买票。

10. 他们做作业做_____很慢。

**II. Turn statements 1-3 into negative statements, and turn statements 4-6 into two
forms of questions (A-not-A and** 吗**).**

1. 星期五我给了我哥哥三十块美元。

2. 今天早上的公共汽车来晚了。

3. 一月五号王教授坐了飞机。

4. 约翰换了7号车。

5. 八点钟小新打了电话。

6. 二零零一年我们都没有去夏威夷旅行。

III. Correct the errors, if there are any, in the following sentences.

1. 昨天我姐姐买了东西就回家。

2. 明天一年级的留学生去了旅行社就练了会话。

3. 我记得谢先生星期一没有喝了酒。

4. 一九八八年他哥哥是了学生，不是老师。

5. 这个俱乐部以前有了很多会员。

6. 下个星期 (next week) 毛先生去纽约就去波士顿。

▶ 練習 Exercises

I. Fill in the blanks with 的, 得, **or** 地.

1. 妹妹一共買了二十塊錢＿＿＿＿＿東西。

2. 我想快快＿＿＿＿＿去時代廣場。

3. 我們＿＿＿＿＿新老師發音發＿＿＿＿＿特別准。

4. 這件衣服＿＿＿＿＿顏色很好看。

5. 媽媽叫我慢慢＿＿＿＿＿吃東西。

6. 平時他喝牛奶喝＿＿＿＿＿比較快。

7. 這件衣服＿＿＿＿＿大小(dàxiǎo, size)不合適。

8. 對不起，我不知道小黃＿＿＿＿＿電話號碼。

9. 因為買機票＿＿＿＿＿人很多，所以我只好早早 (zǎozǎo, early)＿＿＿＿＿
   買票。

10. 他們做作業做＿＿＿＿＿很慢。

II. Turn statements 1-3 into negative statements, and turn statements 4-6 into two forms of questions (A-not-A and 嗎**).**

1. 星期五我給了我哥哥三十塊美元。

2. 今天早上的公共汽車來晚了。

3. 一月五號王教授坐了飛機。

4. 約翰換了7號車。

5. 八點鐘小新打了電話。

6. 二零零一年我們都沒有去夏威夷旅行。

III. Correct the errors, if there are any, in the following sentences.

1. 昨天我姐姐買了東西就回家。

2. 明天一年級的留學生去了旅行社就練了會話。

3. 我記得謝先生星期一沒有喝了酒。

4. 一九八八年他哥哥是了學生，不是老師。

5. 這個俱樂部以前有了很多會員。

6. 下個星期(next week)毛先生去紐約就去波士頓。

IV. Translate the sentences into Chinese.

1. Did you take a taxi last Monday?

2. Tomorrow I'll go to the airport right after I have dinner.

3. Last Friday, they bought two tickets after they had been to the supermarket.

4. Now he knows how to write Chinese characters. (He didn't know how to write them before.)

5. They have not paid the fine yet.

6. Didn't he give you the money?

7. Don't you like the color black?

V. Use 是……的 to rewrite the following sentences, focusing on the underlined parts.

Example: 我在时代广场坐了地铁。→ 我是在时代广场坐的地铁。

1. 他十月一号去了时代广场。

2. 他们打的去了机场。

3. 小王在超市买了餐巾纸。

4. 我们十点钟打了的。

5. 二年级的学生用中文问了问题。

VI. Complete the following dialogue.

A: 今天你是怎么去上班的？

B: ＿＿＿＿＿＿＿＿＿＿＿＿＿＿＿＿。

A: 你平时都坐地铁，今天怎么想坐公共汽车了？

B: ＿＿＿＿＿＿＿＿＿＿＿＿＿＿＿＿。

A: 听说现在坐公共汽车的人多得很。

B: ＿＿＿＿＿＿＿＿＿＿＿＿＿＿＿？ (rhetorical question)

A: 我也不知道。我爸爸今天也坐的公共汽车。

B: ＿＿＿＿＿＿＿＿＿＿＿＿＿＿＿？

A: 他坐66路公共汽车。

B: ＿＿＿＿＿＿＿＿＿＿＿＿＿＿＿。

A: 因为66路是无人售票车，所以车比较好。

IV. Translate the sentences into Chinese.

1. Did you take a taxi last Monday?

2. Tomorrow I'll go to the airport right after I have dinner.

3. Last Friday, they bought two tickets after they had been to the supermarket.

4. Now he knows how to write Chinese characters. (He didn't know how to write them before.)

5. They have not paid the fine yet.

6. Didn't he give you the money?

7. Don't you like the color black?

V. Use 是……的 to rewrite the following sentences, focusing on the underlined parts.

Example: 我在時代廣場坐了地鐵。→ 我是在時代廣場坐的地鐵。

1. 他十月一號去了時代廣場。

2. 他們打的去了機場。

3. 小王在超市買了餐巾紙。

4. 我們十點鐘打了的。

5. 二年級的學生用中文問了問題。

VI. Complete the following dialogue.

A: 今天你是怎麼去上班的？

B: _____ 。

A: 你平時都坐地鐵，今天怎麼想坐公共汽車了？

B: _____ 。

A: 聽說現在坐公共汽車的人多得很。

B: _____ ？ (rhetorical question)

A: 我也不知道。我爸爸今天也坐的公共汽車。

B: _____ ？

A: 他坐66路公共汽車。

B: _____ 。

A: 因為66路是無人售票車, 所以車比較好。

VII. Choose the right words to fill in the blanks, and then read the conversation aloud with a partner.

1.因为……所以 2.地 3.了 4.了 5.了 6.是……的 7.是……的

8.是……的 9.的 10.的

A: 你昨天到哪儿去_____？

B: 我朋友从南京来，我昨天去肯尼迪机场_____。

A: 你_____几点去_____？

B: 我_____晚上八点去_____。

A: 你怎么去_____？

B: 我坐地铁去_____。

A: 纽约的地铁又是数字又是字母，你知道怎么坐吗？

B: 我不知道还不能问吗？我只坐地铁到长途汽车站，然后换机场大巴。

A: 要是你只坐地铁，不是便宜吗？

B: _____只坐地铁很麻烦，要换很多车，_____我坐_____机场 大巴。

A: 那你们_____几点回来_____？

B: 十一点半我们安全_____到家。晚上我们一起吃饭吧。

A: 好，晚上见。

VII. Choose the right words to fill in the blanks, and then read the conversation aloud with a partner.

1.因為……所以　2.地　3.了　4.了　5.了　6.是……的　7.是……的
8.是……的　9.的　10.的

A: 你昨天到哪兒去_____？

B: 我朋友從南京來，我昨天去肯尼迪機場_____。

A: 你_____幾點去_____？

B: 我_____晚上八點去_____。

A: 你怎麼去_____？

B: 我坐地鐵去_____。

A: 紐約的地鐵又是數字又是字母，你知道怎麼坐嗎?

B: 我不知道還不能問嗎？我只坐地鐵到長途汽車站，然後換機場大巴。

A: 要是你只坐地鐵，不是便宜嗎？

B: _____只坐地鐵很麻煩，要換很多車，_____我坐_____機場大巴。

A: 那你們_____幾點回來_____？

B: 十一點半我們安全_____到家。晚上我們一起吃飯吧。

A: 好，晚上見。

第七课
LESSON 7

▶ I. Past Experience with 过
(See Textbook I, Lesson 7)

Selected example from the textbook:

我感恩节才回去过。 (Lesson 7)

The word 过 (guò) can follow a verb to suggest that someone has had the experience of doing something before.

Affirmative sentence

Sentence structure:	S ＋ V ＋ 过 ＋ O

Examples:

Wǒ qù guò Xiàwēiyí.

我去过夏威夷。

I have been to Hawaii before.

Wǒ zuò guò Xīběi Hángkōng Gōngsī de fēijī.

我坐过西北航空公司的飞机。

I have taken Northwest Airlines (flights) before.

To express the idea that someone has never had the experience of doing something before, follow this pattern:

Negative sentence:	S ＋ 没(有) ＋ V ＋ 过 ＋ O

Examples:

Nà wèi xīn lǎoshī méiyǒu qù guò Xiàwēiyí.

那位新老师没有去过夏威夷。

That new teacher has never been to Hawaii.

第七課
LESSON 7

▶ **I. Past Experience with** 過
(See Textbook I, Lesson 7)

Selected example from the textbook:

我感恩節才回去過。(Lesson 7)

The word 過 (guò) can follow a verb to suggest that someone has had the experience of doing something before.

Affirmative sentence

Sentence structure:	S ＋ V ＋ 過 ＋ O

Examples:

Wǒ qù guò Xiàwēiyí.

我去過夏威夷。

I have been to Hawaii before.

Wǒ zuò guò Xīběi Hángkōng Gōngsī de fēijī.

我坐過西北航空公司的飛機。

I have taken Northwest Airlines (flights) before.

To express the idea that someone has never had the experience of doing something before, follow this pattern:

Negative sentence	S ＋ 沒(有) ＋ V ＋ 過 ＋ O

Examples:

Nà wèi xīn lǎoshī méiyǒu qù guò Xiàwēiyí.

那位新老師沒有去過夏威夷。

That new teacher has never been to Hawaii.

Zhè zhǒng diànnǎo tāmen méiyǒu yòng guò.

这种电脑他们没有用过。

They have never used this kind of computer before.

To ask the question "has someone ever done something before?" follow these patterns:

Interrogative sentence:	S ＋ V ＋ 过 ＋ O ＋ 吗
Or:	S ＋ V ＋ 过 ＋ O ＋ 没有

Examples:

Question: Nǐ gǎi guò fēijīpiào ma?

你改过飞机票吗?

Have you ever changed an airline ticket?

Or: Nǐ gǎi guò fēijīpiào méiyǒu?

你改过飞机票没有?

Have you ever changed an airline ticket?

Answers: Gǎi guò, wǒ gǎi guò fēijīpiào.

改过，我改过飞机票。

Yes, I have changed airline ticket(s) (before).

Méiyǒu, wǒ méi(yǒu) gǎi guò fēijīpiào.

没有，我没（有）改过飞机票。

No, I have never changed an airline ticket (before).

Hái méiyǒu, wǒ hái méi (yǒu) gǎi guò fēijīpiào.

还没有，我还没（有）改过飞机票。

Not yet, I have not changed an airline ticket yet (but I intend to do so in the future).

Question: Nǐ zài Zhōngguó zuò guò fēijī ma?

你在中国坐过飞机吗?

Or: Nǐ zài Zhōngguó zuò guò fēijī méiyǒu?

你在中国坐过飞机没有?

Have you ever taken an airplane in China?

Zhè zhǒng diànnǎo tāmen méiyǒu yòng guò.

這種電腦他們沒有用過。

They have never used this kind of computer before.

To ask the question "has someone ever done something before?" follow these patterns:

Interrogative sentence	S ＋ V ＋ 過 ＋ O ＋ 嗎
Or:	S ＋ V ＋ 過 ＋ O ＋ 沒有

Examples:

Question: Nǐ gǎi guò fēijīpiào ma?

你改過飛機票嗎?

Have you ever changed an airline ticket?

Or: Nǐ gǎi guò fēijīpiào méiyǒu?

你改過飛機票沒有?

Have you ever changed an airline ticket?

Answers: Gǎi guò, wǒ gǎi guò fēijīpiào.

改過,我改過飛機票。

Yes, I have changed airline ticket(s) (before).

Méiyǒu, wǒ méi(yǒu) gǎi guò fēijīpiào.

沒有,我沒(有) 改過飛機票。

No, I have never changed an airline ticket (before).

Hái méiyǒu, wǒ hái méi (yǒu) gǎi guò fēijīpiào.

還沒有,我還沒(有) 改過飛機票。

Not yet, I have not changed an airline ticket yet (but I intend to do so in the future).

Question: Nǐ zài Zhōngguó zuò guò fēijī ma?

你在中國坐過飛機嗎？

Or: Nǐ zài Zhōngguó zuò guò fēijī méiyǒu?

你在中國坐過飛機沒有？

Have you ever taken an airplane in China?

Answers: Zuò guò, wǒ zài Zhōngguó zuò guò fēijī.

坐过，我在中国坐过飞机。

Yes, I have taken an airplane in China.

Méiyǒu, wǒ méi(yǒu) zài Zhōngguó zuò guò fēijī.

没有，我没（有）在中国坐过飞机。

No, I have never taken an airplane in China (before).

Hái méiyǒu, wǒ hái méi(yǒu) zài Zhōngguó zuò guò fēijī.

还没有，我还没（有）在中国坐过飞机。

Not yet, I have not taken (an) airplane in China yet.

Note: To express a certain experience in the past, one can place 过 after the verb. The object should be placed after the verb + 过 phrase. In the negative form, 过 must be kept. In this type of sentence a time word indicating a particular time in the past can be used, however, a time word expressing frequency cannot be applied. For example: It is right to say "我去年去过夏威夷" or "我去过夏威夷," but it is incorrect to say "我常常去过夏威夷" or "去年我常常去过夏威夷。"

了 Versus 过

Although both 了 and 过 can denote past actions or events, in a 了 sentence, the speaker's focus is often on the action or event completed at a particular time, whereas in a 过 sentence, the speaker is more interested in the result or the experience of the past action or event.

Compare the differences between the following sentences:

Xiǎo Wén zuótiān zài Niǔyuē zuò le dìtiě.

小文昨天在纽约坐了地铁。

Little Wen took the subway in New York yesterday.

Xiǎo Wén zài Niǔyuē zuò guò dìtiě.

小文在纽约坐过地铁。

Little Wen has taken the subway in New York (before).

Qùnián wǒ xué le Yīngwén.

去年我学了英文。

I studied English last year.

Answers: Zuò guò, wǒ zài Zhōngguó zuò guò fēijī.

坐過，我在中國坐過飛機。

Yes, I have taken an airplane in China.

Méiyǒu, wǒ méi(yǒu) zài Zhōngguó zuò guò fēijī.

沒有，我沒(有)在中國坐過飛機。

No, I have never taken an airplane in China (before).

Hái méiyǒu, wǒ hái méi(yǒu) zài Zhōngguó zuò guò fēijī.

還沒有，我還沒(有)在中國坐過飛機。

Not yet, I have not taken (an) airplane in China yet.

Note: To express a certain experience in the past, one can place 過 after the verb. The object should be placed after the verb + 過 phrase. In the negative form, 過 must be kept. In this type of sentence a time word indicating a particular time in the past can be used, however, a time word expressing frequency cannot be applied. For example: It is right to say "我去年去過夏威夷" or "我去過夏威夷," but it is incorrect to say "我常常去過夏威夷" or "去年我常常去過夏威夷。"

了 Versus 過

Although both 了 and 過 can denote past actions or events, in a 了 sentence, the speaker's focus is often on the action or event completed at a particular time, whereas in a 過 sentence, the speaker is more interested in the result or the experience of the past action or event.

Compare the differences between the following sentences:

Xiǎo Wén zuótiān zài Niǔyuē zuò le dìtiě.

小文昨天在紐約坐了地鐵。

Little Wen took the subway in New York yesterday.

Xiǎo Wén zài Niǔyuē zuò guò dìtiě.

小文在紐約坐過地鐵。

Little Wen has taken the subway in New York (before).

Qùnián wǒ xué le Yīngwén.

去年我學了英文。

I studied English last year.

Wǒ xué guò Yīngwén.

我学过英文。

I have studied English (before).

▶ II. Changes in the Near Future with 了
(See Textbook I, Lesson 1)

Selected example from the textbook:

要上课了，一会儿见。 (Lesson 1)

The particle 了 can be applied to suggest that something is about to happen in the near future. Commonly seen expressions or variations include: 要……了 (yào...le), 就要……了 (jiùyào...le), 快……了 (kuài....le) and 快要……了 (kuàiyào...le). Comparatively speaking, out of all the patterns listed here, 就要……了 often indicates the most imminent action or state.

Note that this function of 了 does not apply to negative sentences.

Affirmative sentence

Sentence structure:	S ＋ （就/快） 要 ＋ V ＋ O ＋ 了

Examples:

Wǒ jiù yào qù Shànghǎi le.

我就要去上海了。

I will go to Shanghai very soon.

Chén jiàoshòu kuài yào lái le.

陈教授快要来了。

Professor Chen will come soon.

Fēijī yào qǐfēi le.

飞机要起飞了。

The airplane is going to take off.

Wǒ xué guò Yīngwén.

我學過英文。

I have studied English (before).

▶ II. Changes in the Near Future with 了
(See Textbook I, Lesson 1)

Selected example from the textbook:

要上課了，一會兒見。(Lesson 1)

The particle 了 can be applied to suggest that something is about to happen in the near future. Commonly seen expressions or variations include: 要……了 (yào...le), 就要……了 (jiùyào...le), 快……了 (kuài....le) and 快要……了 (kuàiyào...le). Comparatively speaking, out of all the patterns listed here, 就要……了 often indicates the most imminent action or state.

Note that this function of 了 does not apply to negative sentences.

Affirmative sentence

Sentence structure:	S ＋ (就/快) 要 ＋ V ＋ O ＋ 了

Examples:

Wǒ jiù yào qù Shànghǎi le.

我就要去上海了。

I will go to Shanghai very soon.

Chén jiàoshòu kuài yào lái le.

陳教授快要來了。

Professor Chen will come soon.

Fēijī yào qǐfēi le.

飛機要起飛了。

The airplane is going to take off.

Interrogative sentence

Sentence structure: S ＋ （就 or 快）要 ＋ V ＋ O ＋ 了 ＋ 吗

Examples:

Question: Nǐ kuài yào shàngkè le ma?

你快要上课了吗？

Are you going to class soon?

Answer: Wǒ kuài yào shàngkè le.

我快要上课了。

I am going to class soon.

Question: Tāmen jiù yào qù lǚxíng le ma?

他们就要去旅行了吗？

Are they about to go traveling?

Answer: Tāmen jiù yào qù lǚxíng le.

他们就要去旅行了。

They are about to go traveling.

Note: The affirmative answer may be made by using 对 or 是 only. The negative answer usually takes the phrase: 还没（有）呢.

Examples:

Question: Nǐ kuài yào qù Nánjīng le ma?

你快要去南京了吗？

Are you going to Nanjing very soon?

Answer: Duì.

对。

Yes.

Hái méi(yǒu) ne.

还没（有）呢。

Not yet.

Interrogative sentence

<table>
<tr><td>Sentence structure:</td><td>S ＋ (就 or 快) 要 ＋ V ＋ O ＋ 了 ＋ 嗎</td></tr>
</table>

Examples:

Question: Nǐ kuài yào shàngkè le ma?

你快要上課了嗎？

Are you going to class soon?

Answer: Wǒ kuài yào shàngkè le.

我快要上課了。

I am going to class soon.

Question: Tāmen jiù yào qù lǚxíng le ma?

他們就要去旅行了嗎？

Are they about to go traveling?

Answer: Tāmen jiù yào qù lǚxíng le.

他們就要去旅行了。

They are about to go traveling.

Note: The affirmative answer may be made by using 對 or 是 only. The negative answer usually takes the phrase: 還沒(有)呢.

Examples:

Question: Nǐ kuài yào qù Nánjīng le ma?

你快要去南京了嗎？

Are you going to Nanjing very soon?

Answer: Duì.

對。

Yes.

Hái méi(yǒu) ne.

還沒(有)呢。

Not yet.

Question: Tāmen jiù yào qù Běijīng le ma?

他们就要去北京了吗？

Are they about to go to Beijing?

Answer: Shì.

是。

Yes.

Hái méi(yǒu) ne.

还没（有）呢。

Not yet.

▶ III. Progressive Aspect or Ongoing Action
(See Textbook I, Lesson 4)

Selected examples from the textbook:

（我）现在还在上中文课。(Lesson 4)
南京等城市正在修建地铁。(Lesson 6)

To express the ongoing process of an action at a certain point of time, add the adverbs 在 (zài) or 正在 (zhèngzài) before the action verb. On an informal occasion, one can simply add the word 呢 (ne) to the end of a statement. One can also use 在 or 正在 together with 呢 in an affirmative statement.

Note that the "certain point of time" can be in the present, as the speaker is speaking, a particular time in the past, or a time in the future. 正在……呢 itself only shows an ongoing action, and does not distinguish whether it happens in the past, the present or the future.

Although all the patterns below are acceptable for expressing ongoing action, the first two are used in written Chinese, while the last two are used in spoken Chinese.

Affirmative sentence

Sentence structure:	S ＋ 在 ＋ V ＋ O
	S ＋ 正在 ＋ V ＋ O
	S ＋ V ＋ O ＋ 呢
	S ＋ （正）在 ＋ V ＋ O ＋ 呢

Question: Tāmen jiù yào qù Běijīng le ma?

他們就要去北京了嗎？

Are they about to go to Beijing?

Answer: Shì.

是。

Yes.

Hái méi(yǒu) ne.

還沒(有)呢。

Not yet.

▶ III. Progressive Aspect or Ongoing Action
(See Textbook I, Lesson 4)

Selected examples from the textbook:

（我）現在還在上中文課。 (Lesson 4)

南京等城市正在修建地鐵。 (Lesson 6)

To express the ongoing process of an action at a certain point of time, add the adverbs 在 (zài) or 正在 (zhèngzài) before the action verb. On an informal occasion, one can simply add the word 呢 (ne) to the end of a statement. One can also use 在 or 正在 together with 呢 in an affirmative statement.

Note that the "certain point of time" can be in the present, as the speaker is speaking, a particular time in the past, or a time in the future. 正在……呢 itself only shows an ongoing action, and does not distinguish whether it happens in the past, the present or the future.

Although all the patterns below are acceptable for expressing ongoing action, the first two are used in written Chinese, while the last two are used in spoken Chinese.

Affirmative sentence

Sentence structure:	S ＋ 在 ＋ V ＋ O
	S ＋ 正在 ＋ V ＋ O
	S ＋ V ＋ O ＋ 呢
	S ＋ (正)在 ＋ V ＋ O ＋ 呢

Examples:

Sūshān de bàba zhèngzài dǎ diànhuà.

苏珊的爸爸正在打电话。

Susan's father is making a phone call (now).

Tā zài liànxí xiězuò ne.

他在练习写作呢。

He is practicing writing (now).

Tā qù fēijīchǎng de shíhòu, wǒ zhèngzài yóuyǒng ne.

他去飞机场的时候，我正在游泳呢。

While he went to the airport, I was swimming.

Zuótiān wǎnshàng qī diǎn, nǐ gēge zài kàn diànshì.

昨天晚上七点，你哥哥在看电视。

At 7:00 p.m. yesterday, your elder brother was watching television.

Míngtiān tāmen chī wǎnfàn de shíhòu, wǒ huì zài shàngkè.

明天他们吃晚饭的时候，我会在上课。

When they eat dinner tomorrow, I'll be attending a class.

To express the idea that someone is not or was not in the process of doing something at a certain time, add 不在 or 没(有)在 before the verb.

Note that in a negative sentence, the words 正 and 呢 are omitted.

Negative sentence

Sentence structure:	S ＋ 不在 ＋ V ＋ O
	S ＋ 没(有)在 ＋ V ＋ O

Examples:

Gāo xiānshēng xiànzài bù zài kàn péngyou.

高先生现在不在看朋友。

Mr. Gao is not visiting his friends now.

(Incorrect: 高先生现在不正在看朋友；or 高先生现在不看朋友呢)

Examples:

Sūshān de bàba zhèngzài dǎ diànhuà.

蘇珊的爸爸正在打電話。

Susan's father is making a phone call (now).

Tā zài liànxí xiězuò ne.

他在練習寫作呢。

He is practicing writing (now).

Tā qù fēijīchǎng de shíhòu, wǒ zhèngzài yóuyǒng ne.

他去飛機場的時候，我正在游泳呢。

While he went to the airport, I was swimming.

Zuótiān wǎnshàng qī diǎn, nǐ gēge zài kàn diànshì.

昨天晚上七點，你哥哥在看電視。

At 7:00 p.m. yesterday, your elder brother was watching television.

Míngtiān tāmen chī wǎnfàn de shíhòu, wǒ huì zài shàngkè.

明天他們吃晚飯的時候，我會在上課。

When they eat dinner tomorrow, I'll be attending a class.

To express the idea that someone is not or was not in the process of doing something at a certain time, add 不在 or 沒(有)在 before the verb.

Note that in a negative sentence, the words 正 and 呢 are omitted.

Negative sentence

Sentence structure:	S ＋ 不在 ＋ V ＋ O
	S ＋ 沒(有)在 ＋ V ＋ O

Examples:

Gāo xiānshēng xiànzài bù zài kàn péngyou.

高先生現在不在看朋友。

Mr. Gao is not visiting his friends now.

(Incorrect: 高先生現在不正在看朋友; or 高先生現在不看朋友呢)

Shànggè xīngqīwǔ wǒ dào tā jiā de shíhou, tā méi zài shuìjiào.

上个星期五我到他家的时候，他没在睡觉。

When I arrived at his house last Friday, he was not sleeping.

（Incorrect: 上个星期五我到他家的时候，他没正在睡觉；
or 上个星期五我到他家的时候，他没睡觉呢）

Interrogative sentence

Sentence structure:	S ＋ 在 ＋ V ＋ O ＋ 吗
Or:	S ＋ 正在 ＋ V ＋ O ＋吗

Examples:

Nǐmen zhèngzài shàngkè ma?

你们正在上课吗？

Are you having class (now)?

Nǐ māma lǚxíng de shíhou, nǐ zhèngzài Zhōngguó gōngzuò ma?

你妈妈旅行的时候，你正在中国工作吗？

When your mother was traveling, were you working in China?

Tā zài kàn shénme bào?

他在看什么报？

What newspaper is he reading?

Note: The meaning of the adverbs 正, 在 and 正在 is essentially the same, but they have different emphases. 正 emphasizes a certain period or time, and 在 emphasizes being in the state of progression, while 正在 refers to both time and state. Only action verbs can be used with 正在……呢. Some verbs that indicate state, psychological activities, directions, such as 是，在，有，懂，知道，喜欢，来，去, etc., cannot be used in the 正在……呢 pattern.

Examples:

Zuótiān xiàwǔ sān diǎn tāmen zhèngzài kàn yīshēng.

昨天下午三点他们正在看医生。

At 3:00 p.m. yesterday they were seeing a doctor.

Shànggè xīngqīwǔ wǒ dào tā jiā de shíhou, tā méi zài shuìjiào.

上個星期五我到他家的時候，他沒在睡覺。

When I arrived at his house last Friday, he was not sleeping.

(Incorrect: 上個星期五我到他家的時候，他沒正在睡覺;

or 上個星期五我到他家的時候，他沒睡覺呢)

Interrogative sentence

Sentence structure:	S ＋ 在 ＋ V ＋ O ＋ 嗎
Or:	S ＋ 正在 ＋ V ＋ O ＋嗎

Examples:

Nǐmen zhèngzài shàngkè ma?

你們正在上課嗎？

Are you having class (now)?

Nǐ māma lǚxíng de shíhou, nǐ zhèngzài Zhōngguó gōngzuò ma?

你媽媽旅行的時候，你正在中國工作嗎？

When your mother was traveling, were you working in China?

Tā zài kàn shénme bào?

他在看什麼報？

What newspaper is he reading?

Note: The meaning of the adverbs 正, 在 and 正在 is essentially the same, but they have different emphases. 正 emphasizes a certain period or time, and 在 emphasizes being in the state of progression, while 正在 refers to both time and state. Only action verbs can be used with 正在……呢. Some verbs that indicate state, psychological activities, directions, such as 是, 在, 有, 懂, 知道, 喜歡, 來, 去, etc., cannot be used in the 正在……呢 pattern.

Examples:

Zuótiān xiàwǔ sān diǎn tāmen zhèngzài kàn yīshēng.

昨天下午三點他們正在看醫生。

At 3:00 p.m. yesterday they were seeing a doctor.

Xià xīngqī nǐ qù zhǎo tā de shíhòu, tā huì zài xuéxí yǔfǎ.

下星期你去找他的时候，他会在学习语法。

When you go to look for him next week, perhaps he will be studying grammar.

▶ IV. A Continued Action or Situation with 着

Selected example from the textbook:

先挂号，然后在候诊区等着叫号。(Lesson 9)

When the particle 着 (zhe) follows a verb, it signifies the continuation of an action or situation.

Affirmative sentence

Sentence structure:	S ＋ V ＋ 着 ＋ 0

Examples:

Tā māma chuānzhe yī jiàn hóng máoyī.

他妈妈穿着一件红毛衣。

His mother is wearing a red sweater.

Bié zhànzhe, zuò xià ba.

别站着，坐下吧。

Don't stand (there), sit down.

Mén kāizhe.

门开着。

The door is open.

In a negative sentence, the words 没有 or 没 are usually inserted before the verb.

Negative sentence

Sentence structure:	S ＋ 没有 ＋ V ＋ 着

Xià xīngqī nǐ qù zhǎo tā de shíhòu, tā huì zài xuéxí yǔfǎ.

下星期你去找他的時候，他會在學習語法。

When you go to look for him next week, perhaps he will be studying grammar.

▶ IV. A Continued Action or Situation with 著

Selected example from the textbook:

先掛號，然後在候診區等著叫號。(Lesson 9)

When the particle 著 (zhe) follows a verb, it signifies the continuation of an action or situation.

Affirmative sentence

Sentence structure:	S ＋ V ＋ 著 ＋ O

Examples:

Tā māma chuānzhe yī jiàn hóng máoyī .

他媽媽穿著一件紅毛衣。

His mother is wearing a red sweater.

Bié zhànzhe, zuò xià ba.

別站著，坐下吧。

Don't stand (there), sit down.

Mén kāizhe.

門開著。

The door is open.

In a negative sentence, the words 沒有 or 沒 are usually inserted before the verb.

Negative sentence

Sentence structure:	S ＋ 沒有 ＋ V ＋ 著

Examples:

Wǒ de mén méiyǒu kāizhe.

我的门没有开着。

My door is not open.

Diànshì méiyǒu kāizhe.

电视没有开着。

The TV is not on.

Interrogative sentence

Sentence structure:	S ＋ V ＋ 着 ＋ O ＋ 吗
	S ＋ V ＋ 着 ＋ O ＋ 没有

Examples:

Question: Chuānghu kāizhe ma?

窗户开着吗?

Is the window open?

Answers: Kāizhe ne.

开着呢。

Yes, it is.

Méiyǒu, méi kāizhe.

没有，没开着。

No, it is not open.

Question: Nǐ dàizhe xiànjīn méiyǒu?

你带着现金没有?

Have you brought cash with you?

Answers: Dàizhe ne.

带着呢。

Yes, I have.

Examples:

Wǒ de mén méiyǒu kāizhe.

我的門沒有開著。

My door is not open.

Diànshì méiyǒu kāizhe.

電視沒有開著。

The TV is not on.

Interrogative sentence

Sentence structure:	S + V + 著 + O + 嗎
	S + V + 著 + O + 沒有

Examples:

Question: Chuānghu kāizhe ma?

窗戶開著嗎?

Is the window open?

Answers: Kāizhe ne.

開著呢。

Yes, it is.

Méiyǒu, méi kāizhe.

沒有, 沒開著。

No, it is not open.

Question: Nǐ dàizhe xiànjīn méiyǒu?

你帶著現金沒有?

Have you brought cash with you?

Answers: Dàizhe ne.

帶著呢。

Yes, I have.

Méiyǒu, méi dàizhe.

没有，没带着。

No, I've not.

Note: The continuation of the action may take place in the past, present or future, but the form should remain unchanged.

Examples:

Yuēhàn zuótiān shàngxué de shíhòu dàizhe xìnyòngkǎ.

约翰昨天上学的时候带着信用卡。

John brought his credit card with him when he went to school yesterday.

Yuēhàn jīntiān shàngxué de shíhòu dàizhe xìnyòngkǎ.

约翰今天上学的时候带着信用卡。

John has his credit card with him in school today.

Yuēhàn míngtiān shàngxué de shíhòu yào dàizhe xìnyòngkǎ.

约翰明天上学的时候要带着信用卡。

John will bring his credit card with him when he goes to school tomorrow.

Note: Now we have learned all three aspectual particles 了, 着 and 过. In summary, the aspectual particle 了 is generally placed immediately after the verb to indicate that an action has been completed. 着 is placed immediately after the verb to indicate a range of meanings related to a continuing state or action. 过 occurs after a verb or adjective to express a past experience or state.

Examples:

Wǒ mǎi le liǎng dài miànbāo.

我买了两袋面包。

I bought two bags of bread.

Gélín chuānzhe yī jiàn hēi xīzhuāng.

格林穿着一件黑西装。

Green is wearing a black suit.

Bǐdé qù guò Xī'ān.

彼得去过西安。

Peter has been to Xi'an.

Méiyǒu, méi dàizhe.

沒有，沒帶著。

No, I've not.

Note: The continuation of the action may take place in the past, present or future, but the form should remain unchanged.

Examples:

Yuēhàn zuótiān shàngxué de shíhòu dàizhe xìnyòngkǎ.

約翰昨天上學的時候帶著信用卡。

John brought his credit card with him when he went to school yesterday.

Yuēhàn jīntiān shàngxué de shíhòu dàizhe xìnyòngkǎ.

約翰今天上學的時候帶著信用卡。

John has his credit card with him in school today.

Yuēhàn míngtiān shàngxué de shíhòu yào dàizhe xìnyòngkǎ.

約翰明天上學的時候要帶著信用卡。

John will bring his credit card with him when he goes to school tomorrow.

Note: Now we have learned all three aspectual particles 了, 著 and 過. In summary, the aspectual particle 了 is generally placed immediately after the verb to indicate that an action has been completed. 著 is placed immediately after the verb to indicate a range of meanings related to a continuing state or action. 過 occurs after a verb or adjective to express a past experience or state.

Examples:

Wǒ mǎi le liǎng dài miànbāo.

我買了兩袋麵包。

I bought two bags of bread.

Gélín chuānzhe yī jiàn hēi xīzhuāng.

格林穿著一件黑西裝。

Green is wearing a black suit.

Bǐdé qù guò Xī'ān.

彼得去過西安。

Peter has been to Xi'an.

▶ V. Simultaneous Actions with 一边……一边

一边……一边 (yībiān…yībiān) can describe two actions taking place simultaneously. The second verb often suggests the main action, and the first verb denotes the accompanying action.

> **Sentence structure:** S ＋ 一边 ＋ V1 ＋ 01 ＋ 一边 ＋ V2 ＋ 02

Examples:

Wǒ xǐhuān yībiān zuò gōnggòng qìchē yībiān dǎ diànhuà.

我喜欢一边坐公共汽车一边打电话。

I like to make phone calls while taking the bus.

Tā chángcháng yībiān kàn diànshì yībiān shuōhuà.

他常常一边看电视一边说话。

He often talks while watching TV.

▶ V. Simultaneous Actions with 一邊……一邊

一邊……一邊 (yībiān…yībiān) can describe two actions taking place simultaneously. The second verb often suggests the main action, and the first verb denotes the accompanying action.

Sentence structure: S ＋ 一邊 ＋ V1 ＋ O1 ＋ 一邊 ＋ V2 ＋ O2

Examples:

Wǒ xǐhuān yībiān zuò gōnggòng qìchē yībiān dǎ diànhuà.

我喜歡一邊坐公共汽車一邊打電話。

I like to make phone calls while taking the bus.

Tā chángcháng yībiān kàn diànshì yībiān shuōhuà.

他常常一邊看電視一邊說話。

He often talks while watching TV.

▶ 练习 Exercises

I. Fill in the blanks with 了 or 过.

虽然王先生以前去_____中国，但是他没有去_____北京。他听朋友说北京特别好玩，所以今年寒假他旅行去_____北京。一月的北京特别冷(lěng, cold)，但是王先生不怕。在北京，他去_____很多地方，还跟一些北京人练_____会话。王先生在北京认识_____一个美国朋友。因为那个朋友以前只吃_____日本饭，没有吃_____中国饭，所以王先生带他去_____一个很好的中国餐厅，请他吃_____中国饭。

II. Fill in the blanks with 正在 or 着 according to the English given within the brackets.

昨天我从超市回家的时候，王小年_____(was going to the supermarket)。我跟他说了再见，就_____(was holding)我买的东西，快快地进(jìn, to enter) 了地铁站。到家的时候正好是晚上七点。妈妈_____(was cooking) 晚饭，爸爸_____(was watching TV)。因为哥哥房间(fángjiān, room) 的门_____(was closed)，所以我以为(yǐwéi, thought)哥哥还没有回家。其实(qíshí, in fact)哥哥昨天不忙，下午五点就回家了，他_____(was sleeping)。

III. Rewrite the sentences using 要……了, 就要……了, 快……了, **or** 快要……了

Example: 电影票剩的不多了。　→　电影票快没有了。

1. 飞机五分钟以后起飞。
2. 现在是八点。药房九点关门 (to be closed)。
3. 今天是十二月十号。我们十二月二十号放寒假。
4. 旅行社说我的飞机票过两天会到。
5. 老师说一年级的学生下个星期开始学中文语法。

IV. Fill in the blanks with 了 **or** (正)在 **according to the English provided.**

上个星期六下午苏珊给彼得打电话的时候，彼得_____(was reserving an airline ticket)。她听说彼得要回夏威夷过圣诞节，她也想去。可是她爸爸已经给她_____(bought)12月18日回家的飞机票。苏珊想问爸爸、妈妈能不能改票。她打电话回家的时候，妈妈_____(was watching TV)，爸爸_____(was cooking)。妈妈说："爸爸给你_____(reserved)回家的飞机票了，你别

▶ 練習 Exercises

I. Fill in the blanks with 了 or 過.

雖然王先生以前去＿＿＿＿＿中國，但是他沒有去＿＿＿＿＿北京。他聽朋友說北京特別好玩，所以今年寒假他旅行去＿＿＿＿＿北京。一月的北京特別冷(lěng, cold)，但是王先生不怕。在北京，他去＿＿＿＿＿很多地方，還跟一些北京人練＿＿＿＿＿會話。王先生在北京認識＿＿＿＿＿一個美國朋友。因為那個朋友以前只吃＿＿＿＿＿日本飯，沒有吃＿＿＿＿＿中國飯，所以王先生帶他去＿＿＿＿＿一個很好的中國餐廳，請他吃＿＿＿＿＿中國飯。

II. Fill in the blanks with 正在 or 著 according to the English given within the brackets.

昨天我從超市回家的時候，王小年＿＿＿＿＿＿(was going to the supermarket)。我跟他說了再見，就＿＿＿＿＿＿(was holding) 我買的東西，快快地進(jìn, to enter) 了地鐵站。到家的時候正好是晚上七點。媽媽＿＿＿＿＿＿(was cooking) 晚飯，爸爸＿＿＿＿＿＿ (was watching TV)。因為哥哥房間(fángjiān, room) 的門＿＿＿＿＿＿(was closed)，所以我以為(yǐwéi, thought)哥哥還沒有回家。其實(qíshí, in fact) 哥哥昨天不忙，下午五點就回家了，他＿＿＿＿＿＿(was sleeping)。

III. Rewrite the sentences using 要……了, 就要……了, 快……了, or 快要……了

Example: 電影票剩的不多了。 → 電影票快沒有了。

1. 飛機五分鐘以後起飛。
2. 現在是八點。藥房九點關門 (to be closed)。
3. 今天是十二月十號。我們十二月二十號放寒假。
4. 旅行社說我的飛機票過兩天會到。
5. 老師說一年級的學生下個星期開始學中文語法。

IV. Fill in the blanks with 了 or (正)在 according to the English provided.

上個星期六下午蘇珊給彼得打電話的時候，彼得＿＿＿＿＿＿(was reserving an airline ticket)。她聽說彼得要回夏威夷過聖誕節，她也想去。可是她爸爸已經給她＿＿＿＿＿ (bought) 12月18日回家的飛機票。蘇珊 想問爸爸、媽媽能不能改票。她打電話回家的時候，媽媽＿＿＿＿＿＿(was watching TV)，爸爸＿＿＿＿＿＿ (was cooking)。媽媽說： "爸爸給你＿＿＿＿＿＿(reserved)回家的飛機票了，你別

_____(go to Hawaii) 了。"苏珊说："因为爸爸_____(bought) 飞机票，所以我要请爸爸改票。"她爸爸只好说："好吧，我明天就去给你改票。"

V. Use 一边，……一边 **to write sentences according to the following phrases.**

Example: 跳舞/说话 → 他们喜欢一边跳舞，一边说话。

1. 唱歌/做作业
2. 看电视/吃饭
3. 打电话/写汉字
4. 喝酒/吃中国饭

VI. Correct the errors, if there are any, in the following sentences.

1. 王老师现在不正在上课。
2. 昨天下午他改飞机票。
3. 我学习语法正在。
4. 你改了飞机票没改吗？
5. 他拿要退的衣服着。
6. 我去飞机场的时候他没有正在睡觉。
7. 他拿超市买的东西去着朋友的生日晚会。

VII. Write an essay in Chinese describing an interesting thing you did in the past. Try to use as many new grammatical patterns as you can, such as 过，了，着，(正)在，一边……一边.

VIII. Choose the right words to fill in the blanks, and then read the conversation aloud with a partner.

1.着 2.着 3.在 4.正在 5.要……了 6.快……了 7.了 8.了
9.一边……一边 10.一边……一边

A: 喂，老朋友，你_____做什么呢？

B: 我_____吃饭。一会儿要去飞机场。

A: 还有一个星期就_____放寒假_____，你女儿_____回来_____吧？

_____(go to Hawaii)了。" 蘇珊說："因為爸爸_____(bought)飛機票,所以我要請爸爸改票。" 她爸爸只好說:"好吧,我明天就去給你改票。"

V. Use 一邊,……一邊 to write sentences according to the following phrases.

Example: 跳舞/說話→ 他們喜歡一邊跳舞,一邊說話。

1. 唱歌/做作業
2. 看電視/吃飯
3. 打電話/寫漢字
4. 喝酒/吃中國飯

VI. Correct the errors, if there are any, in the following sentences.

1. 王老師現在不正在上課。
2. 昨天下午他改飛機票。
3. 我學習語法正在。
4. 你改了飛機票沒改嗎?
5. 他拿要退的衣服著。
6. 我去飛機場的時候他沒有正在睡覺。
7. 他拿超市買的東西去著朋友的生日晚會。

VII. Write an essay in Chinese describing an interesting thing you did in the past. Try to use as many new grammatical patterns as you can, such as 過,了,著,(正)在,一邊……一邊.

VIII. Choose the right words to fill in the blanks, and then read the conversation aloud with a partner.

1.著 2.著 3.在 4.正在 5.要……了 6.快……了 7.了 8.了 9.一邊……一邊 10.一邊……一邊

A: 喂,老朋友,你_____做什麼呢?

B: 我_____吃飯。一會兒要去飛機場。

A: 還有一個星期就_____放寒假_____,你女兒_____回來_____吧?

B: 她没去过夏威夷，寒假要先去夏威夷玩儿。我已经给女儿买_____一张从纽约到波士顿的飞机票，可是她现在要从夏威夷回来。我还得改票。

A: 那你改了吗？

B: 还没有。去飞机场的时候，我可以_____开车_____打电话。

A: _____开车_____打电话不安全。你还是先去机场，再去改票吧。

B: 好。可是不知道那时旅行社是不是还开_____。

A: 要是开_____你就改，要是关_____就明天改。

B: 也只好这样了。我得走了，再见。

A: 再见。

B: 她沒去過夏威夷，寒假要先去夏威夷玩兒。我已經給女兒買_____
一張從紐約到波士頓的飛機票，可是她現在要從夏威夷回來。我還得
改票。

A: 那你改了嗎?

B: 還沒有。去飛機場的時候，我可以_____開車_____打電話。

A: _____開車_____打電話不安全。你還是先去機場，再去改票
吧。

B: 好。可是不知道那時旅行社是不是還開_____。

A: 要是開_____你就改，要是關_____就明天改。

B: 也只好這樣了。我得走了，再見。

A: 再見。

第八课
LESSON 8

▶ **I. Comparisons**

(See Textbook I, Lessons 6 and 10)

Selected examples from the textbook:

在中国坐公共汽车跟美国一样吗？(Lesson 6)

有空调的车比没有空调的车贵一块钱。(Lesson 6)

在中国乘公共汽车和美国一样，前门上车，后门下车。(Lesson 6)

北京、广州和上海有(地铁)，比纽约的地铁漂亮多了。(Lesson 6)

有的网站还报半个月的天气，但一般不如近期的准。(Lesson 10)

1. Same-Degree Comparisons

To express the idea that "A is the same as B," use the words 跟 (gēn, and) and 一样 (yíyàng, alike or same). In place of 跟, the words 和 (hé, and), 像 (xiàng, be like) and 同 (tóng, same) may also be used.

Note that in this case, the "A" and "B" can be two nouns or noun phrases, as well as two actions.

Affirmative sentence

| **Sentence structure:** A ＋ 跟 (or 和、像、同) ＋ B ＋ 一样 |

Examples:

Zhōngguó de gōnggòng qìchē gēn Měiguó de (gōnggòng qìchē) yīyàng.

中国的公共汽车跟美国的(公共汽车)一样。

Buses in China are the same as buses in the United States.

Qǔ qián de yínhángkǎ hé cún qián de (yínhángkǎ) yīyàng.

取钱的银行卡和存钱的(银行卡)一样。

The bank card for withdrawing money is the same as (the one) for depositing money.

第八課
LESSON 8

▶ I. Comparisons
(See Textbook I, Lessons 6 and 10)

Selected examples from the textbook:

在中國坐公共汽車跟美國一樣嗎？(Lesson 6)
有空調的車比沒有空調的車貴一塊錢。(Lesson 6)
在中國乘公共汽車和美國一樣，前門上車，後門下車。(Lesson 6)
北京、廣州和上海有(地鐵)，比紐約的地鐵漂亮多了。(Lesson 6)
有的網站還報半個月的天氣，但一般不如近期的準。(Lesson 10)

1. Same-Degree Comparisons

To express the idea that "A is the same as B," use the words 跟 (gēn, and) and 一樣 (yíyàng, alike or same). In place of 跟, the words 和 (hé, and), 像 (xiàng, be like) and 同 (tóng, same) may also be used.

Note that in this case, the "A" and "B" can be two nouns or noun phrases, as well as two actions.

Affirmative sentence

> **Sentence structure:** A ＋ 跟 (or 和、像、同) ＋ B ＋ 一樣

Examples:

Zhōngguó de gōnggòng qìchē gēn Měiguó de (gōnggòng qìchē) yíyàng.

中國的公共汽車跟美國的 (公共汽車) 一樣。

Buses in China are the same as buses in the United States.

Qǔ qián de yínhángkǎ hé cún qián de (yínhángkǎ) yíyàng.

取錢的銀行卡和存 錢的 (銀行卡) 一樣。

The bank card for withdrawing money is the same as (the one) for depositing money.

To say that "A is different from B," add 不 before 一样. Note that the word 像 cannot be used in a negative sentence.

Negative sentence

Sentence structure:	A ＋ 跟 （or 和、同） ＋ B ＋ 不一样

Examples:

Yóujú gēn yínháng bù yīyàng.

邮局跟银行不一样。

The post office is not the same as the bank.

（Incorrect: 邮局像银行不一样。）

Qǔ qián hé cún qián bù yīyàng.

取钱和存钱不一样。

Withdrawing money is different from depositing money.

（Incorrect: 取钱像存钱不一样。）

Zhōngwén yǔfǎ hé Yīngwén yǔfǎ bù yīyàng.

中文语法和英文语法不一样。

Chinese grammar is different from English grammar.

To express the idea that "A is as [adjective] as B," add an adjective after 一样.

Sentence structure:	A ＋ 跟 （or 和、像、同） ＋ B ＋ 一样 ＋ Adjective

Examples:

Zhè zhǒng yóujiàn gēn nà zhǒng (yóujiàn) yīyàng guì.

这种邮件跟那种(邮件)一样贵。

This kind of mail is as expensive as that kind (of mail).

Kàn diànshì hé kàn diànyǐng yīyàng yǒuyìsi.

看电视和看电影一样有意思。

Watching television is as interesting as watching movies.

To say that "A is different from B," add 不 before 一樣. Note that the word 像 cannot be used in a negative sentence.

Negative sentence

Sentence structure:	A ＋ 跟 (or 和、同) ＋ B ＋ 不一樣

Examples:

Yóujú gēn yínháng bù yīyàng.

郵局跟銀行不一樣。

The post office is not the same as the bank.

(Incorrect: 郵局像銀行不一樣。)

Qǔ qián hé cún qián bù yīyàng.

取錢和存錢不一樣。

Withdrawing money is different from depositing money.

(Incorrect: 取錢像存錢不一樣。)

Zhōngwén yǔfǎ hé Yīngwén yǔfǎ bù yīyàng.

中文語法和英文語法不一樣。

Chinese grammar is different from English grammar.

To express the idea that "A is as [adjective] as B," add an adjective after 一樣.

Sentence structure:	A ＋ 跟 (or 和、像、同) ＋ B ＋ 一樣 ＋ Adjective

Examples:

Zhè zhǒng yóujiàn gēn nà zhǒng (yóujiàn) yīyàng guì.

這種郵件跟那種 (郵件) 一樣貴。

This kind of mail is as expensive as that kind (of mail).

Kàn diànshì hé kàn diànyǐng yīyàng yǒuyìsi.

看電視和看電影一樣有意思。

Watching television is as interesting as watching movies.

Tā shuō Zhōngwén shuō de gēn nǐ yīyàng liúlì.

他说中文说得跟你一样流利。

He speaks Chinese as fluently as you do.

Notes: 1. In general, words or phrases before and after 跟 should be of the same type, if one is a noun, both should be nouns; if one is a verbal phrase, both should be verbal phrases. For example, in 邮局跟银行不一样, both 邮局 and 银行 are nouns. In 看电视和看电影一样有意思, both 看电视 and 看电影 are verbal phrases.

2. If the noun phrases before and after 跟 are the same, the one after 跟 can be dropped, but the modifier should be kept. For example: 这种邮件跟那种（邮件）一样贵. The second 邮件 can be dropped, but the modifier 那种 cannot. If the modifier has a possessive particle 的, it should be kept. For example: 中国的公共汽车跟美国的（公共汽车）一样.

2. Different-Degree Comparisons

To say that "A is more or less [adjective] than B," use the word 比 (bǐ, than).

Affirmative sentence

Sentence structure:	A ＋ 比 ＋ B ＋ Adjecitve

Examples:

Zuò dìtiě bǐ zuò gōnggòng qìchē kuài.

坐地铁比坐公共汽车快。

Taking the subway is faster than taking the bus.

Měiguó de yínháng bǐ Zhōngguó de (yínháng) duō.

美国的银行比中国的（银行）多。

There are more banks in America than in China.

Cháng xiānsheng bǐ Gāo xiānsheng kàn bào kàn de kuài.

常先生比高先生看报看得快。

Mr. Chang reads the newspaper faster than Mr. Gao does.

一点儿 (yìdiǎnr, a bit) can be added to the end of the above pattern to mean "A is a bit more or less [adjective] than B."

Tā shuō Zhōngwén shuō de gēn nǐ yīyàng liúlì.

他說中文說得跟你一樣流利。

He speaks Chinese as fluently as you do.

Notes: 1. In general, words or phrases before and after 跟 should be of the same type, if one is a noun, both should be nouns; if one is a verbal phrase, both should be verbal phrases. For example, in 郵局跟銀行不一樣, both 郵局 and 銀行 are nouns. In 看電視和看電影一樣有意思, both 看電視 and 看電影 are verbal phrases.

2. If the noun phrases before and after 跟 are the same, the one after 跟 can be dropped, but the modifier should be kept. For example: 這種郵件跟那種 (郵件) 一樣貴. The second 郵件 can be dropped, but the modifier 那種 cannot. If the modifier has a possessive particle 的, it should be kept. For example: 中國的公共汽車跟美國的 (公共汽車) 一樣.

2. Different-Degree Comparisons

To say that "A is more or less [adjective] than B," use the word 比 (bǐ, than).

Affirmative sentence

Sentence structure:	A ＋ 比 ＋ B ＋ Adjecitve

Examples:

Zuò dìtiě bǐ zuò gōnggòng qìchē kuài.

坐地鐵比坐公共汽車快。

Taking the subway is faster than taking the bus.

Měiguó de yínháng bǐ Zhōngguó de (yínháng) duō.

美國的銀行比中國的 (銀行) 多。

There are more banks in America than in China.

Cháng xiānsheng bǐ Gāo xiānsheng kàn bào kàn de kuài.

常先生比高先生看報看得快。

Mr. Chang reads the newspaper faster than Mr. Gao does.

一點兒 (yìdiǎnr, a bit) can be added to the end of the above pattern to mean "A is a bit more or less [adjective] than B."

Sentence structure:	A ＋ 比 ＋ B ＋ Adjective ＋ 一点儿

Examples:

Měiguó de yóujú bǐ Zhōngguó de (yóujú) shǎo yīdiǎn.

美国的邮局比中国的（邮局）少一点。

There are slightly fewer post offices in America than in China.

Zhège xiànjīnjī bǐ nàge (xiànjīnjī) dà yī diǎn.

这个现金机比那个（现金机）大一点。

This cash machine is a little bigger than that one.

Nǐ kāichē bǐ wǒ kāi de kuài yìdiǎnr.

你开车比我开得快一点儿。

You drive a little faster than I do.

To express the idea "A is much more or much less [adjective] than B," add 得多 (dé duō, much) or 多了 (duō le, much).

Sentence structure:	A ＋ 比 ＋ B ＋ Adjective ＋ 得多 or 多了

Examples:

Zhège yínháng bǐ nà ge (yínháng) xiǎo dé duō.

这个银行比那个（银行）小得多。

This bank is much smaller than that one.

Tā mǎi yóupiào bǐ wǒ mǎi de kuài duō le.

他买邮票比我买得快多了。

He bought stamps much faster than I did.

Zhè jiàn huáng máoyī bǐ nà jiàn hēi máoyī guì dé duō.

这件黄毛衣比那件黑毛衣贵得多。

This yellow sweater is much more expensive than that black one.

To say that "A is not as [adjective] as B," one should use 没有 (méiyǒu), not 不比 (bùbǐ).

Sentence structure:	A ＋ 比 ＋ B ＋ Adjective ＋ 一點兒

Examples:

Měiguó de yóujú bǐ Zhōngguó de (yóujú) shǎo yīdiǎn.

美國的郵局比中國的（郵局）少一點。

There are slightly fewer post offices in America than in China.

Zhège xiànjīnjī bǐ nàge (xiànjīnjī) dà yī diǎn.

這個現金機比那個 (現金機) 大一 點。

This cash machine is a little bigger than that one.

Nǐ kāichē bǐ wǒ kāi de kuài yìdiǎnr.

你開車比我開得快一點兒。

You drive a little faster than I do.

To express the idea "A is much more or much less [adjective] than B," add 得多 (dé duō, much) or 多了 (duō le, much).

Sentence structure:	A ＋ 比 ＋ B ＋ Adjective ＋ 得多 or 多了

Examples:

Zhège yínháng bǐ nà ge (yínháng) xiǎo dé duō.

這個銀行比那個（銀行）小得多。

This bank is much smaller than that one.

Tā mǎi yóupiào bǐ wǒ mǎi de kuài duō le.

他買郵票比我買得快多了。

He bought stamps much faster than I did.

Zhè jiàn huáng máoyī bǐ nà jiàn hēi máoyī guì dé duō.

這件黃毛衣比那件黑毛衣貴得多。

This yellow sweater is much more expensive than that black one.

To say that "A is not as [adjective] as B," one should use 沒有 (méiyǒu), not 不比 (bùbǐ).

Negative sentence

Sentence structure: A ＋ 没有 ＋ B ＋ Adjective

Examples:

Zhè zhǒng xìnfēng méiyǒu nà zhǒng (xìnfēng) piányí.

这种信封没有那种(信封)便宜。

This type of envelope is not as inexpensive as that type (of envelope).

Kàn diànshì méiyǒu kàn diànyǐng yǒuyìsi.

看电视没有看电影有意思。

Watching television is not as interesting as watching a movie.

Note: 不比 is also used in comparisons, but its meaning is very different. It only indicates that "the former is not more or less [adjective] than the latter," it does not have the implication of "the latter is more or less [adjective] than the former." Compare the differences between 没有 (méiyǒu) and 不比 (bùbǐ) in the following sentences:

Examples:

Niǔyuē méiyǒu Xiàwēiyí yuǎn.

纽约没有夏威夷远。

New York is not as far as Hawaii (i.e., New York is closer than Hawaii).

Niǔyuē bù bǐ Xiàwēiyí yuǎn.

纽约不比夏威夷远。

New York is no farther than Hawaii (i.e., New York is about as far as Hawaii).

Xué Zhōngwén méiyǒu xué Rìwén nán.

学中文没有学日文难。

Learning Chinese is not as hard as learning Japanese (i.e., learning Chinese is easier than learning Japanese).

Xué Zhōngwén bù bǐ xué Rìwén nán.

学中文不比学日文难。

Learning Chinese is no harder than learning Japanese (i.e., learning Chinese is about as hard as learning Japanese).

Negative sentence

> **Sentence structure:**   A ＋ 沒有 ＋ B ＋ Adjective

Examples:

Zhè zhǒng xìnfēng méiyǒu nà zhǒng (xìnfēng) piányí.

這種信封沒有那種(信封) 便宜。

This type of envelope is not as inexpensive as that type (of envelope).

Kàn diànshì méiyǒu kàn diànyǐng yǒuyìsi.

看電視沒有看電影有意思。

Watching television is not as interesting as watching a movie.

Note: 不比 is also used in comparisons, but its meaning is very different. It only indicates that "the former is not more or less [adjective] than the latter," it does not have the implication of "the latter is more or less [adjective] than the former." Compare the differences between 沒有 (méiyǒu) and 不比 (bùbǐ) in the following sentences:

Examples:

Niǔyuē méiyǒu Xiàwēiyí yuǎn.

紐約沒有夏威夷遠。

New York is not as far as Hawaii (i.e., New York is closer than Hawaii).

Niǔyuē bù bǐ Xiàwēiyí yuǎn.

紐約不比夏威夷遠。

New York is no farther than Hawaii (i.e., New York is about as far as Hawaii).

Xué Zhōngwén méiyǒu xué Rìwén nán.

學中文沒有學日文難。

Learning Chinese is not as hard as learning Japanese (i.e., learning Chinese is easier than learning Japanese).

Xué Zhōngwén bù bǐ xué Rìwén nán.

學中文不比學日文難。

Learning Chinese is no harder than learning Japanese (i.e., learning Chinese is about as hard as learning Japanese).

Note: 1. Words or phrases both before and after 比 are generally of the same type.

2. The adverbs 更, 还 and 还要 can be used after the 比-phrase and before the verb/adjective to denote a further degree.

Examples:

Zhè zhǒng xìnfēng bǐ nà zhǒng (xìnfēng) gèng piányí.

这种信封比那种(信封)更便宜。

This type of envelope is even cheaper than that type (of envelope).

Měiguó de yínháng bǐ Zhōngguó de (yínháng) hái duō.

美国的银行比中国的(银行)还多。

There are even more banks in America than in China.

3. Complement can be used after the verb/adjective in sentences with the 比-phrase.

Examples:

Cháng xiānsheng bǐ Gāo xiānsheng tiàowǔ tiào de hǎo.

常先生比高先生跳舞跳得好。

Mr. Chang dances better than Mr. Gao.

Jì hǎiyùn bǐ jì hangkōng piányi èrshí kuài qián.

寄海运比寄航空便宜20块钱。

Mail by sea is $20 cheaper than by air.

4. Difference between 跟 and 比 in expressing comparison can be summarized as: 跟 shows only whether the two persons or things being compared are the same or not, whereas 比 can further indicate the concrete differences between them.

Examples:

Hǎiyùn gēn hángkōng bù yīyàng.

海运跟航空不一样。

Mail by sea and by air are not the same.

Hǎiyùn bǐ hángkōng piányí.

海运比航空便宜。

Sea mail is cheaper than airmail. (Tells how they are different in terms of price.)

Note: 1. Words or phrases both before and after 比 are generally of the same type.

2. The adverbs 更, 還 and 還要 can be used after the 比-phrase and before the verb/adjective to denote a further degree.

Examples:

Zhè zhǒng xìnfēng bǐ nà zhǒng (xìnfēng) gèng piányí.

這種信封比那種(信封)更便宜。

This type of envelope is even cheaper than that type (of envelope).

Měiguó de yínháng bǐ Zhōngguó de (yínháng) hái duō.

美國的銀行比中國的(銀行)還多。

There are even more banks in America than in China.

3. Complement can be used after the verb/adjective in sentences with the 比-phrase.

Examples:

Cháng xiānsheng bǐ Gāo xiānsheng tiàowǔ tiào de hǎo.

常先生比高先生跳舞跳得好。

Mr. Chang dances better than Mr. Gao.

Jì hǎiyùn bǐ jì hangkōng piányi èrshí kuài qián.

寄海運比寄航空便宜20塊錢。

Mail by sea is $20 cheaper than by air.

4. Difference between 跟 and 比 in expressing comparison can be summarized as: 跟 shows only whether the two persons or things being compared are the same or not, whereas 比 can further indicate the concrete differences between them.

Examples:

Hǎiyùn gēn hángkōng bù yíyàng.

海運跟航空不一樣。

Mails by sea and by air are not the same.

Hǎiyùn bǐ hángkōng piányí.

海運比航空便宜。

Sea mail is cheaper than airmail. (Tells how they are different in terms of price.)

Hángkōng bǐ hǎiyùn kuài.

航空比海运快。

Airmail is faster than sea mail. (Tells how they are different in terms of speed.)

3. Comparisons with 不如

不如 can be used to show that a person or thing cannot compare favorably with another.

Sentence structure:	A ＋ 不如 ＋ B

Examples:

Gēge bù rú dìdi gāo.

哥哥不如弟弟高。

The elder brother is not as tall as the younger brother.

Jì tèkuài zhuāndì bùrú jì hángkōng xìn.

寄特快专递不如寄航空信。

Express mail is not as good as airmail.

When 不如 is used to denote comparison, it may be followed by an adjective or verb to indicate the aspect of comparison.

Sentence structure:	A ＋ 不如 ＋ B ＋ （那么） ＋ Adjective/Verb

Examples:

Hǎiyùn bùrú hángkōng (nàme) kuài.

海运不如航空(那么)快。

Sea mail is not as fast as airmail.

Zhōngguó de yínháng bùrú Měiguó de (nàme) duō.

中国的银行不如美国的(那么)多。

Banks in China are not as numerous as in America.

Hángkōng bǐ hǎiyùn kuài.

航空比海運快。

Airmail is faster than sea mail. (Tells how they are different in terms of speed.)

3. Comparisons with 不如

不如 can be used to show that a person or thing cannot compare favorably with another.

Sentence structure:	A + 不如 + B

Examples:

Gēge bù rú dìdi gāo.

哥哥不如弟弟高。

The elder brother is not as tall as the younger brother.

Jì tèkuài zhuāndì bùrú jì hángkōng xìn.

寄特快專遞不如寄航空信。

Express mail is not as good as airmail.

When 不如 is used to denote comparison, it may be followed by an adjective or verb to indicate the aspect of comparison.

Sentence structure:	A + 不如 + B + (那麼) + Adjective/Verb

Examples:

Hǎiyùn bùrú hángkōng (nàme) kuài.

海運不如航空(那麼)快。

Sea mail is not as fast as airmail.

Zhōngguó de yínháng bùrú Měiguó de (nàme) duō.

中國的銀行不如美國的(那麼)多。

Banks in China are not as numerous as in America.

▶ II. Questions with 多

The question adverb 多 (duō, many, much) can be used to ask questions, usually about the degree or quantity of an adjective.

Sentence structure:	S ＋ （有） ＋ 多 ＋ Adjective

Examples:

Question: Nàge yóujú yǒu duō yuǎn?

那个邮局有多远？

How far away is that post office?

Answer: Bù yuǎn, zǒulù zhǐ yào shí fēnzhōng.

不远，走路只要十分钟。

Not far, it takes only ten minutes on foot.

Question: Nǐ mèimei jīnnián duō dà?

你妹妹今年多大？

How old is your little sister this year?

Answer: Wǒ mèimei jīnnián jiǔ suì.

我妹妹今年九岁。

My little sister is nine years old this year.

Note: The adverb 多 usually precedes a monosyllabic adjective.

▶ III. Complement of Result
(See Textbook I, Lessons 3, 5, 7 and 10)

Selected examples from the textbook:

他们说好明天下午四点在十四路汽车站见。(Lesson 3)
你拿好了吗？(Lesson 5)
可是我记得你爸爸、妈妈给你买了回家的飞机票。(Lesson 7)
请改成12月24号，从夏威夷到波士顿。(Lesson 7)
害得我淋成了落汤鸡。(Lesson 10)

Complements of result are adjectives or verbs which immediately follow the main verb. They indicate the direct result of an action, either what it achieves or what happens unintentionally.

▶ II. Questions with 多

The question adverb 多 (duō, many, much) can be used to ask questions, usually about the degree or quantity of an adjective.

Sentence structure:	S ＋ (有) ＋ 多 ＋ Adjective

Examples:

Question: Nàge yóujú yǒu duō yuǎn?

那個郵局有多遠？

How far away is that post office?

Answer: Bù yuǎn, zǒulù zhǐ yào shí fēnzhōng.

不遠，走路只要十分鐘。

Not far, it takes only ten minutes on foot.

Question: Nǐ mèimei jīnnián duō dà?

你妹妹今年多大？

How old is your little sister this year?

Answer: Wǒ mèimei jīnnián jiǔ suì.

我妹妹今年九歲。

My little sister is nine years old this year.

Note: The adverb 多 usually precedes a monosyllabic adjective.

▶ III. Complement of Result
(See Textbook I, Lessons 3, 5, 7 and 10)

Selected examples from the textbook:

> 他們說好明天下午四點在十四路汽車站見。(Lesson 3)
> 你拿好了嗎？(Lesson 5)
> 可是我記得你爸爸、媽媽給你買了回家的飛機票。(Lesson 7)
> 請改成12月24號，從夏威夷到波士頓。(Lesson 7)
> 害得我淋成了落湯雞。(Lesson 10)

Complements of result are adjectives or verbs which immediately follow the main verb. They indicate the direct result of an action, either what it achieves or what happens unintentionally.

Sentence structure: S ＋ V ＋ Complement of Result （V/Adj/Prep） ＋ 0

Examples:

Xiǎojiě, nǐ zhǎo cuò qián le.

小姐，你找错钱了。

Miss, you gave me the wrong change.

Wǒ jì hǎo xìn yào qù yínháng.

我寄好信要去银行。

After I have mailed the letter, I am going to the bank.

Lǎoshī jiǎng de yǔfǎ wǒ tīng dǒng le.

老师讲的语法我听懂了。

I understood (by listening) the grammar that the teacher taught.

Interrogative sentence

Sentence structure: S ＋ V ＋ Complement of Result ＋ 0 ＋ 吗

Examples:

Question: Nǐ kànjiàn Wú xiǎojie le ma?

你看见吴小姐了吗？

Have you seen Miss Wu?

Answer: Wǒ kànjiàn Wú xiǎojie le, tā zài jùlèbù.

我看见吴小姐了，她在俱乐部。

I saw Miss Wu. She is in the club.

Question: Huáng Yīng qǔ dào qián le ma?

黄英取到钱了吗？

Has Ying Huang succeeded in withdrawing the money?

Answer: Tā qǔ dào le.

她取到了。

She succeeded in withdrawing it.

Sentence structure:	S + V + Complement of Result (V/Adj/Prep) + O

Examples:

Xiǎojiě, nǐ zhǎo cuò qián le.

小姐，你找錯錢了。

Miss, you gave me the wrong change.

Wǒ jì hǎo xìn yào qù yínháng.

我寄好信要去銀行。

After I have mailed the letter, I am going to the bank.

Lǎoshī jiǎng de yǔfǎ wǒ tīng dǒng le.

老師講的語法我聽懂了。

I understood (by listening) the grammar that the teacher taught.

Interrogative sentence

Sentence structure:	S + V + Complement of Result + O + 嗎

Examples:

Question: Nǐ kànjiàn Wú xiǎojie le ma?

你看見吳小姐了嗎?

Have you seen Miss Wu?

Answer: Wǒ kànjiàn Wú xiǎojie le, tā zài jùlèbù.

我看見吳小姐了，她在俱樂部。

I saw Miss Wu. She is in the club.

Question: Huáng Yīng qǔ dào qián le ma?

黃英取到錢了嗎?

Has Ying Huang succeeded in withdrawing the money?

Answer: Tā qǔ dào le.

她取到了。

She succeeded in withdrawing it.

The verb-complement of result phrase is usually negated by the adverb 没(有), which precedes the verb.

Examples:

Nà ge yóujiàn méi jì zǒu.

那个邮件没寄走。

That piece of mail has not been sent.

Yuēhàn méi zuò duì zuòyè.

约翰没做对作业。

John did not do his homework correctly.

Note: The adverb 不 can only be used to express supposition or an emphatic negative desire.

Examples:

Nǐ bù zuò wán zuòyè, jiù bù néng kàn diànshì.

你不做完作业，就不能看电视。

If you don't finish doing your homework, you cannot watch TV. (You must finish doing your homework, and only then can you watch TV.)

Wǒ bù qǔ dào qián, jiù bù zǒu.

我不取到钱就不走。

I won't leave if I cannot withdraw the money. (I won't leave unless I can withdraw the money.)

Note: The complement of result immediately follows the verb and no element can be inserted between the complement of result and the verb. The object should be placed after the verb-complement of result phrase. For example: 你找错钱了. (Nǐ zhǎo cuò qián le. You gave [me] the wrong change.) Nothing can be inserted between 找 and 错. The object 钱 and aspectual partical 了 should be placed after 找错.

Here are a few verbs commonly used as complements of result.

完 (wán, finish)—写完、吃完、做完
见 (jiàn, catch sight of)—看见、听见
到 (dào, arrive, reach)—找到、看到、买到
开 (kāi, open)—打开、张开
住 (zhù, stay)—站住、停住、记住
懂 (dǒng, understand)—听懂、看懂

The verb-complement of result phrase is usually negated by the adverb 沒(有), which precedes the verb.

Examples:

Nà ge yóujiàn méi jì zǒu.

那個郵件沒寄走。

That piece of mail has not been sent.

Yuēhàn méi zuò duì zuòyè.

約翰沒做對作業。

John did not do his homework correctly.

Note: The adverb 不 can only be used to express supposition or an emphatic negative desire.

Examples:

Nǐ bù zuò wán zuòyè, jiù bù néng kàn diànshì.

你不做完作業，就不能看電視。

If you don't finish doing your homework, you cannot watch TV. (You must finish doing your homework, and only then can you watch TV.)

Wǒ bù qǔ dào qián, jiù bù zǒu.

我不取到錢就不走.

I won't leave if I cannot withdraw the money. (I won't leave unless I can withdraw the money.)

Note: The complement of result immediately follows the verb and no element can be inserted between the complement of result and the verb. The object should be placed after the verb-complement of result phrase. For example: 你找錯錢了. (Nǐ zhǎo cuò qián le. You gave [me] the wrong change.) Nothing can be inserted between 找 and 錯. The object 錢 and aspectual partical 了 should be placed after 找錯.

Here are a few verbs commonly used as complements of result.

完 (wán, finish)—寫完、吃完、做完
見 (jiàn, catch sight of)—看見、聽見
到 (dào, arrive, reach)—找到、看到、買到
開 (kāi, open)—打開、張開
住 (zhù, stay)—站住、停住、記住
懂 (dǒng, understand)—聽懂、看懂

Note: In addition to the complement of result, we will encounter another type of complement when introducing the structural particle 得 in Lesson 5 of this grammar book. For example: 他吃得多. (Tā chī de duō. He eats a lot.) 他说中文说得不流利. (Tā shuō Zhōngwén shuō de bù liúlì. He does not speak Chinese fluently.) This type is called "complement of degree." We will introduce the other types of complements in the next few chapters.

▶ IV. Simple Directional Complements
(See Textbook I, Lesson 4)

Selected example from the textbook:

小王他们上课去了。 (Lesson 4)

When 来 and 去 are attached to the verb to indicate the direction, it is called a "simple directional complement."

Sentence structure:
S ＋ V ＋ 来/去
S ＋ V ＋ O (PW) 来/去
S ＋ V ＋ O (Person/Thing) ＋ 来/去
S ＋ V ＋ 来/去＋ O (Person/Thing)

Examples:

Fāng xiānsheng huí lái le.
方先生回来了。
Mr. Fang has come back.

Wǒ zǒu dào yóujú qù.
我走到邮局去。
I am walking to the post office.
（Incorrect: 我走到去邮局。）

Xiǎo Táng ná le nà běn shū lái.
小唐拿了那本书来。
Little Tang brought the book (here).

Note: In addition to the complement of result, we will encounter another type of complement when introducing the structural particle 得 in Lesson 5 of this grammar book. For example: 他吃得多. (Tā chī de duō. He eats a lot.) 他說中文說得不流利。 (Tā shuō Zhōngwén shuō de bù liúlì. He does not speak Chinese fluently.) This type is called "complement of degree." We will introduce the other types of complements in the next few chapters.

▶ IV. Simple Directional Complements
(See Textbook I, Lesson 4)

Selected example from the textbook:

小王他們上課去了。 (Lesson 4)

When 來 and 去 are attached to the verb to indicate the direction, it is called a "simple directional complement."

Sentence structure:	S ＋ V ＋ 來/去
	S ＋ V ＋ O (PW) 來/去
	S ＋ V ＋ O (Person/Thing) ＋ 來/去
	S ＋ V ＋ 來/去 ＋ O (Person/Thing)

Examples:

Fāng xiānsheng huí lái le.

方先生回來了。

Mr. Fang has come back.

Wǒ zǒu dào yóujú qù.

我走到郵局去。

I am walking to the post office.

(Incorrect: 我走到去郵局。)

Xiǎo Táng ná le nà běn shū lái.

小唐拿了那本書來。

Little Tang brought the book (here).

Interrogative sentence

Sentence structure:	S ＋ V ＋ 来/去 ＋ 吗

Examples:

Question: Yuēhàn huí jiā qù le ma?

约翰回家去了吗？

Has John gone home?

Answers: Yuēhàn huí jiā qù le.

约翰回家去了。

John has gone home.

Yuēhàn méi huí jiā qù.

约翰没回家去。

John did not go home.

Question: Xiǎo Huáng dào méi dào yínháng qù?

小黄到没到银行去？

Did Little Huang go to the bank?

Answers: Tā dào yínháng qù le.

他到银行去了。

He went to the bank.

Tā méi qù.

他没去。

He didn't go.

Question: Nǐ yào dài péngyou lái ma?

你要带朋友来吗？

Do you want to bring friends over?

Answers: Wǒ yào dài.

我要带。

Yes, I do.

Interrogative sentence

Sentence structure:	S ＋ V ＋ 來/去 ＋ 嗎

Examples:

Question: Yuēhàn huí jiā qù le ma?

約翰回家去了嗎?

Has John gone home?

Answers: Yuēhàn huí jiā qù le.

約翰回家去了。

John has gone home.

Yuēhàn méi huí jiā qù.

約翰沒回家去。

John did not go home.

Question: Xiǎo Huáng dào méi dào yínháng qù?

小黃到沒到銀行去?

Did Little Huang go to the bank?

Answers: Tā dào yínháng qù le.

他到銀行去了。

He went to the bank.

Tā méi qù.

他沒去。

He didn't go.

Question: Nǐ yào dài péngyou lái ma?

你要帶朋友來嗎?

Do you want to bring friends over?

Answers: Wǒ yào dài.

我要帶。

Yes, I do.

Wǒ bù dài.

我不带。

No, I don't.

Note: 1. 来 and 去 indicate direction related to the speaker. If the action is moving toward the speaker, 来 is used. If the action is moving away from the speaker, 去 is used. For example: 约翰回家去了. The speaker is probably at school, John is moving away from where the speaker is (school) toward his home. If John is moving toward the speaker, it should be 约翰回学校来了.

2. The object of place is placed between the verb and the simple directional complement 来/去. For example, in "我到邮局去," 邮局 is a place word. It is placed between the verb 到 and the word 去. But if the object refers to a person or thing, it is placed either before or after 来/去.

For example:

Wáng Xiǎonián ná le nà běn shū lái.

王小年拿了那本书来。

Or: Wáng Xiǎonián ná lái le nà běn shū.

王小年拿来了那本书。

Xiaonian Wang brought the book with him.

▶ V. The Adverb 就 for Emphasis
(See Textbook I, Lesson 8)

Selected example from the textbook:

好，我就寄这种。 (Lesson 8)

The adverb 就 is often used before the verb to indicate emphases of various implications, of which the common ones are as follows:

1. Emphasizing "precisely" or "none other than."

Examples:

Yóujú jiù zài nàr.

邮局就在那儿。

The post office is right there.

Wǒ bù dài.

我不帶。

No, I don't.

Note: 1. 來 and 去 indicate direction related to the speaker. If the action is moving toward the speaker, 來 is used. If the action is moving away from the speaker, 去 is used. For example: 約翰回家去了. The speaker is probably at school, John is moving away from where the speaker is (school) toward his home. If John is moving toward the speaker, it should be 約翰回學校來了.

2. The object of place is placed between the verb and the simple directional complement 來/去. For example, in "我到郵局去," 郵局 is a place word. It is placed between the verb 到 and the word 去. But if the object refers to a person or thing, it is placed either before or after 來/去.

For example:

Wáng Xiǎonián ná le nà běn shū lái.

王小年拿了那本書來。

Or: Wáng Xiǎonián ná lái le nà běn shū.

王小年拿來了那本書。

Xiaonian Wang brought the book with him.

▶ V. The Adverb 就 for Emphasis
(See Textbook I, Lesson 8)

Selected example from the textbook:

好，我就寄這種。 (Lesson 8)

The adverb 就 is often used before the verb to indicate emphases of various implications, of which the common ones are as follows:

1. Emphasizing "precisely" or "none other than."

Examples:

Yóujú jiù zài nàr.

郵局就在那兒。

The post office is right there.

Tā jiù shì Bái lǎoshī.

他就是白老师。

He is Professor Bai (rather than anybody else).

2. Emphasizing "immediately" or "at once."

Examples:

Wǒ péngyou jiù lái.

我朋友就来。

My friend will come right away.

Tā jiù gěi nǐ sòng qù.

他就给你送去。

He will send it to you immediately.

3. Emphasizing "only" or "merely."

Examples:

Zhèr jiù yǒu yī ge yóujú.

这儿就有一个邮局。

There is only one post office here.

Wǒ jiù dài le wǔ kuài qián.

我就带了五块钱。

I only brought five dollars with me.

4. Emphasizing that the subject is "resolute" or "determined."

Examples:

Tā jiù bù qù kànbìng.

他就不去看病。

He simply refused to see a doctor.

Wǒ jiù yào kàn diànshì.

我就要看电视。

I must watch (I insist on watching) TV.

Tā jiù shì Bái lǎoshī.

他就是白老師。

He is Professor Bai (rather than anybody else).

2. Emphasizing "immediately" or "at once."

Examples:

Wǒ péngyou jiù lái.

我朋友就來。

My friend will come right away.

Tā jiù gěi nǐ sòng qù.

他就給你送去。

He will send it to you immediately.

3. Emphasizing "only" or "merely."

Examples:

Zhèr jiù yǒu yī ge yóujú.

這兒就有一個郵局。

There is only one post office here.

Wǒ jiù dài le wǔ kuài qián.

我就帶了五塊錢。

I only brought five dollars with me.

4. Emphasizing that the subject is "resolute" or "determined."

Examples:

Tā jiù bù qù kànbìng.

他就不去看病。

He simply refused to see a doctor.

Wǒ jiù yào kàn diànshì.

我就要看電視。

I must watch (I insist on watching) TV.

▶ 练习 **Exercises**

I. Use 比 **or** 没有 **to write sentences according to the information provided.**

Example: 今天是五十度，明天是五十五度。 →
今天比明天冷 or 今天没有明天暖和。

1. 寄平信要8毛3分钱，寄挂号信要5块4毛2分钱。
2. 纽约的航班多，北京的航班少。
3. 小陈一分钟能写十个汉字，他哥哥一分钟能写十二个汉字。
4. 他每天去一次邮局，我每天去两次。
5. 你英文说得很流利，但是中文说得不流利。

II. Fill in the blanks with 跟……一样 **and** 不如.

1. 和……一样 2. 跟……一样 3. 跟……不一样 4. 不一样 5. 不如 6. 不如

我在中国的时候常常去邮局。我在美国的时候常常去银行。中国的邮局
_____美国的邮局_____，都可以寄邮件。可是中国的邮局_____美
国的邮局也_____。中国的邮局可以存钱，可以订报纸和杂志(zázhì,
magazine)。美国的邮局_____中国的邮局方便，不能存钱。可是中国的银
行_____美国的方便，存钱和取钱都要存折。中国_____美国的邮局
_____，也不一样。中国的银行跟美国的银行一样，也_____。

III. Translate the following sentences into Chinese.

1. Of course, New York is much bigger than Boston.
2. How busy have you been recently?
3. Learning English is a little bit easier than learning French (fǎwén, 法文).
4. The Chinese banks are not as convenient as American banks.
5. You write Chinese characters no faster than he does.
6. How boring is that movie?
7. Going there today is the same as going there tomorrow.
8. Ying Huang went back home.
9. Xiaonian Wang brought a few friends here.

▶ 練習 Exercises

I. Use 比 or 沒有 to write sentences according to the information provided.

Example: 今天是五十度，明天是五十五度。 →
今天比明天冷 or 今天沒有明天暖和。

1. 寄平信要8毛3分錢，寄挂號信要5塊4毛2分錢。
2. 紐約的航班多，北京的航班少。
3. 小陳一分鐘能寫十個漢字，他哥哥一分鐘能寫十二個漢字。
4. 他每天去一次郵局，我每天去兩次。
5. 你英文說得很流利，但是中文說得不流利。

II. Fill in the blanks with 跟……一樣 and 不如.

1.和……一樣　2.跟……一樣　3.跟……不一樣　4.不一樣　5.不如　6.不如

我在中國的時候常常去郵局。我在美國的時候常常去銀行。中國的郵局
_____美國的郵局_____，都可以寄郵件。可是中國的郵局_____美
國的郵局也_____。中國的郵局可以存錢，可以訂報紙和雜誌(zázhì,
magazine)。美國的郵局_____中國的郵局方便，不能存錢。可是中國的銀
行_____美國的方便，存錢和取錢都要存折。中國_____美國的郵局
_____，也不一樣。中國的銀行跟美國的銀行一樣，也_____。

III. Translate the following sentences into Chinese.

1. Of course, New York is much bigger than Boston.
2. How busy have you been recently?
3. Learning English is a little bit easier than learning French (fǎwén, 法文).
4. The Chinese banks are not as convenient as American banks.
5. You write Chinese characters no faster than he does.
6. How boring is that movie?
7. Going there today is the same as going there tomorrow.
8. Ying Huang went back home.
9. Xiaonian Wang brought a few friends here.

IV. Use 多 to ask questions, focusing on the underlined parts.

Example: 明天的温度是四度。 → 明天有多冷？

1. 寄挂号信要5块8毛钱。
2. 他爸爸有一米八二。
3. 从这儿到波士顿有二百英哩(英哩，yīnglǐ, mile)。
4. 这件运动衣有两尺长(尺，chǐ, a unit of length, =1/3 meter)。
5. 那台电视要四百五十块钱。
6. 这儿的春天只有一个多月。

V. Correct the errors, if there are any, in the following sentences.

1. 中国的公共汽车不跟美国的一样。
2. 这种邮件比那种(邮件)一样贵。
3. 美国的银行没有比中国的多。
4. 黄英回了来。
5. 约翰回去家了。
6. 你找钱错了。
7. 我寄信好要去银行。

VI. You sent some mail to your parents. Write an essay in Chinese describing when, where, and how you sent the mail. Try to use as many new grammatical patterns as you can.

VII. Choose the right words to fill in the blanks, and then read the conversation aloud with a partner.

1.多 2.来 3.不如 4.跟……一样 5.到 6.到 7.不一样 8.去
9.去 10.去 11.比 12.就

A: 我刚从邮局回_____。我觉得这儿的邮局_____中国的方便。

B: 真的？我想中国的邮局_____美国的_____。

A: _____。在中国的邮局除了可以寄邮件以外，还可以存钱和订报纸。

B: 你为什么去邮局？

A: 我收_____我奶奶从中国来的信，她要看我的照片。我去寄照片了。

B: 你怎么去邮局的？

IV. Use 多 to ask questions, focusing on the underlined parts.

Example: 明天的溫度是四度。 → 明天有多冷？

1. 寄掛號信要5塊8毛錢。
2. 他爸爸有一米八二。
3. 從這兒到波士頓有二百英哩 (英哩， yīnglǐ, mile)。
4. 這件運動衣有兩尺長(尺， chǐ, a unit of length, =1/3 meter)。
5. 那臺電視要四百五十塊錢。
6. 這兒的春天只有一個多月。

V. Correct the errors, if there are any, in the following sentences.

1. 中國的公共汽車不跟美國的一樣。
2. 這種郵件比那種(郵件)一樣貴。
3. 美國的銀行沒有比中國的多。
4. 黃英回了來。
5. 約翰回去家了。
6. 你找錢錯了。
7. 我寄信好要去銀行。

VI. You sent some mail to your parents. Write an essay in Chinese describing when, where, and how you sent the mail. Try to use as many new grammatical patterns as you can.

VII. Choose the right words to fill in the blanks, and then read the conversation aloud with a partner.

1.多　2.來　3.不如　4.跟……一樣　5.到　6.到　7.不一樣　8.去　9.去　10.去
11.比　12.就

A: 我剛從郵局回＿＿＿＿。我覺得這兒的郵局＿＿＿＿中國的方便。

B: 真的？ 我想中國的郵局＿＿＿＿美國的＿＿＿＿。

A: ＿＿＿＿。在中國的郵局除了可以寄郵件以外，還可以存錢和訂報紙。

B: 你為什麼去郵局?

A: 我收＿＿＿＿我奶奶從中國來的信，她要看我的照片。我去寄照片了。

B: 你怎麼去郵局的?

A: 我走_____的。走路_____坐公共汽车快。

B: 有_____快？

A: 我半个小时就走_____了。

B: 还是坐车快，只要二十分钟。

A: 我_____走路，不用等车。

B: 好，下次你走路_____，我坐车_____。

A: 我走＿＿＿＿的。走路＿＿＿＿坐公共汽車快。

B: 有＿＿＿＿快?

A: 我半個小時就走＿＿＿＿了。

B: 還是坐車快，只要二十分鐘。

A: 我＿＿＿＿走路，不用等車。

B: 好，下次你走路＿＿＿＿，我坐車＿＿＿＿。

第九课
LESSON 9

▶ I. Duration of Time
(See Textbook I, Lesson 4.)

Selected example from the textbook:

我在中国学了一年中文。 (Lesson 4)

To express how long an action lasts, we can put the duration of time after the verb. We call this a "complement of duration." Duration of time can be composed of Num + M + Length of Time, such as 一个小时，两天，三十分钟。

Sentence structure:
S ＋ V ＋ Duration of Time
S ＋ V ＋ O ＋ V ＋ Duration of Time
S ＋ V ＋ Duration of Time ＋（的）＋ O

Examples:

Xiǎo Zhāng zài jiā shuì le yī tiān.
小张在家睡了一天。
Little Zhang slept at home for a day.

Wáng Jiāshēng kànbìng kàn le yī gè bàn xiǎoshí.
王家生看病看了一个半小时。
Jiasheng Wang saw the doctor for an hour and a half.

Wǒ zuótiān shàng le yī tiān (de) kè.
我昨天上了一天(的)课。
Yesterday I had classes all day long.

Wǒ kàn le wǔ fēnzhōng (de) yīshēng.
我看了五分钟(的)医生。
I saw the doctor for five minutes.

第九課
LESSON 9

▶ **I. Duration of Time**
(See Textbook I, Lesson 4.)

Selected example from the textbook:

我在中國學了一年中文。 (Lesson 4)

To express how long an action lasts, we can put the duration of time after the verb. We call this a "complement of duration." Duration of time can be composed of Num + M + Length of Time, such as 一個小時，兩天，三十分鐘。

Sentence structure:	S + V + Duration of Time
	S + V + O + V + Duration of Time
	S + V + Duration of Time + (的) + O

Examples:

Xiǎo Zhāng zài jiā shuì le yī tiān.

小張在家睡了一天。

Little Zhang slept at home for a day.

Wáng Jiāshēng kànbìng kàn le yī gè bàn xiǎoshí.

王家生看病看了一個半小時。

Jiasheng Wang saw the doctor for an hour and a half.

Wǒ zuótiān shàng le yī tiān (de) kè.

我昨天上了一天(的)課。

Yesterday I had classes all day long.

Wǒ kàn le wǔ fēnzhōng (de) yīshēng.

我看了五分鐘(的)醫生。

I saw the doctor for five minutes.

To express for how long an action has not been or was not carried out, the following sentence pattern can be used.

> **Sentence structure:**　S ＋（有）＋ Duration of Time ＋ 没有 ＋ V ＋ (0) ＋（了）

Examples:

Gélín (yǒu) yī gè yuè méiyǒu kànbìng le.

格林（有）一个月没有看病了。

Green has not seen a doctor for a month.

Wáng Jiāshēng (yǒu) yī gè xīngqī méi chīyào le.

王家生（有）一个星期没吃药了。

Jiasheng Wang has not taken medicine for a week.

To express non-occurrence in the future or in a habitual sense, the following sentence pattern can be used.

> **Sentence structure:**　S ＋（有）＋ Duration of Time ＋ 不 ＋ V ＋ (0)

Examples:

Měi nián xuéshēng yǒu sān gè yuè bù shàngxué.

每年学生有三个月不上学。

Every year students have no class for three months.

Míngtiān wǒ yǒu wǔ gè xiǎoshí bù shàngkè.

明天我有五个小时不上课。

Tomorrow there will be five hours that I do not have class.

(I will not have class for five hours.)

When verbs preceding expressions of duration are negated, the focus is on a certain amount of time, rather than duration.

To express for how long an action has not been or was not carried out, the following sentence pattern can be used.

Sentence structure: S ＋ (有) ＋ Duration of Time ＋ 沒有 ＋ V ＋ (O) ＋ (了)

Examples:

Gélín (yǒu) yī gè yuè méiyǒu kànbìng le.

格林(有)一個月沒有看病了。

Green has not seen a doctor for a month.

Wáng Jiāshēng (yǒu) yī gè xīngqī méi chīyào le.

王家生(有)一個星期沒吃藥了。

Jiasheng Wang has not taken medicine for a week.

To express non-occurrence in the future or in a habitual sense, the following sentence pattern can be used.

Sentence structure: S ＋ (有) ＋ Duration of Time ＋ 不 ＋ V ＋ (O)

Examples:

Měi nián xuésheng yǒu sān gè yuè bù shàngxué.

每年學生有三個月不上學。

Every year students have no class for three months.

Míngtiān wǒ yǒu wǔ gè xiǎoshí bù shàngkè.

明天我有五個小時不上課。

Tomorrow there will be five hours that I do not have class.

(I will not have class for five hours.)

When verbs preceding expressions of duration are negated, the focus is on a certain amount of time, rather than duration.

> **Sentence structure:** S ＋ Negation ＋ V ＋ Duration of Time ＋ (的 ＋ O)

Examples:

Wáng Jiāshēng méi kàn yī ge bàn xiǎoshí de bìng, zhǐ kàn le yī ge xiǎoshí (de bìng).

王家生没看一个半小时的病，只看了一个小时（的病）。

Jiasheng Wang did not see the doctor for an hour and a half; he saw (the doctor) for only an hour.

Wǒ méi kàn yī gè xiǎoshí (de) diànshì. Wǒ zhǐ kàn le wǔ fēnzhōng (de diànshì).

我没看一个小时（的）电视，我只看了五分钟（的电视）。

I did not watch TV for an hour. I only watched (TV) for five minutes.

Note: The adverbs should precede the verb, and should not be placed between the verb and the complement. For example: 我只看了五分钟（的）电视. If the sentence structure with a repeated verb is used as in 王家生看病看了一个半小时, the adverb comes before the repeated verb. For example: 王家生看病已经看了一个半小时. When the object is long and definite, it is usually mentioned first.

Examples:

Yīshēng kāi de nà zhǒng yào wǒ chī le yī gè xīngqī le.

医生开的那种药我吃了一个星期了。

I have taken the medicine that the doctor prescribed for a week.

Note: Time expressions can be divided into two major groups in Chinese. The time expressions we learned before belong to the "time-when" group, which indicates when an action takes place and is positioned before the verb. The time expressions we are learning in this lesson belong to the "time-duration" group, which shows for how long an action lasts and is placed after the verb. Following are examples of the "time-when" and "time-duration" groups for comparison.

<table>
<tr><td>Sentence structure:</td><td>S ＋ Negation ＋ V ＋ Duration of Time ＋
(的 ＋ O)</td></tr>
</table>

Examples:

Wáng Jiāshēng méi kàn yī ge bàn xiǎoshí de bìng, zhǐ kàn le yī ge xiǎoshí (de bìng).

王家生沒看一個半小時的病, 只看了一個小時(的病)。

Jiasheng Wang did not see the doctor for an hour and a half; he saw (the doctor) for only an hour.

Wǒ méi kàn yī gè xiǎoshí (de) diànshì. Wǒ zhǐ kàn le wǔ fēnzhōng (de diànshì).

我沒看一個小時(的)電視, 我只看了五分鐘(的電視)。

I did not watch TV for an hour. I only watched (TV) for five minutes.

Note: The adverbs should precede the verb, and should not be placed between the verb and the complement. For example: 我只看了五分鐘(的)電視. If the sentence structure with a repeated verb is used as in 王家生看病看了一個半小時, the adverb comes before the repeated verb. For example: 王家生看病已經看了一個半小時. When the object is long and definite, it is usually mentioned first.

Examples:

Yīshēng kāi de nà zhǒng yào wǒ chī le yī gè xīngqī le.

醫生開的那種藥我吃了一個星期了。

I have taken the medicine that the doctor prescribed for a week.

Note: Time expressions can be divided into two major groups in Chinese. The time expressions we learned before belong to the "time-when" group, which indicates when an action takes place and is positioned before the verb. The time expressions we are learning in this lesson belong to the "time-duration" group, which shows for how long an action lasts and is placed after the verb. Following are examples of the "time-when" and "time-duration" groups for comparison.

Time-When	Time-Duration
shí diǎn	shí gè xiǎo shí
十点 ten o'clock	十个小时 ten hours
liǎng diǎn bàn	liǎng gè bàn xiǎo shí
两点半 half past two	两个半小时 two and half hours
zuó tiān	yī tiān
昨天 yesterday	一天 one day
xīng qī yī	yī gè xīng qī
星期一 Monday	一个星期 one week
shàng gè yuè	yī gè yuè
上个月 last month	一个月 one month
shí yī yuè	shí yī gè yuè
十一月 November	十一个月 eleven months
qù nián	yī nián
去年 last year	一年 one year

Examples:

Wǒ zuótiān shí diǎn shuìjiào de.

我昨天十点睡觉的。

I went to bed at ten yesterday.

Wǒ zuótiān shuì le shí gè xiǎoshí de jiào.

我昨天睡了十个小时的觉。

I slept for ten hours yesterday.

▶ II. Complement of Frequency
(See Textbook I, Lesson 9)

Selected example from the textbook:

一天吃三次，一次一片。 (Lesson 9)

To express frequency of an action, a "complement of frequency" can be used. It is usually composed of number + verbal measure word.

Time-When	Time-Duration
shí diǎn	shí gè xiǎo shí
十点 ten o'clock	十个小时 ten hours
liǎng diǎn bàn	liǎng gè bàn xiǎo shí
两点半 half past two	两个半小时 two and half hours
zuó tiān	yī tiān
昨天 yesterday	一天 one day
xīng qī yī	yī gè xīng qī
星期一 Monday	一个星期 one week
shàng gè yuè	yī gè yuè
上个月 last month	一个月 one month
shí yī yuè	shí yī gè yuè
十一月 November	十一个月 eleven months
qù nián	yī nián
去年 last year	一年 one year

Examples:

Wǒ zuótiān shí diǎn shuìjiào de.

我昨天十點睡覺的。

I went to bed at ten yesterday.

Wǒ zuótiān shuì le shí gè xiǎoshí de jiào.

我昨天睡了十個小時的覺。

I slept for ten hours yesterday.

▶ II. Complement of Frequency
(See Textbook I, Lesson 9)

Selected example from the textbook:

一天吃三次，一次一片。(Lesson 9)

To express frequency of an action, a "complement of frequency" can be used. It is usually composed of number + verbal measure word.

Sentence structure: S + V + frequency

S + V + frequency + 0

Examples:

Yīshēng jiǎnchá le yī cì.

医生检查了一次。

The doctor checked (him) once.

Zhège xīngqī tā qù le sān cì yīyuàn.

这个星期他去了三次医院。

He has been to the hospital three times this week.

Zhège diànyǐng wǒ kàn guò liǎng cì.

这个电影我看过两次。

I have seen the movie twice.

(Incorrect: 这个电影我两次看过。)

Fāng lǎoshī gěi wǒ bǔ le sān cì kè.

方老师给我补了三次课。

Professor Fang made up lessons for me three times. (tutored me three times)

(Incorrect: 方老师给我三次补课了。)

If the object is a pronoun or a person's name, the object is placed before the expression of frequency.

Examples:

Gāo lǎoshī zhǎo le wǒ sān cì.

高老师找了我三次。

Professor Gao asked me to see him three times.

(Incorrect: 高老师找了三次我。)

Tā dǎ le wǒ liǎng xià.

他打了我两下。

He hit me twice.

Tā kàn le Wáng Jiāshēng yī cì.

她看了王家生一次。

She visited Jiasheng Wang once.

Sentence structure:	S + V + frequency
	S + V + frequency + 0

Examples:

Yīshēng jiǎnchá le yī cì.

醫生檢查了一次。

The doctor checked (him) once.

Zhège xīngqī tā qù le sān cì yīyuàn.

這個星期他去了三次醫院。

He has been to the hospital three times this week.

Zhège diànyǐng wǒ kàn guò liǎng cì.

這個電影我看過兩次。

I have seen the movie twice.

(Incorrect: 這個電影我兩次看過。)

Fāng lǎoshī gěi wǒ bǔ le sān cì kè.

方老師給我補了三次課。

Professor Fang made up lessons for me three times. (tutored me three times)

(Incorrect: 方老師給我三次補課了。)

If the object is a pronoun or a person's name, the object is placed before the expression of frequency.

Examples:

Gāo lǎoshī zhǎo le wǒ sān cì.

高老師找了我三次。

Professor Gao asked me to see him three times.

(Incorrect: 高老師找了三次我。)

Tā dǎ le wǒ liǎng xià.

他打了我兩下。

He hit me twice.

Tā kàn le Wáng Jiāshēng yī cì.

她看了王家生一次。

She visited Jiasheng Wang once.

▶ III. Compound Directional Complements
(See Textbook I, Lesson 8)

Selected example from the textbook:

只要把你的银行卡从这个口放进去，输入你的密码……(Lesson 8)

A compound directional complement is composed by combining one of seven specific verbs (listed below) and 来 or 去. The compound directional complement after a verb indicates a dual direction in which the action moves. The following is the list of the 13 compound directional complements.

Verbs

shàng	xià	jìn	chū	huí	guò	qǐ
上	下	进	出	回	过	起

Compound Directional Complements

来： 上来 下来 进来 出来 回来 过来 起来
去： 上去 下去 进去 出去 回去 过去

In a sentence with a verb and a compound directional complement, the verb states the action (to run, to walk, to bring, to fall, etc.) while the complement indicate the dual direction of the action. We use C1 to represent 上、下、进、出、回、过、起, and C2 to represent 来 or 去 in the sentence structure.

Sentence structure:
$$S + V + C1 + C2$$
$$S + V + C1 + 0 + C2$$
$$S + V + C1 + C2 + 0$$

Examples:

Zuò qǐlai, bié zhànzhe.

坐起来，别站着。

Sit up, don't stand (there).

Nǐ zǒu guòqu, bù yào kāichē.

你走过去，不要开车。

You (should) walk over, not drive.

▶ III. Compound Directional Complements
(See Textbook I, Lesson 8)

Selected example from the textbook:

只要把你的銀行卡從這個口放進去，輸入你的密碼……(Lesson 8)

A compound directional complement is composed by combining one of seven specific verbs (listed below) and 來 or 去. The compound directional complement after a verb indicates a dual direction in which the action moves. The following is the list of the 13 compound directional complements.

Verbs

shàng	xià	jìn	chū	huí	guò	qǐ
上	下	進	出	回	過	起

Compound Directional Complements

來: 上來 下來 進來 出來 回來 過來 起來
去: 上去 下去 進去 出去 回去 過去

In a sentence with a verb and a compound directional complement, the verb states the action (to run, to walk, to bring, to fall, etc.) while the complement indicate the dual direction of the action. We use C1 to represent 上、下、進、出、回、過、起, and C2 to represent 來 or 去 in the sentence structure.

Sentence structure: S + V + C1 + C2
  S + V + C1 + O + C2
  S + V + C1 + C2 + O

Examples:

Zuò qǐlai, bié zhànzhe.

坐起來，別站著。

Sit up, don't stand (there).

Nǐ zǒu guòqu, bù yào kāichē.

你走過去，不要開車。

You (should) walk over, not drive.

Xiǎo Lǐ zǒu jìn yīyuàn qù le.

小李走进医院去了。

Little Li walked into the hospital.

Tā mǎi huílai le yīxiē shuǐguǒ.

他买回来了一些水果。

He bought some fruit and brought it back.

Tā mǎi huí yīxiē shuǐguǒ lái.

他买回一些水果来。

He bought some fruit and brought it back.

If the object is a place word, it should be inserted between C1 and C2, such as 小张走进医院去。

More examples:

Tā zǒu shàng lóu qù huàyàn xiě le.

她走上楼去化验血了。

She walked upstairs to do a blood test.

Jīntiān tā zǒu huí xuéxiào qù.

今天他走回学校去。

He will walk back to school today.

来 and 去 in the compound directional complement have the same meaning as in the simple directional complement. When the motion is proceeding towards the speaker, 来 is used. When the action is moving away from the speaker, 去 is used.

Examples:

Nǐ gěi wǒ mǎi yīxiē chī de dōngxi lái.

你给我买一些吃的东西来。

You buy (and bring here) something for me to eat,

Nǐ gěi tā dài diǎnr chī de dōngxi qù.

你给他带点儿吃的东西去。

You take (over there) something for him to eat.

Note: The aspectual particle 了 can be placed between the compound directional complement and the main verb or after the complement.

Xiǎo Lǐ zǒu jìn yīyuàn qù le.

小李走進醫院去了。

Little Li walked into the hospital.

Tā mǎi huílai le yìxiē shuǐguǒ.

他買回來了一些水果。

He bought some fruit and brought it back.

Tā mǎi huí yìxiē shuǐguǒ lái.

他買回一些水果來。

He bought some fruit and brought it back.

If the object is a place word, it should be inserted between C1 and C2, such as 小張走進醫院去。

More examples:

Tā zǒu shàng lóu qù huàyàn xiě le.

她走上樓去化驗血了。

She walked upstairs to do a blood test.

Jīntiān tā zǒu huí xuéxiào qù.

今天他走回學校去。

He will walk back to school today.

來 and 去 in the compound directional complement have the same meaning as in the simple directional complement. When the motion is proceeding towards the speaker, 來 is used. When the action is moving away from the speaker, 去 is used.

Examples:

Nǐ gěi wǒ mǎi yìxiē chī de dōngxi lái.

你給我買一些吃的東西來。

You buy (and bring here) something for me to eat,

Nǐ gěi tā dài diǎnr chī de dōngxi qù.

你給他帶點兒吃的東西去。

You take (over there) something for him to eat.

Note: The aspectual particle 了 can be placed between the compound directional complement and the main verb or after the complement.

Examples:

Lǐ Lǎoshī cóng běi xiàomén zǒu le jìnlái.

李老师从北校门走了进来。

Professor Li came in through the north entrance of the school.

Tā gěi mèimei sòng guò qù le yīxiē shuǐguǒ.

他给妹妹送过去了一些水果。

He delivered some fruit over to his younger sister.

Some compound directional complements have extended uses. The following are the more commonly used ones.

1a. 起来 Indicating the start of an action.

Examples:

Chī le bīngxiāng lǐ de shèngcài, Gélín de dùzi téng qǐlái le.

吃了冰箱里的剩菜，格林的肚子疼起来了。

After eating the leftovers in the refrigerator, Green's stomach started hurting.

Tīng le tā de huà, wǒmen dōu xiào qǐlái le.

听了他的话，我们都笑起来了。

Hearing what he said, we all started laughing.

1b. 起来 Expressing the meaning "when doing something, (you will find...)."

Examples:

Diànnǎo yòng qǐlai hěn fāngbiàn.

电脑用起来很方便。

It is very convenient to use a computer. (When using a computer, it is very convenient.)

Shuō qǐlai róngyì, zuò qǐlai nán.

说起来容易，做起来难。

It's easier said than done. (When one talks about it, it is easy. When one does it, it is difficult.)

Note: If there is an object, it is placed between 起 and 来.

Examples:

Lǐ Lǎoshī cóng běi xiàomén zǒu le jìnlái.

李老師從北校門走了進來。

Professor Li came in through the north entrance of the school.

Tā gěi mèimei sòng guò qù le yīxiē shuǐguǒ.

他給妹妹送過去了一些水果。

He delivered some fruit over to his younger sister.

Some compound directional complements have extended uses. The following are the more commonly used ones.

1a. 起來 Indicating the start of an action.

Examples:

Chī le bīngxiāng lǐ de shèngcài, Gélín de dùzi téng qǐlái le.

吃了冰箱裡的剩菜，格林的肚子疼起來了。

After eating the leftovers in the refrigerator, Green's stomach started hurting.

Tīng le tā de huà, wǒmen dōu xiào qǐlái le.

聽了他的話，我們都笑起來了。

Hearing what he said, we all started laughing.

1b. 起來 Expressing the meaning "when doing something, (you will find...)."

Examples:

Diànnǎo yòng qǐlai hěn fāngbiàn.

電腦用起來很方便。

It is very convenient to use a computer. (When using a computer, it is very convenient.)

Shuō qǐlai róngyì, zuò qǐlai nán.

說起來容易，做起來難。

It's easier said than done. (When one talks about it, it is easy. When one does it, it is difficult.)

Note: If there is an object, it is placed between 起 and 來.

Example:

Zài Xiǎo Wáng de shēngrì wǎnhuì shàng, tóngxuémen tiào qǐ wǔ lái.

在小王的生日晚会上，同学们跳起舞来。

At Little Wang's birthday party, the students began dancing.

2. 下去 Indicating continuation of an action.

Examples:

Chén xiānsheng hái děi zài yīyuàn zhù xiàqù.

陈先生还得在医院住下去。

Mr. Chen has to continue to be hospitalized.

Wǒ míngnián hái yào zài Zhōngguó xuéxí xiàqù.

我明年还要在中国学习下去。

I will continue studying in China next year.

Note: In this sense, the object never takes a complement. You have to move the object to the front in order to use 下去.

Examples:

Zhèxiē wèntí wǒmen hái yào tǎolùn xiàqù.

这些问题我们还要讨论下去。

We will continue discussing these issues.

Wǒmen tǎolùn zhèxiē wèntí xiàqù.

（Incorrect: 我们讨论这些问题下去。）

3a. 出来 Expressing something coming into being as a result of an action.

Examples:

Jīntiān de zuòyè tā dōu zuò chūlai le.

今天的作业他都做出来了。

He managed to do all the homework today.

Gāo lǎoshī néng jiào chū wǒmen de míngzì lái.

高老师能叫出我们的名字来。

Professor Gao can say all our names.

Example:

Zài Xiǎo Wáng de shēngrì wǎnhuì shàng, tóngxuémen tiào qǐ wǔ lái.

在小王的生日晚會上，同學們跳起舞來。

At Little Wang's birthday party, the students began dancing.

2. 下去 Indicating continuation of an action.

Examples:

Chén xiānsheng hái děi zài yīyuàn zhù xiàqù.

陳先生還得在醫院住下去。

Mr. Chen has to continue to be hospitalized.

Wǒ míngnián hái yào zài Zhōngguó xuéxí xiàqù.

我明年還要在中國學習下去。

I will continue studying in China next year.

Note: In this sense, the object never takes a complement. You have to move the object to the front in order to use 下去.

Examples:

Zhèxiē wèntí wǒmen hái yào tǎolùn xiàqù.

這些問題我們還要討論下去。

We will continue discussing these issues.

Wǒmen tǎolùn zhèxiē wèntí xiàqù.

(Incorrect: 我們討論這些問題下去。)

3a. 出來 Expressing something coming into being as a result of an action.

Examples:

Jīntiān de zuòyè tā dōu zuò chūlai le.

今天的作業他都做出來了。

He managed to do all the homework today.

Gāo lǎoshī néng jiào chū wǒmen de míngzì lái.

高老師能叫出我們的名字來。

Professor Gao can say all our names.

3b. 出来 **Expressing the identification of a person or thing through the action.**

Examples:

Wǒ tīng chūlai le, nǐ shì Wáng Míng.

我听出来了，你是王明。

I can tell (by listening) that you are Ming Wang.

Wǒ rèn chūlai le, tā shì Sūshān.

我认出来了，她是苏珊。

I recognize (her); she is Susan.

4a. 下来 **Expressing the gradual change from an active state to a static state or from brightness into darkness.**

Examples:

Tiān hēi xiàlai le.

天黑下来了。

It's getting dark.

Fēijī mànman de tíng xiàlai le.

飞机慢慢地停下来了。

The airplane gradually stopped.

4b. 下来 **Indicating something being fixed to or remaining at a certain place so that it will not disappear, leave or be forgotten.**

Examples:

Xià jiàoshòu jiǎng de yǔfǎ wǒmen dōu xiě xiàlai le.

夏教授讲的语法我们都写下来了。

We have taken down the notes of the grammar taught by Professor Xia.

Nǐ néng bǎ dàjiā de míngzi xiě xiàlai ma?

你能把大家的名字写下来吗？

Can you write down everyone's name?

3b. 出來 Expressing the identification of a person or thing through the action.

Examples:

Wǒ tīng chūlai le, nǐ shì Wáng Míng.

我聽出來了，你是王明。

I can tell (by listening) that you are Ming Wang.

Wǒ rèn chūlai le, tā shì Sūshān.

我認出來了，她是蘇珊。

I recognize (her); she is Susan.

4a. 下來 Expressing the gradual change from an active state to a static state or from brightness into darkness.

Examples:

Tiān hēi xiàlai le.

天黑下來了。

It's getting dark.

Fēijī mànman de tíng xiàlai le.

飛機慢慢地停下來了。

The airplane gradually stopped.

4b. 下來 Indicating something being fixed to or remaining at a certain place so that it will not disappear, leave or be forgotten.

Examples:

Xià jiàoshòu jiǎng de yǔfǎ wǒmen dōu xiě xiàlai le.

夏教授講的語法我們都寫下來了。

We have taken down the notes of the grammar taught by Professor Xia.

Nǐ néng bǎ dàjiā de míngzi xiě xiàlai ma?

你能把大家的名字寫下來嗎?

Can you write down everyone's name?

▶ IV. The Conjunction 一……就

一……就 (yī...jiù) is used together with a pair of verbs to denote two actions occurring in succession. It means "as soon as."

Examples:

Gélín yī dào yīyuàn jiù jìnle jízhěnshì.

格林一到医院就进了急诊室。

As soon as Green got to the hospital, he went into the emergency room.

Xiǎo Lín yī kànwán bìng jiù qù yàofáng qǔle yào.

小林一看完病就去药房取了药。

As soon as Little Lin saw the doctor, she went to the pharmacy to get the medicine.

It may also indicate conditional relations or habitual actions.

Examples:

Xiè lǎoshī yī shēng bìng jiù shuìjiào.

谢老师一生病就睡觉。

Every time Professor Xie gets sick, he sleeps.

Yuēhàn yī kànshū jiù xiǎng shuìjiào.

约翰一看书就想睡觉。

Whenever John reads a book, he wants to sleep.

▶ V. The Conjunction 不但……而且

不但……而且 (bú dàn...érqiě) is a pair of conjunctions used to connect two clauses of a complex sentence. It means "besides A, also B," or "not only A, but also B."

Examples:

Jīntiān wǒ māma bú dàn yào qù yīyuàn, érqiě yào qù yínháng.

今天我妈妈不但要去医院，而且要去银行。

Besides going to the hospital, my mother also needs to go to the bank today.

Jì kuàijiàn bú dàn kuài, érqiě ānquán.

寄快件不但快，而且安全。

To send mail express is not only fast, but also safe.

▶ IV. The Conjunction 一……就

一……就 (yī...jiù) is used together with a pair of verbs to denote two actions occurring in succession. It means "as soon as."

Examples:

Gélín yī dào yīyuàn jiù jìnle jízhěnshì.

格林一到醫院就進了急診室。

As soon as Green got to the hospital, he went into the emergency room.

Xiǎo Lín yī kànwán bìng jiù qù yàofáng qǔle yào.

小林一看完病就去藥房取了藥。

As soon as Little Lin saw the doctor, she went to the pharmacy to get the medicine.

It may also indicate conditional relations or habitual actions.

Examples:

Xiè lǎoshī yī shēng bìng jiù shuìjiào.

謝老師一生病就睡覺。

Every time Professor Xie gets sick, he sleeps.

Yuēhàn yī kànshū jiù xiǎng shuìjiào.

約翰一看書就想睡覺。

Whenever John reads a book, he wants to sleep.

▶ V. The Conjunction 不但……而且

不但……而且 (bú dàn...érqiě) is a pair of conjunctions used to connect two clauses of a complex sentence. It means "besides A, also B," or "not only A, but also B."

Examples:

Jīntiān wǒ māma bú dàn yào qù yīyuàn, érqiě yào qù yínháng.

今天我媽媽不但要去醫院，而且要去銀行。

Besides going to the hospital, my mother also needs to go to the bank today.

Jì kuàijiàn bú dàn kuài, érqiě ānquán.

寄快件不但快，而且安全。

To send mail express is not only fast, but also safe.

▶ 练习 Exercises

I. Combine the phrases into sentences with duration of time expressions.

Example:

看　病　　半天→我看病看了半天。→我看了半天的病。

没　跳舞　　三个月→我有三个月没跳舞了。

1. 吃　饭　　一个小时
2. 病　　　　三天
3. 看　医生　两个小时
4. 买　东西　四个小时
5. 看　电视　二十分钟
6. 没　生病　一年
7. 不　上课　三天
8. 没　吃饭　一天

II. Find a partner to do the following exercise. Each of you can choose four "time-when" and four "time-duration" phrases from the list below to make up sentences. See who can complete the exercise first.

Example:

四点→我四点上课。

四个小时→我看了四个小时的电影。

	Time-When	Time-Duration
1.	十点	十个小时
2.	两点半	两个半小时
3.	昨天	一天
4.	明天	半天
5.	星期一	一个星期
6.	上个月	一个月
7.	十一月	十一个月
8.	去年	一年

▶ 練習 Exercises

I. Combine the phrases into sentences with duration of time expressions.

Example:

看	病	半天→我看病看了半天。→我看了半天的病。
沒	跳舞	三個月→我有三個月沒跳舞了。

1. 吃　　飯　　　　一個小時
2. 病　　　　　　　三天
3. 看　　醫生　　　兩個小時
4. 買　　東西　　　四個小時
5. 看　　電視　　　二十分鐘
6. 沒　　生病　　　一年
7. 不　　上課　　　三天
8. 沒　　吃飯　　　一天

II. Find a partner to do the following exercise. Each of you can choose four "time-when" and four "time-duration" phrases from the list below to make up sentences. See who can complete the exercise first.

Example:

四點→我四點上課。

四個小時→我看了四個小時的電影。

	Time-When	Time-Duration
1.	十點	十個小時
2.	兩點半	兩個半小時
3.	昨天	一天
4.	明天	半天
5.	星期一	一個星期
6.	上個月	一個月
7.	十一月	十一個月
8.	去年	一年

III. Fill in the blanks with duration of time or complement of frequency expressions.

1.一下 2.一天 3.一天 4.三次 5.三次 6.五次

昨天我＿＿＿＿没上课。我上吐下泻，拉了＿＿＿＿肚子。一个小时上了＿＿＿＿厕所(cèsuǒ, bathroom)。我只好去看医生。医生检查了＿＿＿＿我的肚子，叫我去化验血和大便。我得了急性肠炎。医生给我开了药，让我一天吃＿＿＿＿，一次两片。回家的时候，我的好朋友黄友看见我说："我给你打了＿＿＿＿电话，你都不接。你到哪儿去了？"我说："肚子疼，哎哟！我要上厕所。"

IV. Fill in the blanks with 来/去 based on the location of the speaker.

Location of the speaker

1. 小高进医院＿＿＿＿了。   (outside the hospital)
2. 他跑上楼＿＿＿＿了。   (upstairs)
3. 地铁开过＿＿＿＿了。   (behind the subway)
4. 妈妈买回＿＿＿＿几个水果。   (at home)
5. 他从中国带回＿＿＿＿几件毛衣。   (in China)

V. Fill in the blanks with appropriate compound directional complements.

1. 吃了药以后，她的病好＿＿＿＿了。
2. 他们高兴(gāoxìng, happy)地跳＿＿＿＿舞＿＿＿＿。
3. 你说的很好，请说＿＿＿＿。
4. 快到站了，公共汽车慢＿＿＿＿。
5. 黄英的病还没好，还要在医院住＿＿＿＿。
6. 你能听＿＿＿＿是谁吗？
7. 请写＿＿＿＿大家的名字。

VI. Translate the following sentences with 一……就 and 不但……而且.

1. You must go to see the doctor as soon as you get sick.

2. As soon as he got to the hospital, he went into the emergency room.

3. Whenever he goes to the supermarket, he buys cola.

4. She was not only coughing but also had a fever.

III. Fill in the blanks with duration of time or complement of frequency expressions.

1.一下　2.一天　3.一天　4.三次　5.三次　6.五次

昨天我＿＿＿＿＿＿＿沒上課。我上吐下瀉，拉了＿＿＿＿＿＿＿肚子。一個小時上了＿＿＿＿＿＿＿廁所(cèsuǒ, bathroom)。我只好去看醫生。醫生檢查了＿＿＿＿＿＿＿我的肚子，叫我去化驗血和大便。我得了急性腸炎。醫生給我開了藥，讓我一天吃＿＿＿＿＿＿＿，一次兩片。回家的時候，我的好朋友黃友看見我說："我給你打了＿＿＿＿＿＿＿電話，你都不接。你到哪兒去了？"我說:"肚子疼，哎喲! 我要上廁所。"

IV. Fill in the blanks with 來/去 based on the location of the speaker.

Location of the speaker

1. 小高進醫院＿＿＿＿＿＿＿了。　　　　　　(outside the hospital)
2. 他跑上樓＿＿＿＿＿＿＿了。　　　　　　　(upstairs)
3. 地鐵開過＿＿＿＿＿＿＿了。　　　　　　　(behind the subway)
4. 媽媽買回＿＿＿＿＿＿＿幾個水果。　　　　(at home)
5. 他從中國帶回＿＿＿＿＿＿＿幾件毛衣。　　(in China)

V. Fill in the blanks with appropriate compound directional complements.

1. 吃了藥以後，她的病好＿＿＿＿＿＿＿了。
2. 他們高興(gāoxìng, happy)地跳＿＿＿＿＿＿＿舞＿＿＿＿＿＿＿。
3. 你說的很好，請說＿＿＿＿＿＿＿。
4. 快到站了，公共汽車慢＿＿＿＿＿＿＿。
5. 黃英的病還沒好，還要在醫院住＿＿＿＿＿＿＿。
6. 你能聽＿＿＿＿＿＿＿是誰嗎？
7. 請寫＿＿＿＿＿＿＿大家的名字。

VI. Translate the following sentences with 一……就 and 不但……而且.

1. You must go to see the doctor as soon as you get sick.
2. As soon as he got to the hospital, he went into the emergency room.
3. Whenever he goes to the supermarket, he buys cola.
4. She was not only coughing but also had a fever.

5. She not only bought milk and cola, but also bought cups and napkins.

6. As soon as Little Xie saw his elder brother catching a cold, he took him to the school hospital.

VII. Write an essay describing your experience of seeing a doctor. Try to use as many new grammatical patterns from this lesson as you can, such as 一⋯⋯就, 不但⋯⋯而且, **compound directional complements, complement of frequency.**

VIII. Choose the right words to fill in the blanks, and then read the conversation aloud with a partner.

1. 三天　2. 一次　3. 没　4. 过去　5. 不但⋯⋯而且　6. 一⋯⋯就　7. 一年
8. 三次

A: 黄小姐怎么没来上课？

B: 她生病了，病了_____了。

A: 她得什么病了？

B: 她可能感冒了。昨天已经看了_____医生了。

A: 她吃药了吗？

B: 医生给她开了些药，让她一天吃_____，一次三片。现在不发烧了。

A: 她应该_____生病_____看医生。她要多吃点水果和清淡的食物。

B: 我昨天给她送_____一些水果。她妈妈_____给她买了水果，_____做了她喜欢吃的饭。

A: 她常常生病吗？

B: 不，她有_____生病了。这次可能是流感。

A: 好，我今天下午去看看她。

5. She not only bought milk and cola, but also bought cups and napkins.

6. As soon as Little Xie saw his elder brother catching a cold, he took him to the school hospital.

VII. Write an essay describing your experience of seeing a doctor. Try to use as many new grammatical patterns from this lesson as you can, such as 一⋯⋯就, 不但⋯⋯而且, **compound directional complements, complement of frequency.**

VIII. Choose the right words to fill in the blanks, and then read the conversation aloud with a partner.

1. 三天　2. 一次　3. 没　4. 過去　5. 不但⋯⋯而且　6. 一⋯⋯就　7. 一年
8. 三次

A: 黃小姐怎麼沒來上課？

B: 她生病了，病了＿＿＿＿＿＿了。

A: 她得什么麼了？

B: 她可能感冒了。昨天已經看了＿＿＿＿＿＿醫生了。

A: 她吃藥了嗎？

B: 醫生給她開了些藥，讓她一天吃＿＿＿＿＿＿，一次三片。現在不發燒了。

A: 她應該＿＿＿＿＿＿生病＿＿＿＿＿＿看醫生。她要多吃點水果和清淡的食物。

B: 我昨天給她送＿＿＿＿＿＿一些水果。她媽媽＿＿＿＿＿＿給她買了水果，
＿＿＿＿＿＿做了她喜歡吃的飯。

A: 她常常生病嗎？

B: 不，她有＿＿＿＿＿＿＿＿＿生病了。這次可能是流感。

A: 好，我今天下午去看看她。

第十课
LESSON 10

▶ I. Potential Complements

The potential complement expresses capability or potential. It indicates whether the action will possibly achieve a result or reach a state. It is formed by placing a 得 between a verb and a complement of result (CR) or compound directional complement (CD).

Sentence structure:	S ＋ V ＋ 得 ＋ CR/CD
	S ＋ V ＋ 得 ＋ CR/CD ＋ O
	S ＋ O ＋ V ＋得 ＋ CR/CD

Examples:

Xuě bù dà, wǒ zǒu de guòqù.

雪不大，我走得过去。

The snow is not heavy, I can walk over.

Yíhéyuán wǒ qù de liǎo, wǒ yǒu shíjiān.

颐和园我去得了，我有时间。

I can go to the Summer Palace. I have time.

Hái yǒu bàn gè xiǎoshí, wǒmen xiě de wán zuòyè.

还有半个小时，我们写得完作业。

We still have half an hour. We can finish doing (writing) the homework.

Wǒ xiě de chūlai tāmen de míngzi.

我写得出来他们的名字。

I can write out their names.

The negative form is made by replacing 不 between a verb and a complement of result.

第十課
LESSON 10

▶ **I. Potential Complements**

The potential complement expresses capability or potential. It indicates whether the action will possibly achieve a result or reach a state. It is formed by placing a 得 between a verb and a complement of result (CR) or compound directional complement (CD).

Sentence structure:	S ＋ V ＋ 得 ＋ CR/CD
	S ＋ V ＋ 得 ＋ CR/CD ＋ O
	S ＋ O ＋ V ＋得 ＋ CR/CD

Examples:

Xuě bù dà, wǒ zǒu de guòqù.

雪不大，我走得過去。

The snow is not heavy, I can walk over.

Yíhéyuán wǒ qù de liǎo, wǒ yǒu shíjiān.

頤和園我去得了，我有時間。

I can go to the Summer Palace. I have time.

Hái yǒu bàn gè xiǎoshí, wǒmen xiě de wán zuòyè.

還有半個小時，我們寫得完作業。

We still have half an hour. We can finish doing (writing) the homework.

Wǒ xiě de chūlai tāmen de míngzi.

我寫得出來他們的名字。

I can write out their names.

The negative form is made by replacing 不 between a verb and a complement of result.

Negative sentence

```
Sentence structure:    S + V + 不 + CR/CD
                       S + V + 不 + CR/CD + O
                       S + O + V + 不 + CR/CD
```

Examples:

Xià yǔ le, wǒmen tī bù liǎo zúqiú le.

下雨了，我们踢不了足球了。

It is raining. We can't play soccer anymore.

Diànyǐng piào bù gòu, wǒ kàn bù liǎo diànyǐng le.

电影票不够，我看不了电影了。

There are not enough movie tickets. I can't see the movie (anymore).

Fàn tài duō, wǒ chī bù liǎo le.

饭太多，我吃不了了。

There is too much food. I can't eat anymore.

Interrogative sentence

Both 吗 and A-not-A types of questions can be used. But when using the A-not-A question, the affirmative and negative forms of the Verb + Complement (V + C) phrase should be used.

```
Sentence structure:   S + V + 得 + CR/CD + (O) + 吗
                      S + V + 得 + CR/CD + V + 不 + CR/CD
                      + (O)
```

Examples:

Question: Nǐ zhè xiē fàn chī de wán ma?

你这些饭吃得完吗？

Can you eat the entire meal?

Answer: Wǒ zhè xiē fàn chī bù wán.

我这些饭吃不完。

I can't eat the entire meal.

Negative sentence

Sentence structure:	S + V + 不 + CR/CD
	S + V + 不 + CR/CD + O
	S + O + V + 不 + CR/CD

Examples:

Xià yǔ le, wǒmen tī bù liǎo zúqiú le.

下雨了，我們踢不了足球了。

It is raining. We can't play soccer anymore.

Diànyǐng piào bù gòu, wǒ kàn bù liǎo diànyǐng le.

電影票不夠，我看不了電影了。

There are not enough movie tickets. I can't see the movie (anymore).

Fàn tài duō, wǒ chī bù liǎo le.

飯太多，我吃不了了。

There is too much food. I can't eat anymore.

Interrogative sentence

Both 嗎 and A-not-A types of questions can be used. But when using the A-not-A question, the affirmative and negative forms of the Verb + Complement (V + C) phrase should be used.

Sentence structure:	S + V + 得 + CR/CD + (O) + 嗎
	S + V + 得 + CR/CD + V + 不 + CR/CD + (O)

Examples:

Question: Nǐ zhè xiē fàn chī de wán ma?

你這些飯吃得完嗎？

Can you eat the entire meal?

Answer: Wǒ zhè xiē fàn chī bù wán.

我這些飯吃不完。

I can't eat the entire meal.

Question: Nǐ zài hùliánwǎng shàng kàn de dào tiānqì yùbào ma?

你在互联网上看得到天气预报吗？

Can you see the weather forecast on the Internet?

Answer: Wǒ (zài hùliánwǎng shàng) kàn de dào (tiānqì yùbào).

我（在互联网上）看得到（天气预报）。

I can see (the weather forecast on the Internet).

Question: Nǐ zuò de wán zuò bù wán zuòyè?

你做得完做不完作业？

Can you finish doing your homework?

Answer: Wǒ zuò de wán (zuòyè).

我做得完（作业）。

I can finish doing my homework.

Question: Xiànzài nǐ kàn de dào kàn bù dào tiānqì yùbào?

现在你看得到看不到天气预报？

Can you see the weather forecast now?

Answer: Xiànzài wǒ kàn bù dào (tiānqì yùbào).

现在我看不到（天气预报）。

No, I can't see (the weather forecast) now.

Note: Another way to express capability is through the use of 能 + V. Although 能 + V and the potential complement mean essentially the same thing, the potential complement is generally a more idiomatic way to express capability. Although not necessary, auxiliary verbs of possibility (such as 能 and 可以) can be placed before the verb with an affirmative potential complement, and the meaning remains the same.

Examples:

Wǒ (néng) chī de wán zhè xiē fàn.

我（能）吃得完这些饭。

I can eat the entire meal.

Wǒ (kěyǐ) zhǎo de zháo tā.

我（可以）找得着她。

I can find her.

Question: Nǐ zài hùliánwǎng shàng kàn de dào tiānqì yùbào ma?

你在互聯網上看得到天氣預報嗎?

Can you see the weather forecast on the Internet?

Answer: Wǒ (zài hùliánwǎng shàng) kàn de dào (tiānqì yùbào).

我(在互聯網上)看得到(天氣預報)。

I can see (the weather forecast on the Internet).

Question: Nǐ zuò de wán zuò bù wán zuòyè?

你做得完做不完作業?

Can you finish doing your homework?

Answer: Wǒ zuò de wán (zuòyè).

我做得完(作業)。

I can finish doing my homework.

Question: Xiànzài nǐ kàn de dào kàn bù dào tiānqì yùbào?

現在你看得到看不到天氣預報?

Can you see the weather forecast now?

Answer: Xiànzài wǒ kàn bù dào (tiānqì yùbào).

現在我看不到(天氣預報)。

No, I can't see (the weather forecast) now.

Note: Another way to express capability is through the use of 能 + V. Although 能 + V and the potential complement mean essentially the same thing, the potential complement is generally a more idiomatic way to express capability. Although not necessary, auxiliary verbs of possibility (such as 能 and 可以) can be placed before the verb with an affirmative potential complement, and the meaning remains the same.

Examples:

Wǒ (néng) chī de wán zhè xiē fàn.

我(能)吃得完這些飯。

I can eat the entire meal.

Wǒ (kěyǐ) zhǎo de zháo tā.

我(可以)找得著她。

I can find her.

Complement of Degree versus Potential Complement

Both the complement of degree (Lesson 5) and the potential complement use 得 before the complement. The differences between these two types of complements are listed below.

(1) The complement of degree assesses how well or how fast, etc., an action is or was carried out.

The potential complement tells whether or not an action will possibly achieve a result or reach a state. The complement of degree can be modified by placing an adverb before it, while the potential complement cannot be modified.

Examples:

Tā kàn de hěn qīngchǔ.

他看得很清楚。 (complement of degree, emphasizes how he saw it)

He saw it very clearly.

Tā kàn de qīngchǔ.

他看得清楚。 (potential complement, emphasizes that he has the ability to see it clearly)

He can see it clearly.

(2) They have different negative forms.

Examples:

Tā kàn de bù qīngchǔ.

他看得不清楚。 (complement of degree)

He did not see it clearly.

Tā kàn bù qīngchǔ.

他看不清楚。 (potential complement)

He can not see it clearly.

(3) They have different A-not-A question forms.

Examples:

Xuě xià de dà bù dà?

雪下得大不大？ (complement of degree)

Is it snowing heavily?

Complement of Degree versus Potential Complement

Both the complement of degree (Lesson 5) and the potential complement use 得 before the complement. The differences between these two types of complements are listed below.

(1) The complement of degree assesses how well or how fast, etc., an action is or was carried out.

The potential complement tells whether or not an action will possibly achieve a result or reach a state. The complement of degree can be modified by placing an adverb before it, while the potential complement cannot be modified.

Examples:

> Tā kàn de hěn qīngchǔ.
>
> 他看得很清楚。 (complement of degree, emphasizes how he saw it)
> He saw it very clearly.

> Tā kàn de qīngchǔ.
>
> 他看得清楚。 (potential complement, emphasizes that he has the ability to see it clearly)
> He can see it clearly.

(2) They have different negative forms.

Examples:

> Tā kàn de bù qīngchǔ.
>
> 他看得不清楚。 (complement of degree)
> He did not see it clearly.

> Tā kàn bù qīngchǔ.
>
> 他看不清楚。 (potential complement)
> He can not see it clearly.

(3) They have different A-not-A question forms.

Examples:

> Xuě xià de dà bù dà?
>
> 雪下得大不大? (complement of degree)
> Is it snowing heavily?

Xuě xià de dà xià bù dà?

雪下得大下不大？ (potential complement)

Might it snow heavily?

(4) The objects are positioned differently.

Examples:

Wáng Xiǎonián zuò Zhōngguó fàn zuò de hǎo.

王小年做中国饭做得好。 (complement of degree)

Xiaonian Wang cooks Chinese food well.

Wáng Xiǎonián zuò de hǎo Zhōngguó fàn.

王小年做得好中国饭。 (potential complement)

Xiaonian Wang can cook Chinese food well.

Note: The aspectual particles 了, 着 and 过 (See Lesson 7) never occur after the verb with a potential complement. In the sentence 我们踢不了足球, 了 reads as liǎo, and it means "can." In 我可以找得着她, 着 reads as zháo, indicating the goal or result of the action is achieved.

II. Reduplication of Verbs
(See Textbook I, Lesson 9)

Selected example from the textbook:

下了课我陪她去学校医院看看。 (Lesson 9)

Reduplication of verbs implies a short, quick and informal action. It is often used to soften the tone of the statement.

Formulas of reduplicated verbs:

Monosyllabic verbs: A A

When monosyllabic verbs are reduplicated, the reduplicated verb is in the neutral tone.

Examples:

zuò   zuòzuo

坐 → 坐坐

Xuě xià de dà xià bù dà?

雪下得大下不大? (potential complement)

Might it snow heavily?

(4) The objects are positioned differently.

Examples:

Wáng Xiǎonián zuò Zhōngguó fàn zuò de hǎo.

王小年做中國飯做得好。 (complement of degree)

Xiaonian Wang cooks Chinese food well.

Wáng Xiǎonián zuò de hǎo Zhōngguó fàn.

王小年做得好中國飯。 (potential complement)

Xiaonian Wang can cook Chinese food well.

Note: The aspectual particles 了, 著 and 過 (See Lesson 7) never occur after the verb with a potential complement. In the sentence 我們踢不了足球, 了 reads as liǎo, and it means "can." In 我可以找得著她, 著 reads as zháo, indicating the goal or result of the action is achieved.

II. Reduplication of Verbs
(See Textbook I, Lesson 9)

Selected example from the textbook:

下了課我陪她去學校醫院看看。 (Lesson 9)

Reduplication of verbs implies a short, quick and informal action. It is often used to soften the tone of the statement.

Formulas of reduplicated verbs:

Monosyllabic verbs: A A

When monosyllabic verbs are reduplicated, the reduplicated verb is in the neutral tone.

Examples:

zuò   zuòzuo

坐 → 坐坐

kàn   kànkan

看 → 看看

wán wánwan

玩 → 玩玩

Nǐ zuòzuo, wǒ qù guàhào.

你坐坐，我去挂号。

Take a seat. I am going to register. (It won't take long.)

Wǒ kěyǐ kànkan zhè běn shū ma?

我可以看看这本书吗？

May I take a look at the book? (Just look briefly.)

Nǐ xiǎngxiang, nǐ bǎ huìyuánzhèng fàng zài nǎr le?

你 想 想，你把会员证放在哪儿了？

Please think (please try to recall), where did you put the membership card?

(The reduplication makes the question indirect and the tone less strong.)

Disyllabic verbs: ABAB

Examples:

liànxí liànxí liànxí

练习 → 练习练习

xuéxí xuéxí xuéxí

学习 → 学习学习

Zhège wèntí wǒmen yào tǎolùn tǎolùn.

这个问题我们要讨论讨论。

We should discuss this question. (The discussion won't be too long or serious.)

Nǐ yìnggāi qù yīyuàn jiǎnchá jiǎnchá.

你应该去医院检查检查。

You should go to the hospital to have an examination. (The exam is not long.)

Jīntiān xiàwǔ wǒmen liànxí liànxí fāyīn ba.

今天下午我们练习练习发音吧。

Let's practice pronunciation this afternoon. (Do it lightly.)

kàn　　kànkan

看 → 看看

wán　　wánwan

玩 → 玩玩

Nǐ zuòzuo, wǒ qù guàhào.

你坐坐，我去掛號。

Take a seat. I am going to register. (It won't take long.)

Wǒ kěyǐ kànkan zhè běn shū ma?

我可以看看這本書嗎？

May I take a look at the book? (Just look briefly.)

Nǐ xiǎngxiang, nǐ bǎ huìyuánzhèng fàng zài nǎr le?

你 想 想，你把會員證放在哪兒了？

Please think (please try to recall), where did you put the membership card?

(The reduplication makes the question indirect and the tone less strong.)

Disyllabic verbs: ABAB

Examples:

liànxí liànxí liànxí

練習 → 練習練習

xuéxí xuéxí xuéxí

學習 → 學習學習

Zhège wèntí wǒmen yào tǎolùn tǎolùn.

這個問題我們要討論討論。

We should discuss this question. (The discussion won't be too long or serious.)

Nǐ yìnggāi qù yīyuàn jiǎnchá jiǎnchá.

你應該去醫院檢查檢查。

You should go to the hospital to have an examination. (The exam is not long.)

Jīntiān xiàwǔ wǒmen liànxí liànxí fāyīn ba.

今天下午我們練習練習發音吧。

Let's practice pronunciation this afternoon. (Do it lightly.)

Note: In a verb-object phrase, only the verb can be reduplicated.

Examples:

Wǎnshang tā chángcháng kànkan bào, tiàotiao wǔ.

晚上他常常看看报、跳跳舞。

In the evening he often reads the newspaper and dances.

(Incorrect: 晚上他常常看报看报、跳舞跳舞。)

Wǒ gěi nǐ bǔbu kè.

我给你补补课。

Let me make up the missed lesson for you.

(Incorrect: 我给你补课补课。)

Note: When monosyllabic verbs are reduplicated, there is another way to express the same meaning, by inserting "一" between the verbs.

Examples:

Nǐ zuò yī zuò, wǒ qù guàhào.

你坐一坐，我去挂号。(same as 坐坐)

You take a seat, I am going to register.

Ràng wǒ xiǎng yī xiǎng.

让我想一想。(same as 想想)

Let me think about it.

Note: If the aspectual particle 了 is used to emphasize the completion of an action, 了 must be placed between the two parts of the reduplicated verb.

Examples:

Tā zuò le zuò, jiù qù guàhào le.

他坐了坐，就去挂号了。

He sat for a little while, then went to register.

Dàjiā xiūxí le xiūxí.

大家休息了休息。

Everybody took a rest.

Note: In a verb-object phrase, only the verb can be reduplicated.

Examples:

Wǎnshang tā chángcháng kànkan bào, tiàotiao wǔ.

晚上他常常看看報、跳跳舞。

In the evening he often reads the newspaper and dances.

(Incorrect: 晚上他常常看報看報、跳舞跳舞。)

Wǒ gěi nǐ bǔbu kè.

我給你補補課。

Let me make up the missed lesson for you.

(Incorrect: 我給你補課補課。)

Note: When monosyllabic verbs are reduplicated, there is another way to express the same meaning, by inserting "一" between the verbs.

Examples:

Nǐ zuò yī zuò, wǒ qù guàhào.

你坐一坐，我去掛號。(same as 坐坐)

You take a seat, I am going to register.

Ràng wǒ xiǎng yī xiǎng.

讓我想一想。(same as 想 想)

Let me think about it.

Note: If the aspectual particle 了 is used to emphasize the completion of an action, 了 must be placed between the two parts of the reduplicated verb.

Examples:

Tā zuò le zuò, jiù qù guàhào le.

他坐了坐，就去掛號了。

He sat for a little while, then went to register.

Dàjiā xiūxí le xiūxí.

大家休息了休息。

Everybody took a rest.

▶ III. 把 Sentences

(See Textbook I, Lessons 7 and 8)

Selected examples from the textbook:

他得把12月18日的票改到25日。 (Lesson 7)

只要把你的银行卡从这个口放进去，输入你的密码⋯⋯(Lesson 8)

把 sentence is used to show the result of an action (verb) directed by the subject to some definite person or thing. It is composed of a 把 + object phrase before the verb.

Sentence structure: S ＋ 把 ＋ O ＋ V ＋ Other Elements

Examples:

Wǒ bǎ yào dài lái le.

我把药带来了。

I have brought the medicine.

Wǒ bǎ jīntiān de tiānqì yùbào chāo zài zhǐ shàng le.

我把今天的天气预报抄在纸上了。

I copied (wrote) today's weather forecast on the newspaper.

Tā bǎ wǒ mǎi de shuǐguǒ chī le.

他把我买的水果吃了。

He ate the fruit that I bought.

Note: Notionally the object of 把 in a 把 sentence is the receiver of the action indicated by the verb. For example, in 他把我买的水果吃了, 水果 is the object of 把, and it is also receiver of the action 吃. In a 把 sentence, the object of 把 should be definite, not a general referral. Compare the following sentences:

Wǒ qù mǎi máoyī.

我去买毛衣。

I am going to buy a sweater. (any sweater)

Wǒ qù bǎ máoyī mǎi huílái.

我去把毛衣买回来。

I am going to buy the sweater. (the one that both the speaker and listener know about)

▶ III. 把 Sentences
(See Textbook I, Lessons 7 and 8)

Selected examples from the textbook:

他得把12月18日的票改到25日。 (Lesson 7)

只要把你的銀行卡從這個口放進去，輸入你的密碼⋯⋯ (Lesson 8)

把 sentence is used to show the result of an action (verb) directed by the subject to some definite person or thing. It is composed of a 把 + object phrase before the verb.

Sentence structure:	S ＋ 把 ＋ O ＋ V ＋ Other Elements

Examples:

Wǒ bǎ yào dài lái le.

我把藥帶來了。

I have brought the medicine.

Wǒ bǎ jīntiān de tiānqì yùbào chāo zài zhǐ shàng le.

我把今天的天氣預報抄在紙上了。

I copied (wrote) today's weather forecast on the newspaper.

Tā bǎ wǒ mǎi de shuǐguǒ chī le.

他把我買的水果吃了。

He ate the fruit that I bought.

Note: Notionally the object of 把 in a 把 sentence is the receiver of the action indicated by the verb. For example, in 他把我買的水果吃了, 水果 is the object of 把, and it is also receiver of the action 吃. In a 把 sentence, the object of 把 should be definite, not a general referral. Compare the following sentences:

Wǒ qù mǎi máoyī.

我去買毛衣。

I am going to buy a sweater. (any sweater)

Wǒ qù bǎ máoyī mǎi huílái.

我去把毛衣買回來。

I am going to buy the sweater. (the one that both the speaker and listener know about)

In a 把 sentence the verb is usually followed by other elements.

Examples:

Nǐ bǎ nà zhāng xìnyòngkǎ dàizhe.

你把那张信用卡带着。(aspectual particle 着)

(You) bring that credit card with you.

Wǒ bǎ yào chī le.

我把药吃了。(aspectual particle 了)

I took the medicine.

Tā bǎ shū fàng zài jiālǐ le.

他把书放在家里了。(aspectual particle 了)

He put the books in his house.

Nǐ bǎ jīntiān de zuòyè zài kànkan.

你把今天的作业再看看。(reduplication of verb 看看)

Take a look at today's homework again.

Nǐ kuài bǎ yào chī xiàqù.

你快把药吃下去。(compound directional complement 下去)

(You) eat the medicine quickly.

Tā bǎ shuǐguǒ chī wán le.

他把水果吃完了。(complement of result 完, aspectual particle 了)

He ate all the fruit.

▶ IV. 被 Sentences
(See Textbook I, Lesson 10)

Selected example from the textbook:

反正天气预报没说有阵雨，我被淋湿了。(Lesson 10)

The 被 sentence in Chinese is similar to the passive voice in English, though it is not as commonly used. The 被 sentence expresses that a person or thing (the subject) is subject to a certain result of the action. The subject is the receiver of the action and the object of 被 is the doer of the action. Very

In a 把 sentence the verb is usually followed by other elements.

Examples:

Nǐ bǎ nà zhāng xìnyòngkǎ dàizhe.

你把那張信用卡帶著。(aspectual particle 著)

(You) bring that credit card with you.

Wǒ bǎ yào chī le.

我把藥吃了。(aspectual particle 了)

I took the medicine.

Tā bǎ shū fàng zài jiālǐ le.

他把書放在家裏了。(aspectual particle 了)

He put the books in his house.

Nǐ bǎ jīntiān de zuòyè zài kànkan.

你把今天的作業再看看。(reduplication of verb 看看)

Take a look at today's homework again.

Nǐ kuài bǎ yào chī xiàqù.

你快把藥吃下去。(compound directional complement 下去)

(You) eat the medicine quickly.

Tā bǎ shuǐguǒ chī wán le.

他把水果吃完了。(complement of result 完, aspectual particle 了)

He ate all the fruit.

▶ IV. 被 Sentences
(See Textbook I, Lesson 10)

Selected example from the textbook:

反正天氣預報沒說有陣雨，我被淋濕了。(Lesson 10)

The 被 sentence in Chinese is similar to the passive voice in English, though it is not as commonly used. The 被 sentence expresses that a person or thing (the subject) is subject to a certain result of the action. The subject is the receiver of the action and the object of 被 is the doer of the action. Very often it conveys the sense that something has gone wrong. It is composed of a 被 + object phrase before the verb.

Sentence structure: S ＋ 被 ＋ O ＋ V ＋ Other Elements

Examples:

Wáng Jiāshēng bèi yǔ lín chéngle luò tāng jī.

王家生被雨淋成了落汤鸡。

Jiasheng Wang was soaked (like a drenched chicken) by the rain.

Sǎn bèi Zhāng Wén ná huí jiā le.

伞被张文拿回家了。

The umbrella was taken home by Wen Zhang.

Fàn bèi Bāo xiǎojiě chī le.

饭被包小姐吃了。

(The entire) meal was eaten by Miss Bao.

The negative form of the 被 sentence is generally made by placing the negative adverb 没（有） before the preposition 被.

Examples:

Shū méi bèi Wáng Xiǎonián ná zǒu.

书没被王小年拿走。

The book was not taken away by Xiaonian Wang.

Tā méi bèi yǔ lín shī.

他没被雨淋湿。

He was not soaked by the rain.

Sometimes the object of 被 can be omitted if the context is understood.

Examples:

Yuēhàn de chē bèi kāi zǒu le.

约翰的车被开走了。

John's car was driven away (by somebody).

often it conveys the sense that something has gone wrong. It is composed of a 被 + object phrase before the verb.

Sentence structure: S ＋ 被 ＋ O ＋ V ＋ Other Elements

Examples:

Wáng Jiāshēng bèi yǔ lín chéngle luò tāng jī.

王家生被雨淋成了落湯雞。

Jiasheng Wang was soaked (like a drenched chicken) by the rain.

Sǎn bèi Zhāng Wén ná huí jiā le.

傘被張文拿回家了。

The umbrella was taken home by Wen Zhang.

Fàn bèi Bāo xiǎojiě chī le.

飯被包小姐吃了。

(The entire) meal was eaten by Miss Bao.

The negative form of the 被 sentence is generally made by placing the negative adverb 沒(有) before the preposition 被.

Examples:

Shū méi bèi Wáng Xiǎonián ná zǒu.

書沒被王小年拿走。

The book was not taken away by Xiaonian Wang.

Tā méi bèi yǔ lín shī.

他沒被雨淋濕。

He was not soaked by the rain.

Sometimes the object of 被 can be omitted if the context is understood.

Examples:

Yuēhàn de chē bèi kāi zǒu le.

約翰的車被開走了。

John's car was driven away (by somebody).

Cài bèi chī le.

菜被吃了。

The dish was eaten (by somebody).

In spoken Chinese, the prepositions 叫, 让 and 给 are also often used to indicate the passive, though they must be followed by an object.

Examples:

Zhàopiàn ràng Zhāng Wén dài lái le.

照片让张文带来了。

The photograph was brought here by Wen Zhang.

Wǒ de yóupiào jiào Xiǎo Jīn ná zǒu le.

我的邮票叫小金拿走了。

My stamps were taken away by Little Jin.

Tā gěi lǎoshī jiào chū qù le.

他给老师叫出去了。

He was called out (of class) by the teacher.

Incorrect: Xīn shū ràng jiè zǒu le.

新书让借走了。 (the object 人 must be added after 让.)

The new books were checked out (by somebody).

Note: As in the 把 sentence, the verb in a 被 sentence is normally followed by some other element.

▶ V. The Conjunction 连……都/也
(See Textbook I, Lesson 4)

Selected example from the textbook:

(连)我都说不好。 (Lesson 4)

To emphasize a part of a sentence, put 连 before the element to be emphasized and 都 or 也 before the verb. This sentence can emphasize subject, object or verb.

Cài bèi chī le.

菜被吃了。

The dish was eaten (by somebody).

In spoken Chinese, the prepositions 叫, 讓 and 給 are also often used to indicate the passive, though they must be followed by an object.

Examples:

Zhàopiàn ràng Zhāng Wén dài lái le.

照片讓張文帶來了。

The photograph was brought here by Wen Zhang.

Wǒ de yóupiào jiào Xiǎo Jīn ná zǒu le.

我的郵票叫小金拿走了。

My stamps were taken away by Little Jin.

Tā gěi lǎoshī jiào chū qù le.

他給老師叫出去了。

He was called out (of class) by the teacher.

Incorrect: Xīn shū ràng jiè zǒu le.

新書讓借走了。 (the object 人 must be added after 讓.)

The new books were checked out (by somebody).

Note: As in the 把 sentence, the verb in a 被 sentence is normally followed by some other element.

▶ V. The Conjunction 連······都/也
(See Textbook I, Lesson 4)

Selected example from the textbook:

(連)我都說不好。 (Lesson 4)

To emphasize a part of a sentence, put 連 before the element to be emphasized and 都 or 也 before the verb. This sentence can emphasize subject, object or verb.

连＋S ＋ 都/也 ＋ V ＋ (O)
S ＋连 ＋ O ＋都/也 ＋ V
S ＋ 连 ＋ V ＋ (O) ＋都/也 ＋
Negation ＋ V

Examples:

Xiànzài lián Běijīng xiàtiān yě rè le.

现在连北京夏天也热了。

Now even summer in Beijing is hot. (emphasizes the subject)

Lián lǎoshī dōu bù rènshí zhège zì.

连老师都不认识这个字。

Even the teacher doesn't know this word. (emphasizes the subject)

Tā lián bīngxiāng lǐ de shèngcài dōu chī wán le.

他连冰箱里的剩菜都吃完了。

He even ate all the leftovers in the refrigerator. (emphasizes the object)

Tā lián fàn yě méi chī, jiù péi mèimei qù yīyuàn le.

他连饭也没吃，就陪妹妹去医院了。

He did not even eat (his meal), just went straight to the hospital with his younger sister. (emphasizes the object)

Nánjīng tā lián qù dōu méi qù guò.

南京他连去都没去过。

He has not even been to Nanjing. (emphasizes the verb)

Zuótiān tā lián kàn yě méi kàn, jiù bǎ shū gěi wǒ le.

昨天他连看也没看，就把书给我了。

Yesterday he did not even take a look at the book before he gave it to me. (Emphasize the verb)

连 can be omitted, while the adverb 都 or 也 can never be dropped.

Examples:

Jīntiān (lián) Lín lǎoshī dōu lái le.

今天(连)林老师都来了。

Even Professor Lin came today.

<table>
<tr><td>**Sentence structure:**</td><td>連 + S + 都/也 + V + (O)
S + 連 + O + 都/也 + V
S + 連 + V + (O) + 都/也 +
Negation + V</td></tr>
</table>

Examples:

Xiànzài lián Běijīng xiàtiān yě rè le.

現在連北京夏天也熱了。

Now even summer in Beijing is hot. (emphasizes the subject)

Lián lǎoshī dōu bù rènshí zhège zì.

連老師都不認識這個字。

Even the teacher doesn't know this word. (emphasizes the subject)

Tā lián bīngxiāng lǐ de shèngcài dōu chī wán le.

他連冰箱里的剩菜都吃完了。

He even ate all the leftovers in the refrigerator. (emphasizes the object)

Tā lián fàn yě méi chī, jiù péi mèimei qù yīyuàn le.

他連飯也沒吃，就陪妹妹去醫院了。

He did not even eat (his meal), just went straight to the hospital with his younger sister. (emphasizes the object)

Nánjīng tā lián qù dōu méi qù guò.

南京他連去都沒去過。

He has not even been to Nanjing. (emphasizes the verb)

Zuótiān tā lián kàn yě méi kàn, jiù bǎ shū gěi wǒ le.

昨天他連看也沒看，就把書給我了。

Yesterday he did not even take a look at the book before he gave it to me. (Emphasize the verb)

連 can be omitted, while the adverb 都 or 也 can never be dropped.

Examples:

Jīntiān (lián) Lín lǎoshī dōu lái le.

今天(連)林老師都來了。

Even Professor Lin came today.

Tā (lián) huà yě méi shuō, jiù chūqù le.

他（连）话也没说，就出去了。

He went out without even saying a word.

Note: If the object is emphasized, it should be moved from after the verb to before the verb, such as: 他连饭也没吃。 When 连 is followed by a verb or V + O phrase, the verb after 都 or 也 is most often in negative form. For example: 昨天他连看也没看，就把书给我了。

▶ VI. The Conjunction 虽然⋯⋯但是 or 虽然⋯⋯可是

Selected example from the textbook:

现在虽然学生生病还是先去学校的医务室，但是不付钱拿药的数量少了。

(Lesson 9, reading exercises)

The pair of conjunctions 虽然⋯⋯但是 or 虽然⋯⋯可是 (suīrán...dànshì or suīrán... kěshì; although) can combine two clauses in a complex sentence. It means that the speaker admits that the first clause is a fact, however, s/he thinks that the second clause is still reasonable.

Note that 虽然 (suīrán, although) can be omitted, but 但是 or 可是 should be kept. 虽然 should be put at the beginning of a sentence.

Examples:

Suīrán zhè bǎ yǔsǎn hěn piányi, dànshì tài xiǎo le.

虽然这把雨伞很便宜，但是太小了。

Although this umbrella is cheap, it's too small.

(Incorrect: 虽然这把雨伞很便宜，太小了，or 这把雨伞太小了，虽然很便宜。)

(Suīrán) tā shì Zhōngguó rén, kěshì tā bù huì shuō Zhōngwén.

（虽然）他是中国人，可是他不会说中文。

He is Chinese, however he doesn't know how to speak Chinese.

(Incorrect: 虽然他是中国人，他不会说中文，or 他不会说中文，虽然他是中国人。)

Tā (lián) huà yě méi shuō, jiù chūqù le.

他(連) 話也沒說，就出去了。

He went out without even saying a word.

Note: If the object is emphasized, it should be moved from after the verb to before the verb, such as: 他連飯也沒吃。 When 連 is followed by a verb or V + O phrase, the verb after 都 or 也 is most often in negative form. For example: 昨天他連看也沒看，就把書給我了。

▶ VI. The Conjunction 雖然……但是 or 雖然……可是

Selected example from the textbook:

現在雖然學生生病還是先去學校的醫務室，但是不付錢拿藥的數量少了。

(Lesson 9, reading exercises)

The pair of conjunctions 雖然……但是 or 雖然……可是 (suīrán...dànshì or suīrán... kěshì; although) can combine two clauses in a complex sentence. It means that the speaker admits that the first clause is a fact, however, s/he thinks that the second clause is still reasonable.

Note that 雖然 (suīrán, although) can be omitted, but 但是 or 可是 should be kept. 雖然 should be put at the beginning of a sentence.

Examples:

Suīrán zhè bǎ yǔsǎn hěn piányi, dànshì tài xiǎo le.

雖然這把雨傘很便宜，但是太小了。

Although this umbrella is cheap, it's too small.

(Incorrect: 雖然這把雨傘很便宜，太小了， or 這把雨傘太小了，雖然很便宜。)

(Suīrán) tā shì Zhōngguó rén, kěshì tā bù huì shuō Zhōngwén.

(雖然) 他是中國人，可是他不會說中文。

He is Chinese, however he doesn't know how to speak Chinese.

(Incorrect: 雖然他是中國人，他不會說中文， or 他不會說中文，雖然他是中國人。)

► 练习 **Exercises**

. . . .

I. Turn the following phrases into potential complements.

Example: 能上去 → 上得去

1. 能吃完
2. 不能看完
3. 能听懂
4. 不能看到
5. 能说清楚
6. 不能找着

II. Underline the complements in the following sentences and state which type of complement each of them is.

1. 今年下雪下得很早。
2. 他买东西买得很快。
3. 他说中文说得不流利。
4. 王小年拿来了那本书。
5. 约翰没做完作业。
6. 你看见王小文了吗？
7. 昨天下了一天的雨。
8. 王家生看病看了一个半小时。
9. 这个星期我去了三次医院。
10. 他买回来了一些水果。
11. 下雨了，我们踢不了足球。
12. 现在看得到看不到天气预报？

III. Change the following sentences into 把 **sentences.**

Example: 他喝完可乐了。 → 他把可乐喝完了。

1. 他做完今天的作业了。
2. 他吃完了我买的水果。
3. 妈妈做好了晚饭。

▶ 練習 Exercises

....

I. Turn the following phrases into potential complements.

Example: 能上去 → 上得去

1. 能吃完
2. 不能看完
3. 能聽懂
4. 不能看到
5. 能說清楚
6. 不能找著

II. Underline the complements in the following sentences and state which type of complement each of them is.

1. 今年下雪下得很早。
2. 他買東西買得很快。
3. 他說中文說得不流利。
4. 王小年拿來了那本書。
5. 約翰沒做完作業。
6. 你看見王小文了嗎?
7. 昨天下了一天的雨。
8. 王家生看病看了一個半小時。
9. 這個星期我去了三次醫院。
10. 他買回來了一些水果。
11. 下雨了,我們踢不了足球。
12. 現在看得到看不到天氣預報?

III. Change the following sentences into 把 sentences.

Example: 他喝完可樂了。 → 他把可樂喝完了。

1. 他做完今天的作業了。
2. 他吃完了我買的水果。
3. 媽媽做好了晚飯。

4. 王家生带来了雨伞。

5. 黄英拿走了今天的报。

6. 我拿药回来了。

IV. Change the 把 sentences you made in Exercise III into 被 sentences.

Example: 他把可乐喝完了。→ 可乐被他喝完了。

1.
2.
3.
4.
5.
6.

V. Change the following sentences into 连……都/也 sentences, emphasizing the underlined parts.

Example: 我家没有电脑。→ 我家连计算机都没有。

1. 他下雨没带伞。

2. 李老师不认识这个字。

3. 小黄忘了女朋友的电话。

4. 波士顿他没去过。

5. 南京12月没有雪。

6. 那个学生找不到学校的体育馆。

7. 那个人没喝过可乐。

8. 格林昨天没学习。

9. 雪他没看过。

10. 王家生不踢足球了。

VI. Choose the appropriate word from the choices given to complete the sentences.

1. 明天我_____(不但、虽然、因为)要练拼音，_____(但是、而且、所以)要抄写汉字。

2. _____(虽然、因为、不但)他的邮件比较多，_____(而且、所以、可是)都是平信。

4. 王家生帶來了雨傘。

5. 黃英拿走了今天的報。

6. 我拿藥回來了。

IV. Change the 把 **sentences you made in Exercise III into** 被 **sentences.**

Example: 他把可樂喝完了。 → 可樂被他喝完了。

1.

2.

3.

4.

5.

6.

V. Change the following sentences into 連……都/也 **sentences, emphasizing the underlined parts.**

Example: 我家沒有電腦。→ 我家連電腦都沒有。

1. 他下雨沒帶傘。

2. 李老師不認識這個字。

3. 小黃忘了女朋友的電話。

4. 波士頓他沒去過。

5. 南京12月沒有雪。

6. 那個學生找不到學校的體育館。

7. 那個人沒喝過可樂。

8. 格林昨天沒學習。

9. 雪他沒看過。

10. 王家生不踢足球了。

VI. Choose the appropriate word from the choices given to complete the sentences.

1. 明天我_____(不但、雖然、因為)要練拼音，_____(但是、而且、所以)要抄寫漢字。

2. _____(雖然、因為、不但)他的郵件比較多，(而且、所以、可是)都是平信。

3. 这个柜台_____(不但、虽然、因为)小，_____(而且、但是、所以)很新。

4. 中文_____(不但、因为、虽然)比较难，_____(但是、所以、而且)很有意思。

5. 海运_____(因为、虽然、不但)便宜，_____(所以、但是、而且)安全。

6. _____(虽然、因为、不但)这些信件很重要，_____(可是、所以、而且)我想寄挂号。

VII. Correct the errors, if there are any, in the following sentences.

1. 你这些饭吃得完不完？

2. 王小年做中国饭得好。

3. 我们今天晚上跳舞跳舞吧。

4. 我把药吃。

5. 他不被雨淋湿。

6. 南京他连去都去过。

7. 这把雨伞太小了，虽然很便宜。

VIII. Choose the right words to fill in the blanks, and then read the conversation aloud with a partner.

1. 虽然……可是 2. 不 3. 得 4. 把 5. 把 6. 把 7. 被 8. 连……都

A: 你明天看_____见黄雪吗？

B: 她好像跟朋友去南京了。你为什么找她？

A: 昨天我们去颐和园玩儿，她_____我的伞拿走了。我周末要用。

B: 她怎么_____你的伞_____拿？

A: 我想她拿错了。她的伞_____我拿来了。

B: 反正你拿了她的，她拿了你的。你们不用换了。

A: 那不行，_____都是伞，_____我的比她的贵多了。

B: 不是一样用吗？反正这个周末前你找_____到她，就先用她的吧。

A: 也只好这样了。等她回来我一定_____我的伞要回来。

B: 你也得_____她的伞给她呀。

A: 那当然，好，再见。

3. 這個櫃檯_____(不但、雖然、因為)小，_____(而且、但是、所以)很新。

4. 中文_____(不但、因為、雖然)比較難，_____(但是、所以、而且)很有意思。

5. 海運_____(因為、雖然、不但) 便宜，_____(所以、但是、而且)安全。

6. _____(雖然、因為、不但)這些信件很重要，_____(可是、所以、而且)我想寄掛號。

VII. Correct the errors, if there are any, in the following sentences.

1. 你這些飯吃得完不完?
2. 王小年做中國飯得好。
3. 我們今天晚上跳舞跳舞吧。
4. 我把藥吃。
5. 他不被雨淋濕。
6. 南京他連去都去過。
7. 這把雨傘太小了，雖然很便宜。

VIII. Choose the right words to fill in the blanks, and then read the conversation aloud with a partner.

1.雖然……可是 2.不 3.得 4.把 5.把 6.把 7.被 8.連……都

A: 你明天看_____見黃雪嗎?

B: 她好像跟朋友去南京了。你為什麼找她?

A: 昨天我們去頤和園玩兒，她_____我的傘拿走了。我週末要用。

B: 她怎麼_____你的傘_____拿?

A: 我想她拿錯了。她的傘_____我拿來了。

B: 反正你拿了她的，她拿了你的。你們不用換了。

A: 那不行，_____都是傘，_____我的比她的貴多了。

B: 不是一樣用嗎? 反正這個週末前你找_____到她，就先用她的吧。

A: 也只好這樣了。等她回來我一定_____我的傘要回來。

B: 你也得_____她的傘給她呀。

A: 那當然，好，再見。

练习答案
Key to Exercises

· ·

▶ 第一课 **Lesson 1**

I. Change the following affirmative sentences into negative ones.

1. 小王不是新学生。
2. 他没有中文名字。
3. 我不是美国人。
4. 李老师没有美国留学生。
5. 我不去欢迎小张。
6. 我不叫王美英。
7. 你不去上课。

II. Change the following statements into questions.

1. 他要去出差吗？
2. 一会儿你去餐厅吗？
3. 新学生有中文名字吗？
4. 你去问王老师吗？
5. 他姓文吗？

III. Correct the errors, if there are any, in the following sentences.

1. 我没有美国饭。
2. 新老师不是英国人。
3. 他姓张，叫张小文。
4. 请问，您是留学生吗？
5. 你快去餐厅吃饭吧！
6. 老师给我起了中文名字。

IV. Rearrange the following words to make correct sentences.

1. 这个人叫什么名字？
2. 这位老师是他的朋友。
3. 他回来了，那太好了。
4. 我要去上课。
5. 你去中国出差吗？

練習答案
Key to Exercises

. . . .

▶ 第一課 Lesson 1

I. Change the following affirmative sentences into negative ones.

1.　小王不是新學生。
2.　他沒有中文名字。
3.　我不是美國人。
4.　李老師沒有美國留學生。
5.　我不去歡迎小張。
6.　我不叫王美英。
7.　你不去上課。

II. Change the following statements into questions.

1.　他要去出差嗎？
2.　一會兒你去餐廳嗎？
3.　新學生有中文名字嗎？
4.　你去問王老師嗎？
5.　他姓文嗎？

III. Correct the errors, if there are any, in the following sentences.

1.　我沒有美國飯。
2.　新老師不是英國人。
3.　他姓張，叫張小文。
4.　請問，您是留學生嗎？
5.　你快去餐廳吃飯吧！
6.　老師給我起了中文名字。

IV. Rearrange the following words to make correct sentences.

1.　這個人叫什麼名字？
2.　這位老師是他的朋友。
3.　他回來了，那太好了。
4.　我要去上課。
5.　你去中國出差嗎？

V. Complete the following dialogue.

A: 你好 ！

B: 你好！

A: 请问，您是美国学生吗？

B: 是，我是美国学生。

A: 太好了！这位是……？

B: 这位是我朋友。

A: 您好！请问您贵姓？

C: 我姓李。

A: 很高兴 (g□oxìng, happy) 认识你们。对不起 (duìbùq□, excuse me)，我要上课。一会儿见。

B: 一会儿见。

VI. Read the following numbers aloud in Chinese and write the first three in Chinese characters.

22 → èrshí'èr, 二十二   38 → sānshíbā, 三十八   45 → sìshíwǔ, 四十五   97 → jiǔshíqī, 九十七

50 → wǔshí, 五十   14 → shísì, 十四   81 → bāshíyī, 八十一   78 → qīshíbā, 七十八

VII. Fill in the blanks with the appropriate measure words.

1. 个   2. 个   3. 个   4. 个   5. 位   6. 位

7. 位

VIII. Choose the right words to fill in the blanks, and then read the conversation aloud with a partner.

1. 是   2. 是   3. 是   4. 吗   5. 吗   6. 吗

7. 有   8. 有   9. 有   10. 没   11. 个   12. 个

V. Complete the following dialogue.

A:　你好！

B:　你好！

A:　請問，您是美國學生嗎？

B:　是，我是美國學生。

A:　太好了！這位是……？

B:　這位是我朋友。

A:　您好！請問您貴姓？

C:　我姓李。

A:　很高興 (gāoxìng, happy) 認識你們。對不起 (duìbùqǐ, excuse me), 我要上課。一會兒見。

B:　一會兒見。

VI. Read the following numbers aloud in Chinese and write the first three in Chinese characters.

22 → èrshí'èr, 二十二　　　38 → sānshíbā, 三十八　　　45 → sìshíwǔ, 四十五　　　97 → jiǔshíqī, 九十七

50 → wǔshí, 五十　　　14 → shísì, 十四　　　81 → bāshíyī, 八十一　　　78 → qīshíbā, 七十八

VII. Fill in the blanks with the appropriate measure words.

1.　個　　　2.　個　　　3.　個　　　4.　個　　　5.　位　　　6.　位

7.　位

VIII. Choose the right words to fill in the blanks, and then read the conversation aloud with a partner.

1.　是　　　2.　是　　　3.　是　　　4.　嗎　　　5.　嗎　　　6.　嗎

7.　有　　　8.　有　　　9.　有　　　10.　沒　　　11.　個　　　12.　個

▶ 第二课 **Lesson 2**

I. Change the following questions into A-not-A questions.

1. 王小年是不是第三代移民？
2. 你有没有兄弟姐妹？
3. 你吃饭没吃饭？
4. 你妹妹学不学会计学？
5. 你朋友有没有中文名字？

II. Translate the following phrases into Chinese.

1. 流利的中文
2. 很好的电脑
3. 美国老师
4. 中国学生们
5. 你爸爸
6. 我朋友的电脑

III. Rearrange the following phrases to make correct sentences.

1. 我们都不想家(or 我们不都想家)，你们呢？
2. 他的老家在北京，可是他不说中文。
3. 他们跟你(or 你跟他们)去中国餐馆吃饭吗？
4. 第二个人和第三个人都是华裔。
5. 和你妹妹都不在学院学英文(or 你和你妹妹不都在学院学英文)。

IV. Correct the errors, if there are any, in the following sentences.

1. 我们都学习中文和英文。
2. 你的老乡在学校帮助你吗？
3. Correct
4. 第七个人叫高大新。
5. 我朋友家有四口人。
6. 这个大学很好。
7. Correct
8. 她姐姐有中国朋友，对不对？

V. Translate the following phrases into Chinese, and then make up sentences of your own using each of the phrases.

1. 第一个留学生
2. 第二个大学
3. 第三代移民
4. 第十个(or 台，tái) 电脑
5. 第五位教授
6. 第二个医生

▶ 第二課 Lesson 2

I. Change the following questions into A-not-A questions.

1. 王小年是不是第三代移民？
2. 你有沒有兄弟姐妹？
3. 你吃飯沒吃飯？
4. 你妹妹學不學會計學？
5. 你朋友有沒有中文名字？

II. Translate the following phrases into Chinese.

1. 流利的中文　　　　2. 很好的電腦　　　　3. 美國老師　　　　4. 中國學生們s
5. 你爸爸　　　　6. 我朋友的電腦

III. Rearrange the following phrases to make correct sentences.

1. 我們都不想家 (or 我們不都想家)，你們呢？
2. 他的老家在北京，可是他不說中文。
3. 他們跟你 (or 你跟他們) 去中國餐館吃飯嗎？
4. 第二個人和第三個人都是華裔。
5 和你妹妹都不在學院學英文 (or 你和你妹妹不都在學院學英文)。

IV. Correct the errors, if there are any, in the following sentences.

1. 我們都學習中文和英文。
2. 你的老鄉在學校幫助你嗎？
3. Correct
4. 第七個人叫高大新。
5. 我朋友家有四口人。
6. 這個大學很好。
7. Correct
8. 她姐姐有中國朋友，對不對？

V. Translate the following phrases into Chinese, and then make up sentences of your own using each of the phrases.

1. 第一個留學生　　　　2. 第二個大學　　　　3. 第三代移民
4. 第十個 (or 台，tái) 電腦　　　5. 第五位教授　　　6. 第二個醫生

VI. Read the following passage and answer the questions.

1. Does Zhang Kai speak Chinese well? Why or why not?

    No, he does not speak Chinese well because he was born and raised in the United States.

2. Where are Zhang Kai's grandfather and grandmother?

    They are in Beijing.

3. Are both Zhang Kai's father and his mother college professors?

    No, they are not both college professors.

4. Is Zhang Kai going to Beijing this year? Why or why not?

    Yes, he is going to Beijing this year, because he wants to go to a college to learn Chinese with professors there, and he would like to ask his grandparents to help him study Chinese.

5. Do Zhang Kai's grandparents know Chinese?

    Yes, they know Chinese.

VII. Choose the right words to fill in the blanks, and then read the conversation aloud with a partner.

1. 有没有   2. 很好   3. 都   4. 吗   5. 不   6. 在

7. 对不对   8. 好吗

VI. Read the following passage and answer the questions.

1.   Does Zhang Kai speak Chinese well? Why or why not?

     No, he does not speak Chinese well because he was born and raised in the United States.

2.   Where are Zhang Kai's grandfather and grandmother?

     They are in Beijing.

3.   Are both Zhang Kai's father and his mother college professors?

     No, they are not both college professors.

4.   Is Zhang Kai going to Beijing this year? Why or why not?

     Yes, he is going to Beijing this year, because he wants to go to a college to learn Chinese with professors

     there, and he would like to ask his grandparents to help him study Chinese.

5.   Do Zhang Kai's grandparents know Chinese?

     Yes, they know Chinese.

VII. Choose the right words to fill in the blanks, and then read the conversation aloud with a partner.

1.   有沒有   2.   很好   3.   都   4.   嗎   5.   不   6.   在

7.   對不對   8.   好嗎

▶ 第三课 **Lesson 3**

I. Translate the following phrases into Chinese. If there are several possible ways of saying a phrase, suggest as many possibilities as you can.

1. 九元八角六分(钱)；九块八毛六分(钱)
2. 五十元零五分(钱)；五十块零五分(钱)
3. 七十八路公共汽车；七十八号公共汽车
4. 下午两点零三分
5. 上午十点五十八分；十一点差两分；差两分十一点
6. 二零零二年十一月三日星期一
7. 一九九八年十月十一日星期五下午四点四十五分；一九九八年十月十一日星期五下午四点三刻
8. 七一八三九二五四三六
9. 六四五房间；六四五号房间

II. Answer questions 1–3 affirmatively, and questions 4–6 negatively.

1. 这个星期一我去电影院。
2. 明天小王的爸爸出差。
3. 我和我弟弟都有八十块钱。
4. 六月十五号我不坐公共汽车。
5. 他们今天晚上十二点不睡觉。
6. 五月三号他妹妹不去电影院。

III. Correct the errors, if there are any, in the following sentences.

1. 我和我朋友这个星期天去玩。
2. 他妈妈给他四十一块五毛钱。
3. 我们十一点二十分去看晚会。
4. 王教授今天下午四点半教学生英文。
5. 现在是八点差三分。
6. 这个星期天小张想去跳舞。
7. 那个美国大片没有意思。

IV. Rearrange the following phrases to make meaningful sentences, and then translate your sentences into English.

1. 星期五上午九点我想出门。I want to go out on Friday morning at nine o'clock.
2. 这本英文书是十八块九毛六分钱。This English book costs $18.96.
3. 我想晚上十点和我爸爸在家看电影。I want to watch a movie at home with my dad tonight at 10 o'clock.

▶ 第三課 Lesson 3

I. Translate the following phrases into Chinese. If there are several possible ways of saying a phrase, suggest as many possibilities as you can.

1.　九元八角六分(錢)；九塊八毛六分(錢)
2.　五十元零五分(錢)；五十塊零五分(錢)
3.　七十八路公共汽車；七十八號公共汽車
4.　下午兩點零三分
5.　上午十點五十八分；十一點差兩分；差兩分十一點
6.　二零零二年十一月三日星期一
7.　一九九八年十月十一日星期五下午四點四十五分；一九九八年十月十一日星期五下午四點三刻
8.　七一八三九二五四三六
9.　六四五房間；六四五號房間

II. Answer questions 1–3 affirmatively, and questions 4–6 negatively.

1.　這個星期一我去電影院。
2.　明天小王的爸爸出差。
3.　我和我弟弟都有八十塊錢。
4.　六月十五號我不坐公共汽車。
5.　他們今天晚上十二點不睡覺。
6.　五月三號他妹妹不去電影院。

III. Correct the errors, if there are any, in the following sentences.

1.　我和我朋友這個星期天去玩。
2.　他媽媽給他四十一塊五毛錢。
3.　我們十一點二十分去看晚會。
4.　王教授今天下午四點半教學生英文。
5.　現在是八點差三分。
6.　這個星期天小張想去跳舞。
7.　那個美國大片沒有意思。

IV. Rearrange the following phrases to make meaningful sentences, and then translate your sentences into English.

1.　星期五上午九點我想出門。I want to go out on Friday morning at nine o'clock.
2.　這本英文書是十八塊九毛六分錢。This English book costs $18.96.
3.　我想晚上十點和我爸爸在家看電影。I want to watch a movie at home with my dad tonight at 10 o'clock.

4. 你的英文和中文都说得很流利。Your English and Chinese are both very fluent.

5. 这个十字路口没有红绿灯。There is no traffic light at this intersection.

V. With a partner, ask each other questions about your telephone numbers, room numbers, etc.

VI. Rewrite the following sentences using 呢.

1. 我喜欢看美国大片。他呢?

2. 小高的工作很好。小王的呢?

3. 苏珊不去体育馆。约翰呢?

4. 这个电影院大。那个电影院呢?

VII. Fill in the blanks with 吗 or 呢.

1. 呢	2. 吗	3. 呢	4. 吗	5. 呢	6. 呢
7. 吗	8. 吗	9. 呢	10. 呢		

VIII. Choose the right words to fill in the blanks, and then read the conversation aloud with a partner.

1. 下午	2. 四点	3. 吗	4. 下午	5. 两点	6. 呢
7. 明天	8. 2005年8月	9. 1986年9月1号	10. 吗		

4. 你的英文和中文都說得很流利。Your English and Chinese are both very fluent.
5. 這個十字路口沒有紅綠燈。There is no traffic light at this intersection.

V. With a partner, ask each other questions about your telephone numbers, room numbers, etc.

VI. Rewrite the following sentences using 呢.

1. 我喜歡看美國大片。他呢？
2. 小高的工作很好。小王的呢？
3. 蘇珊不去體育館。約翰呢？
4. 這個電影院大。那個電影院呢？

VII. Fill in the blanks with 嗎 or 呢.

1. 呢　　　　2. 嗎　　　　3. 呢　　　　4. 嗎　　　　5. 呢　　　6. 呢
7. 嗎　　　　8. 嗎　　　　9. 呢　　　　10. 呢

VIII. Choose the right words to fill in the blanks, and then read the conversation aloud with a partner.

1. 下午　　2. 四點　　　　3. 嗎　　　　4. 下午　　5. 兩點　　6. 呢
7. 明天　　8. 2005年8月　　9. 1986年9月1號　　10. 嗎

▶ 第四课 **Lesson 4**

I. Answer the following questions.

1. 他觉得会话比较容易。

2. 第三课有一点难。

3. 他明天在家练中文发音。

4. 老师问学生问题。

5. 我哥哥十二点睡觉。

6. 我觉得那家中餐馆很好。

II. Make questions from these statements, focusing on the underlined parts.

Examples:

1. 谁是美国留学生？

2. 你哥哥喜欢看什么电影？

3. 谁是第三代移民？

4. 第几位老师是北京人？

5. 星期天你想看什么电影？

6. 今天下午几点他练唱歌？

7. 明天晚上你想在哪儿做作业？

8. 老师要你们抄写多少(个)汉字？

9. 你哥哥觉得输入拼音怎么样？

10. 他觉得什么特别有意思？

III. Complete the pivotal sentences by using the hints in parentheses.

1. 王小年请那个中国学生吃中国饭。

2. 王小年的爸爸、妈妈叫王小年去他们开的中餐馆吃饭。

3. 王家生的女朋友请王家生看美国大片。

4. 约翰叫苏珊在北校门等她。

5. 老师叫我们问他问题。

IV. Change the following sentences into topic-comment sentences.

1. 中文名字我们都有。

2. 喝酒的年龄我们还没到。

3. 中文的语法格林觉得不太难。

4. 抄写汉字我也练习。

5. 中文王小年说得不流利。

304   **Key to Exercises**

I. Answer the following questions.

1. 他覺得會話比較容易。
2. 第三課有一點難。
3. 他明天在家練中文發音。
4. 老師問學生問題。
5. 我哥哥十二點睡覺。
6. 我覺得那家中餐館很好。

II. Make questions from these statements, focusing on the underlined parts.

Examples:

1. 誰是美國留學生？
2. 你哥哥喜歡看什麼電影？
3. 誰是第三代移民？
4. 第幾位老師是北京人？
5. 星期天你想看什麼電影？
6. 今天下午幾點他練唱歌？
7. 明天晚上你想在哪兒做作業？
8. 老師要你們抄寫多少(個)漢字？
9. 你哥哥覺得輸入拼音怎麼樣？
10. 他覺得什麼特別有意思？

III. Complete the pivotal sentences by using the hints in parentheses.

1. 王小年請那個中國學生吃中國飯。
2. 王小年的爸爸、媽媽叫王小年去他們開的中餐館吃飯。
3. 王家生的女朋友請王家生看美國大片。
4. 約翰叫蘇珊在北校門等她。
5. 老師叫我們問他問題。

IV. Change the following sentences into topic-comment sentences.

1. 中文名字我們都有。
2. 喝酒的年齡我們還沒到。
3. 中文的語法格林覺得不太難。
4. 抄寫漢字我也練習。
5. 中文王小年說得不流利。

V. Translate the following phrases into Chinese and then use them to make up your own sentences.

1. 明天的电影
2. 一加仑的牛奶
3. 十块钱的现金
4. 我的英文老师
5. 你妈妈的汽车
6. 做作业的学生
7. 教中文的王老师
8. 他用的电脑

VI. Fill in the blanks with 的 where necessary.

星期一上午我和我____妹妹想去超级市场买东西。我除了要买五加仑____的____牛奶、十块钱____的____乳酪以外，还要买一件蓝色____的____西装。我____妹妹想买一些便宜____的____刀、叉，还想买一些减价____的____日用品。下午三点，我们想去看一个中国_____电影，因为下午____的____电影比较便宜_____。晚上，我们想去吃美国_____饭。

VII. Form questions with (是)……还是, and then provide answers using the phrases below.

1. 你是练习发音还是练习会话？练习发音。
2. 你是用拼音输入汉字还是手写汉字？用拼音输入汉字。
3. 你是去体育馆还是去电影院？去电影院。
4. 你是问一个问题还是问两个问题？两个问题。
5. 你是在家睡觉还是去生日晚会？去生日晚会。

VIII. Choose the right words to fill in the blanks, and then read the conversation aloud with a partner.

1. 吧
2. 抄写汉字和会话
3. 哪
4. 叫
5. 吧
6. 什么
7. 是
8. 还是

V. Translate the following phrases into Chinese and then use them to make up your own sentences.

1. 明天的电影　　　2. 一加仑的牛奶
3. 十块钱的现金　　4. 我的英文老师
5. 你妈妈的汽车　　6. 做作业的学生
7. 教中文的王老师　8. 他用的电脑

VI. Fill in the blanks with 的 where necessary.

星期一上午我和我_____妹妹想去超级市场买东西。我除了要买五加仑___的___牛奶、十块钱___的___乳酪以外，还要买一件蓝色___的___西装。我_____妹妹想买一些便宜___的___刀、叉，还想买一些减价___的___日用品。下午三点，我们想去看一个中国_____电影，因为下午___的___电影比较便宜_____。晚上，我们想去吃美国_____饭。

VII. Form questions with (是)…… 還是, and then provide answers using the phrases below.

1. 你是練習發音還是練習會話? 練習發音。
2. 你是用拼音輸入漢字還是手寫漢字? 用拼音輸入漢字。
3. 你是去體育館還是去電影院？去電影院。
4. 你是問一個問題還是問兩個問題? 兩個問題。
5. 你是在家睡覺還是去生日晚會? 去生日晚會。

VIII. Choose the right words to fill in the blanks, and then read the conversation aloud with a partner.

1. 吧　　2. 抄写汉字和会话　　3. 哪　　4. 叫　　5. 吧　　6. 什么
7. 是　　8. 还是

▶ 第五课 **Lesson 5**

I. Fill in the blanks with 的 **or** 得.

1. 的   2. 得   3. 的   4. 的   5. 的，得   6. 得   7. 的，的   8. 得

II. Correct the errors, if there are any, in the following sentences.

1. 小王学语法学得很快，但是写汉字写得很慢。
2. 这个超市的面包很好。
3. 他只喝牛奶，不喝别的。
4. 退衣服很容易。
5. 我们想在体育馆下车。
6. 这个电脑很棒。
7. 那件很新的衣服不是我哥哥的。

III. Translate the following sentences into Chinese.

1. 今天肥皂不减价吧？
2. 你想买哪件西装？黑的还是黄的（or 你想买黑西装还是黄西装）？
3. 我用的塑料杯子很大。
4. 我朋友没有看这个星期的电影。
5. 这件毛衣很贵吧？
6. 蓝色的汽车是我老师的。
7. 谁想看那个美国电影？你还是他（or 是你还是他想看那个美国电影）？

IV. Underline the auxiliary verb of each sentence, then change the sentences into questions. (Use the A-not-A pattern to ask questions for the first five sentences, and use 吗 **to ask questions for the last five sentences.)**

1. 牛奶不能退。
   能   牛奶能不能退？
2. 能   明天我能不能去王小年的生日晚会？
3. 会   会不会跟我们去超市？
4. 会   格林会不会？
5. 可以   我明天可以不可以去问高老师问题？
6. 要   你想喝可乐吗？
7. 要   我要发准每一个音吗？
8. 想   你想去超市买日用品吗？
9. 得   两点了，你得上课了吗？
10. 应该   你应该去酒吧吗？

▶ 第五課 Lesson 5

I. Fill in the blanks with 的 or 得.

1. 的   2. 得   3. 的   4. 的   5. 的，得   6. 得   7. 的，的   8. 得

II. Correct the errors, if there are any, in the following sentences.

1. 小王學語法學得很快，但是寫漢字寫得很慢。
2. 這個超市的麵包很好。
3. 他只喝牛奶，不喝別的。
4. 退衣服很容易。
5. 我們想在體育館下車。
6. 這個電腦很棒。
7. 那件很新的衣服不是我哥哥的。

III. Translate the following sentences into Chinese.

1. 今天肥皂不減價吧？
2. 你想買哪件西裝？黑的還是黃的（or 你想買黑西裝還是黃西裝）？
3. 我用的塑料杯子很大。
4. 我朋友沒有看這個星期的電影。
5. 這件毛衣很貴吧？
6. 藍色的汽車是我老師的。
7. 誰想看那個美國電影？你還是他（or 是你還是他想看那個美國電影）？

IV. Underline the auxiliary verb of each sentence, then change the sentences into questions. (Use the A-not-A pattern to ask questions for the first five sentences, and use 嗎 to ask questions for the last five sentences.)

1. 牛奶不能退。
    能　牛奶能不能退?
2. 能　明天我能不能去王小年的生日晚會?
3. 會　會不會跟我們去超市?
4. 會　格林會不會?
5. 可以　我明天可以不可以去問高老師問題?
6. 要　你想喝可樂嗎?
7. 要　我要發準每一個音嗎?
8. 想　你想去超市買日用品嗎?
9. 得　兩點了，你得上課了嗎?
10. 應該　你應該去酒吧嗎?

V. Fill in the blanks with the appropriate auxiliary verbs. (You can have more than one answer.)

1. 可以   2. 能   3. 可以   4. 不能   5. 要   6. 要
7. 想   8. 得   9. 会

VI. You went shopping yesterday. Write an essay in Chinese, describing what you bought and how much money you spent. Try to use as many new grammatical patterns from Lessons 1–5 as you can.

(Answers may vary.)

VII. Choose the right words to fill in the blanks, and then read the conversation aloud with a partner.

1. 想   2. 能   3. 得   4. 得   5. 会   6. 可以
7. 得   8. 能   9. 要   10. 应该   11. 得很快   12. 应该

V. Fill in the blanks with the appropriate auxiliary verbs. (You can have more than one answer.)

1. 可以   2. 能   3. 可以   4. 不能   5. 要   6. 要

7. 想   8. 得   9. 會

VI. You went shopping yesterday. Write an essay in Chinese, describing what you bought and how much money you spent. Try to use as many new grammatical patterns from Lessons 1–5 as you can.

(Answers may vary.)

VII. Choose the right words to fill in the blanks, and then read the conversation aloud with a partner.

1. 想   2. 能   3. 得   4. 得   5. 會   6. 可以

7. 得   8. 能   9. 要   10. 應該   11. 得很快   12. 應該

▶ 第六课 **Lesson 6**

I. **Fill in the blanks with** 的, 得, **or** 地.

1. 的	2. 地	3. 的, 得	4. 的	5. 地	6. 得				
7. 的	8. 的	9. 的, 地	10. 得						

II. **Turn statements 1–3 into negative statements, and turn statements 4–6 into two forms of questions (A-not-A and** 吗**).**

1. 星期五我没给我哥哥三十块美元。

2. 今天早上的公共汽车没来晚。

3. 一月五号王教授没坐飞机。

4. 约翰换没换7号车？约翰换了7号车吗？

5. 八点钟小新打没打电话？八点钟小新打了电话吗？

6. 二零零一年你们都去没去夏威夷旅行？二零零一年你们都没有去夏威夷旅行吗？

III. **Correct the errors, if there are any, in the following sentences.**

1. 昨天我姐姐买了东西就回家了。

2. 明天一年级的留学生去了旅行社就练会话。

3. 我记得谢先生星期一没有喝酒。

4. 一九八八年他哥哥是学生，不是老师。

5. 这个俱乐部以前有很多会员。

6. 下个星期 (next week) 毛先生去了纽约就去波士顿。

IV. **Translate the sentences into Chinese.**

1. 你上星期一坐出租汽车了吗？（打的了吗？）

2. 明天我吃了晚饭就去飞机场。

3. 上星期五他们去了超市就买了两张票。

4. 现在他会写汉字了。

5. 他们还没付罚金。

6. 他没给你钱吗？

7. 你不喜欢黑颜色吗？

V. **Use** 是……的 **to rewrite the following sentences, focusing on the underlined parts.**

1. 他是十月一号去时代广场的。or 他是十月一号去的时代广场。

2. 他们是打的去的机场。or 他们是打的去机场的。

3. 小王是在超市买餐巾纸的。or 小王是在超市买的餐巾纸。

▶ 第六課 **Lesson 6**

I. Fill in the blanks with 的, 得, or 地.

1. 的   2. 地   3. 的, 得   4. 的   5. 地   6. 得

7. 的   8. 的   9. 的, 地   10. 得

II. Turn statements 1–3 into negative statements, and turn statements 4–6 into two forms of questions (A-not-A and 嗎).

1. 星期五我沒給我哥哥三十塊美元。

2. 今天早上的公共汽車沒來晚。

3. 一月五號王教授沒坐飛機。

4. 約翰換沒換7號車? 約翰換了7號車嗎?

5. 八點鐘小新打沒打電話? 八點鐘小新打了電話嗎?

6. 二零零一年你們都去沒去夏威夷旅行? 二零零一年你們都沒有去夏威夷旅行嗎?

III. Correct the errors, if there are any, in the following sentences.

1. 昨天我姐姐買了東西就回家了。

2. 明天一年級的留學生去了旅行社就練會話。

3. 我記得謝先生星期一沒有喝酒。

4. 一九八八年他哥哥是學生,不是老師。

5. 這個俱樂部以前有很多會員。

6. 下個星期 (next week) 毛先生去了紐約就去波士頓。

IV. Translate the sentences into Chinese.

1. 你上星期一坐出租汽車了嗎? (打的了嗎?)

2. 明天我吃了晚飯就去飛機場。

3. 上星期五他們去了超市就買了兩張票。

4. 現在他會寫漢字了。

5. 他們還沒付罰金。

6. 他沒給你錢嗎?

7. 你不喜歡黑顏色嗎?

V. Use 是……的 to rewrite the following sentences, focusing on the underlined parts.

1. 他是十月一號去時代廣場的。or 他是十月一號的時代廣場。

2. 他們是打的去的機場。or 他們是打的去機場的。

3. 小王是在超市買餐巾紙的。or 小王是在超市買的餐巾紙。

4. 我们是十点钟打的(dī)的(de)。 or 我们是十点钟打的(de)的(dī)。

5. 二年级的学生是用中文问的问题。 or 二年级的学生是用中文问问题的。

VI. Complete the following dialogue.

A: 今天你是怎么去上班的？

B: _____我是坐公共汽车去上班的_____。

A: 你平时都坐地铁，今天怎么想坐公共汽车了？

B: _____因为听说坐公共汽车很有意思_____。

A: 听说现在坐公共汽车的人多得很。

B: _____你怎么知道的_____？ (rhetorical question)

A: 我也不知道。我爸爸今天也坐的公共汽车。

B: _____你爸爸坐几路公共汽车_____？

A: 他坐66路公共汽车。

B: _____他为什么坐66路公共汽车_____？

A: 因为66路是"无人售票"车，所以车比较好_____。

VII. Choose the right words to fill in the blanks, and then read the conversation aloud with a partner.

1. 了	2. 了	3. 是……的	4. 是……的	5. 的	6. 的
7. 因为……所以		8. 了		9. 是……的	10. 地

4. 我們是十點鐘打的(di)的(de)。or 我們是十點鐘打的(de)的(di)。

5. 二年級的學生是用中文問的問題。or 二年級的學生是用中文問問題的。

VI. Complete the following dialogue.

A: 今天你是怎麼去上班的？

B: _____我是坐公共汽車去上班的_____。

A: 你平時都坐地鐵，今天怎麼想坐公共汽車了？

B: _____因為聽說坐公共汽車很有意思_____。

A: 聽說現在坐公共汽車的人多得很。

B: _____你怎麼知道的_____？(rhetorical question)

A: 我也不知道。我爸爸今天也坐的公共汽車。

B: _____你爸爸坐幾路公共汽車_____？

A: 他坐66路公共汽車。

B: _____他為什麼坐66路公共汽車_____？

A: 因為66路是"無人售票"車, 所以車比較好_____。

VII. Choose the right words to fill in the blanks, and then read the conversation aloud with a partner.

1. 了   2. 了   3. 是……的   4. 是……的   5. 的   6. 的

7. 因為……所以   8. 了   9. 是……的   10. 地

▶ 第七课 **Lesson 7**

I. Fill in the blanks with 了 **or** 过.

1. 过   2. 过   3. 了   4. 了   5. 了   6. 了
7. 过   8. 过   9. 了   10. 了

II. Fill in the blanks with 正在 **or** 着 **according to the English given within the brackets.**

1. 正在去超市   2. 拿着   3. 正在做   4. 正在看电视   5. 关着   6. 正在睡觉

III. Rewrite the sentences using 要……了，就要……了，快……了，or 快要……了.

1. 飞机五分钟以后要起飞了。
2. 药房快要关门了。
3. 我们快要放寒假了。
4. 旅行社说我的飞机票就要到了。
5. 老师说一年级的学生要开始学中文语法了。

IV. Fill in the blanks with 了 **or** (正)在 **according to the English provided.**

1. 正在订飞机票   2. 买了   3. 正在看电视   4. 正在做饭   5. 订了
6. 去夏威夷了   7. 买了

V. Use 一边，……一边 **to write sentences according to the following phrases.**

1. 我们常常一边唱歌一边做作业。
2. 有时候我喜欢一边看电视一边吃饭。
3. 她一边打电话一边写汉字。
4. 有的人喜欢一边喝酒一边吃中国饭。

VI. Correct the errors, if there are any, in the following sentences.

1. 王老师现在不在上课。
2. 昨天下午他改了飞机票。
3. 我正在学习语法。
4. 你改了飞机票没改？
5. 他拿着要退的衣服。
6. 我去飞机场的时候他没有在睡觉。
7. 他拿着超市买的东西去朋友的生日晚会。

▶ 第七課 Lesson 7

I. Fill in the blanks with 了 or 過.

1. 過　　　2. 過　　　3. 了　　　4. 了　　　5. 了　　　6. 了
7. 過　　　8. 過　　　9. 了　　　10. 了

II. Fill in the blanks with 正在 or 著 according to the English given within the brackets.

1. 正在去超市　　2. 拿著　　3. 正在做　　4. 正在看電視　　5. 關著　　6. 正在睡覺

III. Rewrite the sentences using 要……了, 就要……了, 快……了, or 快要……了.

1. 飛機五分鐘以後要起飛了。
2. 藥房快要關門了。
3. 我們快要放寒假了。
4. 旅行社說我的飛機票就要到了。
5. 老師說一年級的學生要開始學中文語法了。

IV. Fill in the blanks with 了 or (正)在 according to the English provided.

1. 正在訂飛機票　　2. 買了　　3. 正在看電視　　4. 正在做飯　　5. 訂了
6. 去夏威夷了　　7. 買了

V. Use 一邊, ……一邊 to write sentences according to the following phrases.

1. 我們常常一邊唱歌一邊做作業。
2. 有時候我喜歡一邊看電視一邊吃飯。
3. 她一邊打電話一邊寫漢字。
4. 有的人喜歡一邊喝酒一邊吃中國飯。

VI. Correct the errors, if there are any, in the following sentences.

1. 王老師現在不在上課。
2. 昨天下午他改了飛機票。
3. 我正在學習語法。
4. 你改了飛機票沒改？
5. 他拿著要退的衣服。
6. 我去飛機場的時候他沒有在睡覺。
7. 他拿著超市買的東西去朋友的生日晚會。

VII. Write an essay in Chinese describing an interesting thing you did in the past. Try to use as many new grammatical patterns as you can such as 过, 了, 着, (正)在, 一边······一边.

(Answers may vary.)

VIII. Choose the right words to fill in the blanks, and then read the conversation aloud with a partner.

1. 在   2. 正在   3. 要······了   4. 快······了   5. 了
6. 一边······一边   7. 一边······一边   8. 着   9. 着   10. 了

VII. Write an essay in Chinese describing an interesting thing you did in the past. Try to use as many new grammatical patterns as you can such as 過，了，著，(正)在，一邊……一邊.

(Answers may vary.)

VIII. Choose the right words to fill in the blanks, and then read the conversation aloud with a partner.

1.　在　　　　2.　正在　　　3.　要……了　　4.　快……了　　5.　了
6.　一邊……一邊　　7.　一邊……一邊　　8.　著　　9.　著　　10.　了

▶ 第八课 Lesson 8

I. Use 比 or 没有 to write sentences according to the information provided.

1. 寄平信比寄括号信便宜。寄平信没有寄括号信贵。

2. 纽约的航班比北京的多。纽约的航班没有北京的少。

3. 小陈写汉字比他哥哥写得慢。小陈写汉字没有他哥哥写得快。

4. 他每天比我去邮局少。他每天没有我去邮局多。

5. 你英文说得比中文说得流利。你中文说得没有英文说得流利。

II. Fill in the blanks with 跟……一样 and 不如.

1. 和　　　2. 一样　　　3. 跟　　　4. 不一样　　　5. 不如　　　6. 不如

7. 跟　　　8. 一样　　　9. 不一样

III. Translate the following sentences into Chinese.

1. 纽约当然比波士顿大得多。

2. 你最近多忙？

3. 学英文比学法文容易一点。

4. 中国的银行不如美国的方便。

5. 你写中国字不比他写得快。

6. 那个电影多没有意思？

7. 今天去那儿跟明天去一样。

8. 黄英回家去了。

9. 王小年带来几个朋友。

IV. Use 多 to ask questions, focusing on the underlined parts.

1. 寄挂号信要多贵？

2. 他爸爸有多高？

3. 从这儿到波士顿有多远？

4. 这件运动服有多长？

5. 那台电视机有多贵？

6. 这儿的春天有多长？

V. Correct the errors, if there are any, in the following sentences.

1. 中国的公共汽车跟美国的不一样。

2　 这种邮件跟那种(邮件)一样贵。

3. 美国的银行不比中国的多。

4　 黄英回来了。

▶ 第八課 Lesson 8

I. Use 比 or 沒有 to write sentences according to the information provided.

1. 寄平信比寄括號信便宜。寄平信沒有寄括號信貴。

2. 紐約的航班比北京的多。紐約的航班沒有北京的少。

3. 小陳寫漢字比他哥哥寫得慢。小陳寫漢字沒有他哥哥寫得快。

4. 他每天比我去郵局少。他每天沒有我去郵局多。

5. 你英文說得比中文說得流利。你中文說得沒有英文說得流利。

II. Fill in the blanks with 跟……一樣 and 不如.

1. 和　　　　2.　一樣　　　　3.　跟　　　　4.　不一樣　　　　5.　不如　　　　6.　不如

7. 跟　　　　8.　一樣　　　　9.　不一樣

III. Translate the following sentences into Chinese.

1. 紐約當然比波士頓大得多。

2. 你最近多忙?

3. 學英文比學法文容易一點。

4. 中國的銀行不如美國的方便。

5. 你寫中國字不比他寫得快。

6. 那個電影多沒有意思?

7. 今天去那兒跟明天去一樣。

8. 黃英回家去了。

9. 王小年帶來幾個朋友。

IV. Use 多 to ask questions, focusing on the underlined parts.

1. 寄掛號信要多貴?

2. 他爸爸有多高?

3. 從這兒到波士頓有多遠?

4. 這件運動服有多長?

5. 那台電視機有多貴?

6. 這兒的春天有多長?

V. Correct the errors, if there are any, in the following sentences.

1. 中國的公共汽車跟美國的不一樣。

2. 這種郵件跟那種(郵件)一樣貴。

3. 美國的銀行不比中國的多。

4. 黃英回來了。

5.　约翰回家去了。

6.　你找错钱了。

7.　我寄好信要去银行。

VI. You sent some mail to your parents. Write an essay in Chinese describing when, where, and how you sent the mail. Try to use as many new grammatical patterns as you can.

(Answers may vary.)

VII. Choose the right words to fill in the blanks, and then read the conversation aloud with a partner.

1.　来　　　2.　不如　　　3.　跟……一样　　　4.　不一样　　　5.　到　　　6.　去

7.　比　　　8.　多　　　9.　到　　　　　　　10.　就　　　　　　11.　去　　　12.　去

5.　約翰回家去了。

6.　你找錯錢了。

7.　我寄好信要去銀行。

VI. You sent some mail to your parents. Write an essay in Chinese describing when, where, and how you sent the mail. Try to use as many new grammatical patterns as you can.

(Answers may vary.)

VII. Choose the right words to fill in the blanks, and then read the conversation aloud with a partner.

1. 來	2. 不如	3. 跟……一樣	4. 不一樣	5. 到	6. 去
7. 比	8. 多	9. 到	10. 就	11. 去	12. 去

▶ 第九课 **Lesson 9**

I. Combine the phrases into sentences with duration of time expressions.

1. 我吃饭吃了一个小时。我吃了一个小时的饭。

2. 我病了三天。

3. 我看医生看了两个小时。我看了两个小时的医生。

4. 我买东西买了四个小时。我买了四个小时的东西。

5. 我看电视看了二十分钟。我看了二十分钟的电视。

6. 我有一年没生病了。

7. 我有三天不上课。

8. 我有一天没吃饭。

II. Find a partner to do the following exercise. Each of you can choose four "time-when" and four "time-duration" phrases from the list below to make up sentences. See who can complete the exercise first.

1. 我十点上课。我上了十个小时的课。

2. 我两点半去医院。我去医院去了两个半小时。

3. 昨天他生病了。他生了一天的病。

4. 我明天去买东西。 我买了半天的东西。

5. 星期一不上课。 我们有一个星期不上课。

6. 我上个月没看病。我有一个月没看病了。

7. 十一月我们还上课。我们上了十一个月的课。

8. 去年我在中国学中文。我在中国学了一年中文。

III. Fill in the blanks with "duration of time" or "complement of frequency" expressions.

1. 一天　　2. 天　　3. 三次　　4. 一下　　5. 三次　　6. 五次

IV. Fill in the blanks with 来/去 based on the location of the speaker.

Location of the speaker

1. 去　　2. 来　　3. 去　　4. 来　　5. 去

V. Fill in the blanks with appropriate compound directional complements.

1. 起来　　2. 起，来　　3. 下去　　4. 下来　　5. 下去　　6. 出来　　7. 下来

VI. Translate the following sentences with 一……就 and 不但……而且.

1. 你一生病就要看医生。

2. 他一到医院就进了急诊室。

▶ 第九課 Lesson 9

I. Combine the phrases into sentences with duration of time expressions.

1. 我吃飯吃了一個小時。我吃了一個小時的飯。
2. 我病了三天。
3. 我看醫生看了兩個小時。我看了兩個小時的醫生。
4. 我買東西買了四個小時。 我買了四個小時的東西。
5. 我看電視看了二十分鐘。 我看了二十分鐘的電視。
6. 我有一年沒生病了。
7. 我有三天不上課。
8. 我有一天沒吃飯。

II. Find a partner to do the following exercise. Each of you can choose four "time-when" and four "time-duration" phrases from the list below to make up sentences. See who can complete the exercise first.

1. 我十點上課。我上了十個小時的課。
2. 我兩點半去醫院。我去醫院去了兩個半小時。
3. 昨天他生病了。他生了一天的病。
4. 我明天去買東西。我買了半天的東西。
5. 星期一不上課。我們有一個星期不上課。
6. 我上個月沒看病。我有一個月沒看病了。
7. 十一月我們還上課。我們上了十一個月的課。
8. 去年我在中國學中文。我在中國學了一年中文。

III. Fill in the blanks with "duration of time" or "complement of frequency" expressions.

1. 一天　　　2. 一天　　　3. 三次　　　4. 一下　　　5. 三次　　　6. 五次

IV. Fill in the blanks with 來/去 based on the location of the speaker.

Location of the speaker

1. 去　　　2. 來　　　3. 去　　　4. 來　　　5. 去

V. Fill in the blanks with appropriate compound directional complements.

1. 起來　　2. 起，來　　3. 下去　　4. 下來　　5. 下去　　6. 出來　　7. 下來

VI. Translate the following sentences with 一……就 and 不但……而且.

1. 你一生病就要看醫生。
2. 他一到醫院就進了急診室。

3. 他一去超市就买可乐。

4. 她不但咳嗽，而且发烧。

5. 她不但买了牛奶和可乐，而且买了杯子和餐巾纸。

6. 小谢一看见他哥哥感冒了就带去他校医院了。

VII. Write an essay describing your experience of seeing a doctor. Try to use as many new grammatical patterns from this lesson as you can, such as 一……就, 不但……而且, compound directional complements, complement of frequency.

(Answers may vary.)

VIII. Choose the right words to fill in the blanks, and then read the conversation aloud with a partner.

1. 三天　　　2. 一次　　　3. 三次　　　4. 一……就　　　5. 过去
6. 不但……而且　　　7. 一年　　　8. 没

3. 他一去超市就買可樂。

4. 她不但咳嗽，而且發燒。

5. 她不但買了牛奶和可樂，而且買了杯子和餐巾紙。

6. 小謝一看見他哥哥感冒了就帶去他校醫院了。

VII. Write an essay describing your experience of seeing a doctor. Try to use as many new grammatical patterns from this lesson as you can, such as 一……就, 不但……而且, compound directional complements, complement of frequency.

(Answers may vary.)

VIII. Choose the right words to fill in the blanks, and then read the conversation aloud with a partner.

1. 三天   2. 一次   3. 三次   4. 一……就   5. 過去

6. 不但……而且   7. 一年   8. 沒

▶ 第十课 **Lesson 10**

I. Turn the following phrases into potential complements.

1. 吃得完   2. 看不完   3. 听得懂   4. 看不到   5. 说得清楚

6. 找不着

II. Underline the complements in the following sentences and state which type of complement each of them is.

1. 很早 (complement of degree)

2. 很快 (complement of degree)

3. 不流利 (complement of degree)

4. 来 (simple directional complement)

5. 完 (complement of result)

6. 见 (complement of result)

7. 一天 (complement of duration)

8. 一个半小时 (complement of duration)

9. 三次 (complement of frequency)

10. 回来 (compound directional complement)

11. 不了 (potiential complement)

12. 看得到看不到 (potiential complement)

III. Change the following sentences into 把 sentences.

1. 他把今天的作业做完了。

2. 他把我买的水果吃完了。

3. 妈妈把晚饭做好了。

4. 王家生把雨伞带来了。

5. 黄英把今天的报拿走了。

6. 我把药拿回来了。

IV. Change the 把 sentences you made in Exercise III into 被 sentences.

1. 今天的作业被他做完了。

2. 我买的水果被他吃完了。

3. 晚饭被妈妈做好了。

4. 雨伞被王家生带来了。

5. 今天的报被黄英拿走了。

6. 药被我拿回来了。

▶ 第十課 Lesson 10

I. Turn the following phrases into potential complements.

1. 吃得完   2. 看不完   3. 聽得懂   4. 看不到   5. 說得清楚
6. 找不著

II. Underline the complements in the following sentences and state which type of complement each of them is.

1. 很早 (complement of degree)
2. 很快 (complement of degree)
3. 不流利 (complement of degree)
4. 來 (simple directional complement)
5. 完 (complement of result)
6. 見 (complement of result)
7. 一天 (complement of duration)
8. 一個半小時 (complement of duration)
9. 三次 (complement of frequency)
10. 回來 (compound directional complement)
11. 不了 (potiential complement)
12. 看得到看不到 (potiential complement)

III. Change the following sentences into 把 sentences.

1. 他把今天的作業做完了。
2. 他把我買的水果吃完了。
3. 媽媽把晚飯做好了。
4. 王家生把雨傘帶來了。
5. 黃英把今天的報拿走了。
6. 我把藥拿回來了。

IV. Change the 把 sentences you made in Exercise III into 被 sentences.

1. 今天的作業被他做完了。
2. 我買的水果被他吃完了。
3. 晚飯被媽媽做好了。
4. 雨傘被王家生帶來了。
5. 今天的報被黃英拿走了。
6. 藥被我拿回來了。

V. Change the following sentences into 连……都/也 sentences, emphasizing the underlined parts.

1. 他下雨连伞都没带。
2. 连李老师都不认识这个字。
3. 小黄连女朋友的电话都忘了。
4. 波士顿他连去都没去过。
5. 南京12月连雪都没有。
6. 那个学生连学校的体育馆都找不到。
7. 那个人连可乐都没喝过。
8. 连格林昨天都没学习。
9. 雪他连看都没看过。
10. 连王家生都不踢足球了。

VI. Choose the appropriate word from the choices given to complete the sentences.

1. 明天我不但要练拼音，而且要抄写汉字。
2. 虽然他的邮件比较多，可是都是平信。
3. 这个柜台虽然小，但是很新。
4. 中文虽然比较难，但是很有意思。
5. 海运不但便宜，而且安全。
6. 因为这些信件很重要，所以我想寄挂号。

VII. Correct the errors, if there are any, in the following sentences.

1. 你这些饭吃得完吃不完？
2. 王小年做中国饭做得好。
3. 我们今天晚上跳跳舞吧。
4. 我把药吃了。
5. 他没被雨淋湿。
6. 南京他连去都没去过。
7. 这把雨伞虽然很便宜，可是太小了。

VIII. Choose the right words to fill in the blanks, and then read the conversation aloud with a partner.

1. 得   2. 把   3. 连……都   4. 被   5. 虽然……可是
6. 不   7. 把   8. 把

V. Change the following sentences into 連……都/也 sentences, emphasizing the underlined parts.

1. 他下雨連傘都沒帶。
2. 連李老師都不認識這個字。
3. 小黃連女朋友的電話都忘了。
4. 波士頓他連去都沒去過。
5. 南京12月連雪都沒有。
6. 那個學生連學校的體育館都找不到。
7. 那個人連可樂都沒喝過。
8. 連格林昨天都沒學習。
9. 雪他連看都沒看過。
10. 連王家生都不踢足球了。

VI. Choose the appropriate word from the choices given to complete the sentences.

1. 明天我不但要練拼音，而且要抄寫漢字。
2. 雖然他的郵件比較多，可是都是平信。
3. 這個櫃檯雖然小，但是很新。
4. 中文雖然比較難，但是很有意思。
5. 海運不但便宜，而且安全。
6. 因為這些信件很重要，所以我想寄掛號。

VII. Correct the errors, if there are any, in the following sentences.

1. 你這些飯吃得完吃不完?
2. 王小年做中國飯做得好。
3. 我們今天晚上跳跳舞吧。
4. 我把藥吃了。
5. 他沒被雨淋濕。
6. 南京他連去都沒去過。
7. 這把雨傘雖然很便宜, 可是太小了。

VIII. Choose the right words to fill in the blanks, and then read the conversation aloud with a partner.

1. 得　　2. 把　　3. 連……都　　4. 被　　5. 雖然……可是
6. 不　　7. 把　　8. 把

Index of Grammar Points

Index of Grammar Points